CRM

by Lars Helgeson

CRM For Dummies®

Published by: **John Wiley & Sons, Inc.**, 111 River Street, Hoboken, NJ 07030-5774, www.wiley.com

For general information on our other products and services, please contact our Customer Care Department within the U.S. at 877-762-2974, outside the U.S. at 317-572-3993, or fax 317-572-4002. For technical support, please visit https://hub.wiley.com/community/support/dummies.

Wiley publishes in a variety of print and electronic formats and by print-on-demand. Some material included with standard print versions of this book may not be included in e-books or in print-on-demand. If this book refers to media such as a CD or DVD that is not included in the version you purchased, you may download this material at http://booksupport.wiley.com. For more information about Wiley products, visit www.wiley.com.

Library of Congress Control Number: 2017942394

ISBN 978-1-119-36897-7 (pbk); ISBN 978-1-119-36898-4 (ebk); ISBN 978-1-119-36899-1 (ebk)

Manufactured in the United States of America

C10012525_073019

Contents at a Glance

Table of Contents

Introduction

If you ask ten people what CRM (Customer Relationship Management) is, you'll get ten different answers. Some think of it as a sales tool, some think of it as a culture. Some people see it as a savior for a business, offering accountability and efficiency. Some people are scared to death of CRM for the workload it can create if it isn't done right.

Very, very few people have ever taken a class in CRM. Universities are only now starting to offer it in their curricula. Seminars are often very product-focused. Without standardized definitions and training programs, it's a challenge to bring everyone in an organization up to the same level of proficiency with CRM.

I recently had a conversation with a friend who works in a company that forces all sales reps to manually enter every bit of data into the company's homegrown CRM. He tallied up the hours he spent in a month just doing data entry — 20 hours. It's no wonder some people don't like CRM!

In this book, I talk about the concept of Complete CRM as a way of helping you think of it as part of a bigger picture. A CRM that doesn't capture the information you need to do your job puts data in unreachable silos. A CRM that automatically pulls in sales, marketing, and operational information also pulls a team together. This is what I mean by *complete*.

CRM is not a simple subject. It involves many disciplines; to make it effective, you must have at least a basic knowledge of how those disciplines work. From managing sales people to building emails to running events, CRM reaches across every department in your organization. But like another friend once told me, "How do you climb a mountain? One step at a time."

About This Book

This book is written in plain, simple English. The point is to break down a complex topic (designing and implementing CRM) into manageable pieces. I first cover the basics of sales management, marketing, and operational process. From there, I show you how to apply CRM to each of those fields.

The content of this book has been pulled together from my experience helping hundreds of businesses launch and maintain their CRM initiatives, combined with the research and feedback of leaders in this space.

If you're a CRM expert, there's a good chance you will gain some lessons from the many sources and experiences cited in this book. If you're a business owner looking to get CRM working for you, this book provides you the foundation for managing a team or outsourcing your CRM implementation.

Remember that every business is unique, and the way a CRM is used within that business is also unique. There is no "one size fits all" for any business unless you are a franchisor (and even then, there are variables from franchisee to franchisee).

Icons Used in This Book

This book uses icons to call out special attention to gotchas or little pearls of wisdom you can take with you.

This icon alerts you about information you can apply to your business today. Usually most people overlook these things that can be a surprising benefit to you.

REMEMBER

Don't forget to remember these important points (or at least dog-ear the pages so that you can look them up again a few days later).

When it comes to designing and getting your team using your CRM, you can make costly mistakes. These paragraphs tip you off to those gotchas that can set you back in time, money, or attitude.

Where to Go from Here

Now you're ready for action. Give the pages a quick flip and scan a section or two that you know you'll need later. Remember, this is *your* book — your toolbox of strategies and tactics that gets your team loving and using your CRM. Circle any paragraphs you find useful, highlight key concepts, add your own sticky notes, and doodle in the margins next to the complicated stuff.

This book starts with a background and focus on CRM strategy. When you have that figured out, Chapter 3 helps you find the best vendor. After that, I cover some basic topics about sales, marketing, and operations and how they fit into your CRM. And finally, the book ends with an advanced discussion on how to use the concepts of Complete CRM to bring your business to the next level.

Finally, don't forget to check out the cheat sheet for this book at dummies.com and search for this book's title.

REMEMBER

The more you mark up your book, the easier it is for you to find all the good stuff again.

1

Laying the CRM Foundation

IN THIS PART . . .

Understand the key strategies and components that make up your Complete CRM.

Get your team on board and create a data-driven culture.

Pick the best sales and marketing software for your business

IN THIS CHAPTER

» Finding out how to incorporate the R in CRM

» Integrating CRM into your business

» Understanding the terms around CRM

» Determining your CRM goals

Chapter 1

Embarking on Your Journey to Complete CRM

The first part of getting Customer Relationship Management (CRM) to work for your business is to understand what CRM really is. If you ask ten people, you're likely to get ten different answers, each rooted in their personal experiences.

CRM has only started being taught in colleges and universities, so it's no wonder there is fear, uncertainty, and doubt (also known as FUD) around it. Making CRM work in any business is a challenge, but it's one you can overcome with a grasp of the strategies and tactics.

This chapter introduces the concept of Complete CRM and all the terms and technologies that make it possible. You can then apply all that knowledge to your organization with confidence.

Bringing the R in CRM to the Forefront

Every organization is built on relationships. It doesn't matter how big or small the company is, which industry it serves, or who you are in that organization — relationships drive the success or failure of that group of people and the technology behind them.

The "R" in CRM stands for "relationship," something that everyone — whether in sales, marketing, or operations — in your company contributes to. The more you understand how these relationships work, and how everyone in your organization influences them, the more efficiently your organization runs and the easier you generate revenue.

One key to understanding relationships in the context of CRM is knowing the difference between Complete CRM and Traditional CRM.

Traditional CRM is rooted in cataloging notes that salespeople made when they called their leads. Leads became contacts only after they bought something. These methods quickly became cumbersome and outdated when compared with the modern online, customizable, and mobile solutions available today.

Complete CRM is built for today's business world and requires:

- A holistic view of the relationship between your business and its leads, clients, vendors, and employees
- A comprehensive approach to CRM
- A combination of strategy, practice, and software that brings together everything you know about a lead or client into a single resource

Complete CRM helps you understand what happens in the sales process, record how people engage with your marketing efforts, and track other interactions with your operations staff (for example, customer service, events, projects, and invoicing). Figure 1-1 illustrates how everything works together in a single system.

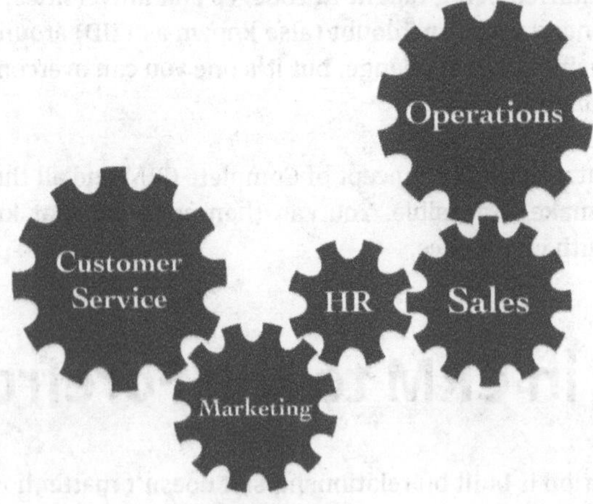

FIGURE 1-1: What Complete CRM does for you.

HIRING A CRM CONSULTANT

Many businesses work with consultants to set up Complete CRM. Not all consultants are created equal — in fact, a lot of consultants call themselves experts without the experience to back up the claim — and when it comes to CRM, most have specific biases based on their experiences installing or using a particular platform.

If you're hiring a consultant, be sure your consultant has experience relative to the size of your business and industry. If a consultant specializes in enterprise business process, don't expect that person to have an understanding of what it takes to run a startup business.

Don't rely on a single story or a gut feeling. CRM is too far-reaching, and the organization you work for is too important, to gamble with. With the right tools, reference material, and data, you'll make an informed decision that you can feel confident about.

Be cognizant of these gotchas that surface often when working with CRM:

- Some consultants will tell you that you must do something in an effort to bring them more work. If someone says "you have to hire this software development company" or "you have to use this system integrator to make your software work," you may be investing in something overly complicated that guarantees more work (and money) for overpriced labor.
- Some vendors will tell you their product (hardware or software) isn't working because you and your staff are misusing it. The vendor may blame the original salesperson. Remember that you're never stuck with a vendor you don't like; sometimes it's better to change strategies and vendors. Even if you've already invested a significant amount of money with a vendor, you're not trapped; you can make a switch to a new and better vendor.
- Many consultants are incentivized to sell businesses on large, complex systems because they're paid to get those systems up and running. Overbuilt CRM platforms can cause huge inefficiencies that may require you to spend thousands of hours and dollars to try to fix them. Be skeptical of falling for the big company line. Remember that bigger is not always better.

It takes an understanding of every piece of your organization to make Complete CRM work. Some concepts may be totally new to you. How some areas work may be totally new to you, and you may have to learn how different departments you've never ventured into work. You need to convince everyone from the top down of your vision of Complete CRM to be successful.

REMEMBER

Transitioning to a Complete CRM mindset can give you a greater perception and empathy for those people who make your organization the best it can be.

Extending CRM to Your Entire Business

CRM is more than just software. It's a mindset. Every business reaches a point, usually early on, when everything that's happening can't be held in someone's brain. People in the organization need to take notes, or they'll forget important things like customer issues, birthdays, or deadlines. With the aid of good tools to organize the information you need, you create a more efficient and effective business.

A good CRM system builds a framework for the information managed in your organization. Sales, marketing, and operations information needs to live in the same system because relationships reach across all those departments, as shown in Figure 1-2. Relationships represent the lifeblood of any organization, even those that don't outright sell products or services. The better you can understand and learn from those relationships, the more valuable and efficient you and your organization are.

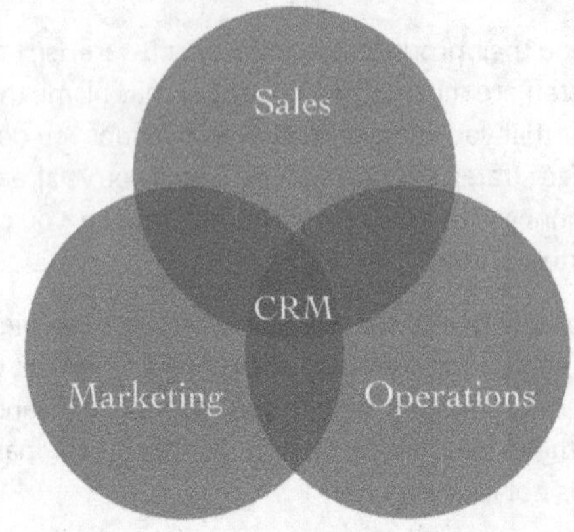

FIGURE 1-2: Sales, marketing, and operations working together.

Disorganization in any business leads to missed deadlines, sloppy work, and uninformed managers. CRM is the cure for these negative effects by creating organization and defining processes, but it doesn't just happen. It takes leadership, focus, and dedication to achieve the vision that you set.

Knowing the Buzzwords

CRM is awash in terms and buzzwords that people like to throw around. This section gives you the background you need to translate the CRM-speak.

You may be already familiar with some of these terms — for example, buyer personas are a tried-and-true marketing technique. But they may have a slightly different meaning in a CRM context than you're used to. Get to know these buzzwords, as they come up in meetings when you communicate your vision.

Content marketing

Content marketing is marketing, except instead of telling people to buy your widget, you're educating them on how great widgets like the ones that you sell are (oh, and by the way, this educational piece was sponsored by ACME Widget Company). It's a subtle way of getting people to read the pieces your marketing people write.

People "consume" content that they find interesting or educational. When you write a paper, record a podcast, or record a video, it's more likely to have an impact if you focus on providing value.

Your Complete CRM is connected to your content marketing pieces; Figure 1-3 shows a blog. Every blog, article, e-book, and whitepaper you write should capture the reader's contact information so you can follow up with relevant, personalized, and targeted messages. Capture all this information within your CRM, and your sales and marketing teams work together to the benefit of both.

Personalized content

Personalized content means that you create content specific to the person reading it. In the old days, this technique was referred to as a *mail merge,* where you would print "Dear Joe" at the top of a letter written to Joe. Nowadays, you can do that with email and webpages. You can even put totally customized pages (known as *personalized URLs,* or PURLs) together based on what you know about the reader. More targeted personalization in your marketing has a direct, positive impact on converting your leads into paying customers.

People listen when they feel someone is speaking directly to them. When you personalize content, you make people feel as though you care enough to make something just for them; see Figure 1-4. It's like hearing a story that was made just for you; you listen when you feel someone is speaking directly to you.

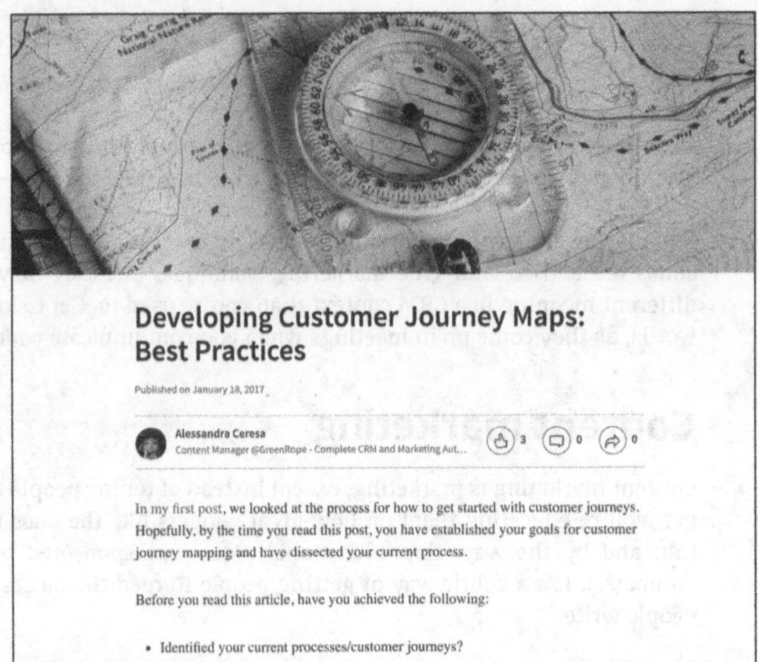

Developing Customer Journey Maps: Best Practices
Published on January 18, 2017
Alessandra Ceresa
Content Manager @GreenRope - Complete CRM and Marketing Aut...
3
0
0
In my first post, we looked at the process for how to get started with customer journeys. Hopefully, by the time you read this post, you have established your goals for customer journey mapping and have dissected your current process.
Before you read this article, have you achieved the following:
• Identified your current processes/customer journeys?

FIGURE 1-3: A blog is a good example of content marketing.

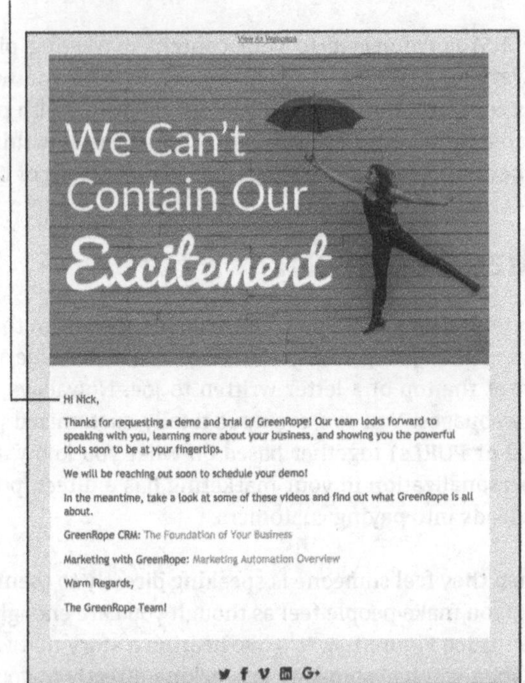

FIGURE 1-4: Personalized emails are better received.

REMEMBER

Personalizing content always brings up privacy considerations, as some people may not want you to know everything about their preferences and characteristics, so be sensitive to your market and how you're personalizing the information you're communicating.

When people engage with your personalized content, your CRM measures how they interact with you. Your salespeople then have access to information they need to have meaningful, direct conversations, while giving your marketing team insight into what resonates with your target market. With your team armed with better information, you can focus on techniques that maximize conversion.

Conversion

Conversion happens when someone does something of value for you. Usually it's when a customer buys your product or service, but conversions also record other actions that don't involve a transaction, such as downloading an e-book or filling out a form.

Conversions can have multiple stages, and are often depicted as a funnel or pipeline. The process of moving through stages toward the final conversion should be measured, if at all possible. This way, you can set up automation around people advancing (or not advancing) to the next stage, and measure your success in driving people toward the conversion at the bottom of your sales funnel. Turn to Chapter 11 to set up an automation process.

Your CRM should give you the ability to track conversions, along with the paths people take to get there. You need to know where weak links are in your conversion process and why they occur, and have ways to easily address your messaging and methods of improving conversion rates. Use buyer journeys to identify and address those weak links.

Data-driven

Decisions made entirely by instinct are inherently riskier. A good CRM provides you with a lot of information, and the platform should help compile that data in a way that's actionable. Require your consultants and employees to show you the numbers that back up their recommendations. While experience is a good teacher, it can also lead you astray in a world of changing market forces and technologies.

Being data-driven is as much a mindset as it is part of an organization's culture. The more everyone relies on data to justify decisions, the more accountable and rational those decisions are. Turn to Chapter 15 for more information about how to measure your CRM data.

For example, my company decided to try Facebook's lead capture system. After four weeks the numbers didn't justify continuing, so the decision was made to stop using it. Had I not analyzed the numbers, my company may still be using a channel that doesn't pay off as well as other channels. (As a side note, Facebook changed its system later, and after trying it again, my company found better success with it.)

Big data

Big data means that people have accessibility to more data now than a few years ago; oftentimes it's unstructured, massive, and hard to understand. You can accumulate all kinds of data if you want to — demographic data about your contacts, website clicks, email opens and clicks, social media, and video, for example. But if you can't make any sense of it, and it isn't actionable, it's useless.

Understanding what to do with all the data you gather is much more important than simply accumulating mountains of data you can't use. Conversely, not enough data may lead you in the wrong direction, too.

Your Complete CRM, because it collects data from all the channels you use for sales, marketing, and operations, generates a lot of data. Make sure the platform you select makes it easy to sift through all that data, so you can be efficient in making strategic and tactical decisions about your business.

Your CRM gives you all the data you can handle through reports and charts. Chapter 15 covers how to capture and track data; Chapter 17 helps you see how the data has an impact on your business.

Segmentation

When marketers talk about segmentation, they mean that they are looking at smaller subsets of the entire potential market of customers. The more granular you can divide your market, the better you can understand each of these segments. The most segmented market is one-to-one personalization, which is possible, but challenging, both from a strategy and technology perspective.

A good CRM helps you understand what your various market segments are and how they interact with your brand. (See Chapter 4.) CRM platforms should make it easy for you to target and send personalized messages to your market segments.

Figure 1-5 shows how you can segment an email targeted toward a specific interest. This particular message is sent to people who expressed interest in email marketing, as opposed to sales, marketing automation, or customer service products. You may send different messages based on interests, demographics such as gender or age, or actions taken, such as if one of your salespeople has already introduced your product to the lead.

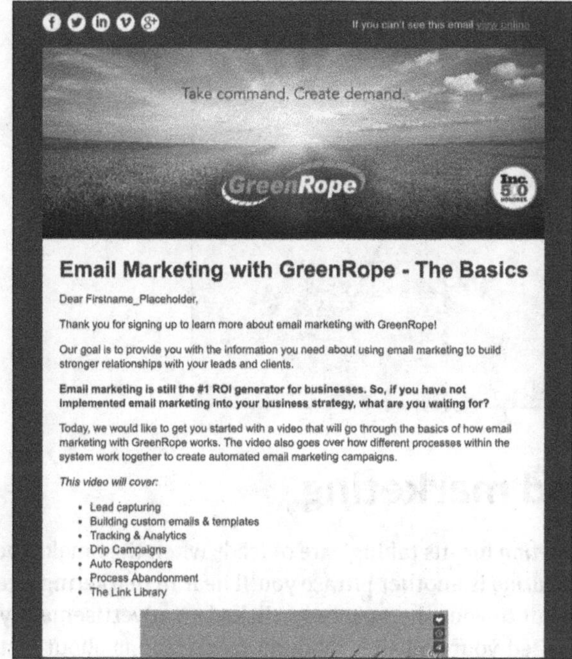

FIGURE 1-5: This email is sent to a specific segment — contacts interested in email marketing.

Buyer persona

A *buyer persona* is a characterization of a particular market segment. If you're targeting middle-aged housewives, you could create Sally, a 42-year-old mother of two who lives in the suburbs and drives a minivan. If you're targeting tall people who might want to buy the pants you're importing, you could create Tom, a 25-year-old, single professional who plays basketball on the weekends. This generalized, stereotypical person is meant to help put context around how customers would use your product or service. If you think about how Sally would react to your marketing message, it's easier to put yourself in her shoes when you can picture an actual person responding to you.

Buyer personas are useful in helping you set up your market segments and personalize messages sent through your CRM. Figure 1-6 shows a template to set up a buyer persona. Your sales and marketing teams can think about how to divide their efforts and resources to sell to the personas you create. Chapter 4 covers how to create buyer personas in your CRM.

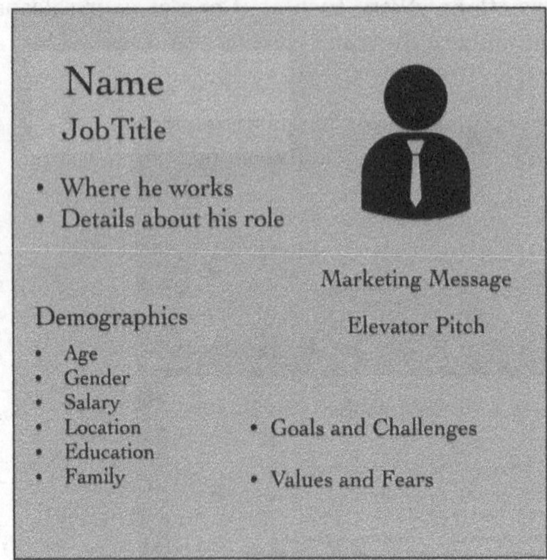

FIGURE 1-6: Set up a template for your buyer personas.

Inbound marketing

Inbound marketing means taking care of leads when they make the effort to contact you. *Lead nurturing* is another phrase you'll hear in marketing circles. When someone reaches out to you, she may have clicked an advertisement you placed, or she may have visited your website. Inbound marketing is about setting up processes to capture those leads and follow them all the way to conversion (the point where they do something you want them to do, like buy your product or service).

Complete CRM focuses on having a process and measuring everything you can about your leads as they learn about your brand and eventually convert into customers. Your CRM collects the behavioral and demographic data throughout the inbound marketing and lead nurturing process and uses automation to help your team communicate with your leads and clients efficiently.

Customer lifecycle/journey

Customer lifecycle is a term that encapsulates the journey people take from the time when they first hear about you, through their decision to purchase from you, to their consuming your product or service and becoming an advocate for your brand; see Figure 1-7. Often this progression isn't linear, as people tend to show varying levels of interest and usage of your product or service. A good manager of this lifecycle can track where people are in various phases of engagement and can set up marketing and automation to encourage movement toward conversion and advocacy.

CRM platforms help you measure this lifecycle. (See Chapter 4.) Knowing how long people spend in various phases and what moves them along the customer journey is critical to improving how you do business. Your team uses your CRM to keep track of who is where in this journey, helping each person effectively reach each individual contact with the right message.

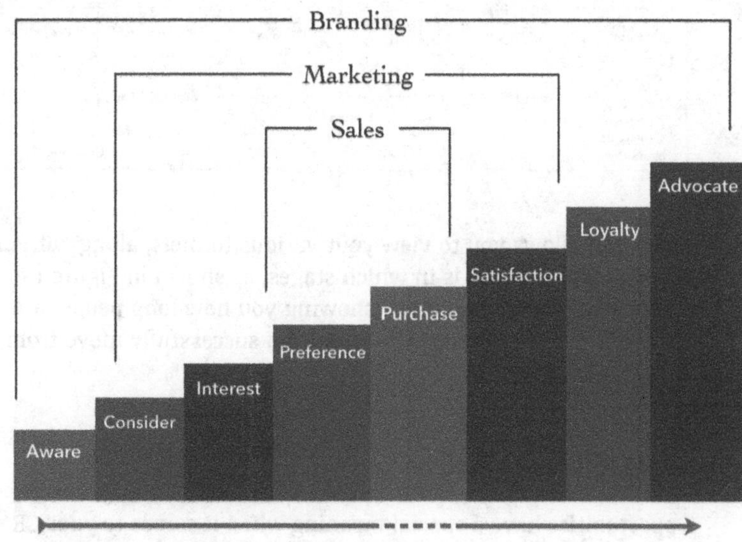

FIGURE 1-7: The customer lifecycle.

Sales pipeline/funnel

When your potential customers move through the process of buying something from you, you can place them into categories along their journey. Often these categories are descriptively named like "lead," "qualified lead," "reviewing proposal," and hopefully "customer." It's called a pipeline because usually people go through a standardized process from stage to stage. Pipelines are often drawn horizontally; see Figure 1-8. Funnels, on the other hand, tend to be drawn vertically, with the neck of the funnel getting smaller to represent the exit of potential buyers as they go from stage to stage. For example, you may start with 100 leads, but only 80 of them qualify to move closer to becoming a customer after they have a conversation with a salesperson.

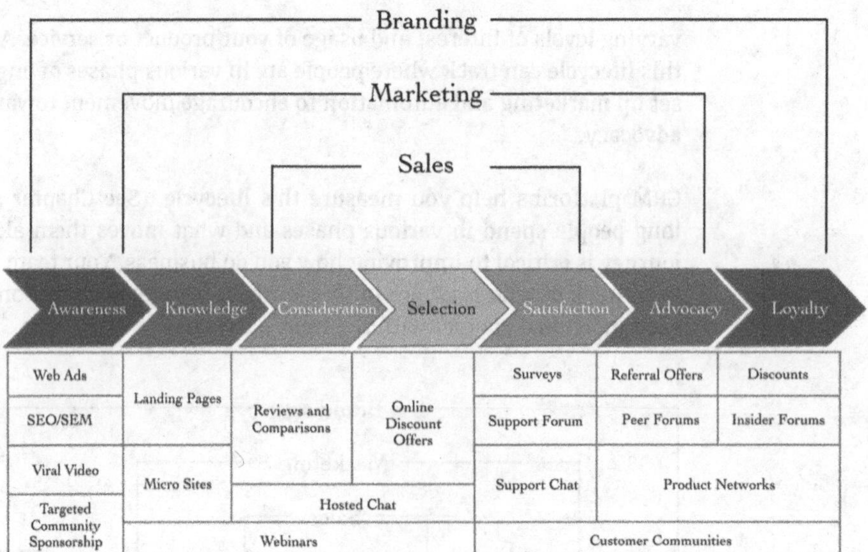

FIGURE 1-8: A sales pipeline.

Your CRM allows you to view your various funnels, along with drilling down into the charts to see who is in which stages, as shown in Figure 1-9. Good CRM platforms also provide analytics, showing you how long people are spending in each stage and the percentage of people who successfully move from stage to stage in a given time period.

Opportunities

Opportunities have a special meaning when it comes to your CRM. Each opportunity represents a chance for a lead to become a client. Because opportunities generally have a longer sales cycle and more interaction with your team, they're typically used for selling high-value products or services.

Each opportunity has characteristics you can use to categorize it. The quality of the opportunity, source, products, and/or services involved, the value of those products and services, date of expected close, and manager of the opportunity are aspects attached to it and can be used for categorizing and segmentation.

Your CRM stores everything about an opportunity in a convenient, easy-to-access place. Contacts and companies associated with the opportunity make it easy to track who the key players are; when you target resources to close that opportunity, you know what to say, and whom to say it to.

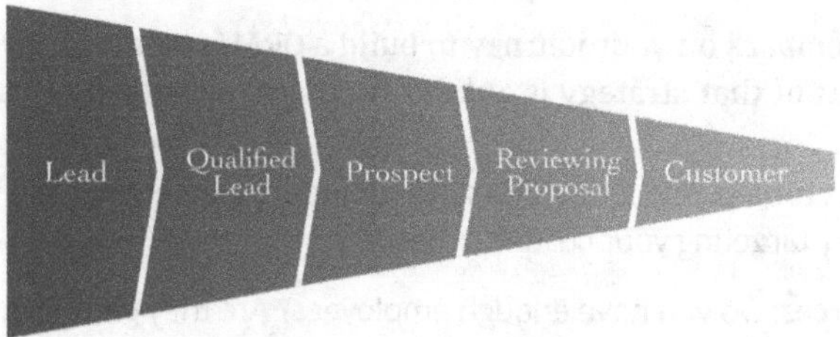

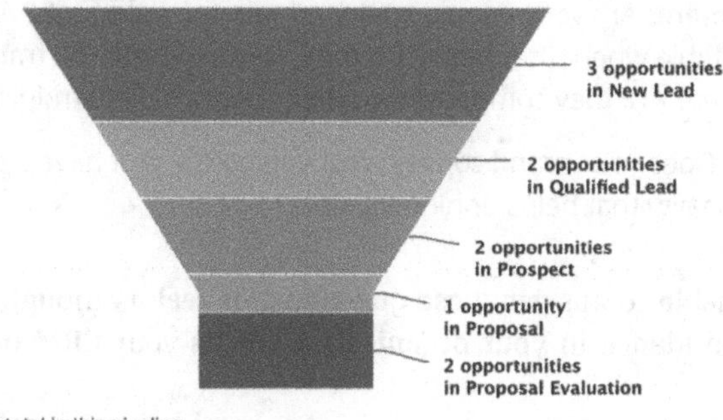

FIGURE 1-9: Different types of sales funnels.

Using Strategies and Tactics

Many people use strategies and tactics interchangeably, but anyone with military experience can tell you they're different. Senior management usually define strategies, while middle managers and those who execute employ tactics. This section covers how to distinguish between strategies and tactics in the design and implementation of your CRM.

It's important to understand how both strategies and tactics work together to build a solid company with principles of Complete CRM. Your leadership guides high-level strategy to unify your team, while knowledge of effective tactics to reach your goals make that happen.

Coming up with effective strategies

Strategies are high-level, macroeconomic ways of looking at how to keep your business competitive. They take larger forces into consideration, and tend to focus on the "why" of the business.

Before you embark on your journey to build a CRM, you must have a solid strategy in place. Part of that strategy is answering these questions:

- **Market forces:** Are competitors in your industry emerging? Are they a threat? Are they targeting your customer base?
- **Resources:** Do you have enough employees? Are they getting enough education and training? Is their morale high? Are they sharing information with each other, guarding it for control over others, or fear for their livelihoods?
- **Investment:** Are your people equipped with the right tools? Are they comfortable where they work? Do they have access to the training materials they need? Are they compensated when they complete training?
- **Brand:** Does your brand convey what you do? Does it have a personality? Is it a personality that helps or hinders sales?

If you're unable to answer these questions, or feel as though the answers don't give you confidence in your organization, focus your CRM on addressing these issues.

Using effective tactics

Tactics, on the other hand, are about what happens every day at your business. They involve the tools people use, and how they use them. Usually they are more about the "how."

These questions focus on the day-to-day operations, and you want to have good answers for them.

- **Customer relationship management (CRM):** Are you managing every aspect of your customer lifecycle? Is it easy for your team to access the data they need to get their jobs done? If your sales and support teams are talking to clients, do they know enough about those clients to provide great service?
- **Outbound communication:** Are you using all the right channels (for example, email, print, pay-per-click ads) to reach your leads and clients? Are you measuring performance?
- **Funnels and conversion:** Are you tracking how people progress through the process of purchasing from you? If they're leaving, why? Are you following up with them? How long is it taking for people to make the purchase decision? Are you able to automate and/or personalize any of these interactions?

» **Access to relevant information:** Can your salespeople track what their leads are doing? Do they get alerted when their leads show signs of wanting to buy? Does your customer service team see how your clients absorb the information you send them? Does your marketing team have access to sales- and support-related data that could help them segment their communication?

Measuring "effective"

The word "effective" can have many different meanings, so it's important to take the time to make sure what it means to you. At an organizational level, it often translates to "efficient," meaning fewer resources to accomplish tasks the company needs done. At an individual level, it can mean giving people the freedom to do their jobs well.

TIP

Take time to think about your overall goals, both as an organization and with your CRM, as those goals relate to being effective. When you know where you want to go with both, and what it means for you to be effective, you can check whether you're on the path for accomplishing both.

In all cases, measuring and reporting lets you know if you're moving your organization in the right direction. An effective Complete CRM means you do more with less, with the data easily accessible to back that up.

Finding Your Success with Complete CRM

Beyond a self-help cliché, success can also have many meanings. This section covers several ways you can apply metrics to gauge how well you are doing.

REMEMBER

Everyone defines "success" a little differently. It's important that you take the time to write down what it means to you, both personally and to your business.

If you have a lifestyle business, your goals may be more driven around giving you free time. If you're growing a for-profit business, your goals may be centered on maximizing top-line revenue or profit. If you manage a non-profit, you may be focused on donations and/or maximizing how much you can deliver to your cause. In every case, success is unique to you, so take the time to be clear on what benefits the CRM can offer both you and your organization.

You can use a few metrics to determine your level of success. These metrics are examples and are suggestions for you, but it is important you consider all these when laying out your plans for your CRM. Your strategy — and therefore the way you set up your Complete CRM — should focus on driving you toward the success metrics that mean the most to you.

Growth

Whether you're measuring over a short time span, or a longer history, you should be able to see numbers that indicate improvement on a large scale:

- **Top-line growth (total revenue):** Revenue is usually measured through actual dollars received, but if you're on an accrual-based accounting system, it can also include total amount of business booked. Your CRM should attach revenue to contacts and companies, and should track each individual buyer journey and what drives that revenue.
- **Number of customers:** If your customers are mostly similar or you sell a limited number of similar products, you may use the raw number of customers as a good metric for measuring success. Your CRM holds all your customer data, including groups of customers to help you segment them for analysis, automation, and marketing.
- **Average revenue per customer:** When you sell a wide range of products or services, you may want to measure the amount of revenue you're collecting from each individual customer. This metric indicates whether you're capitalizing on cross-selling or up-selling opportunities. Your CRM reports show this information and help you see which segments of your market are more valuable to you.
- **Marketing reach:** This metric is usually related to awareness of your brand. The number of brand impressions, the number of followers or likes in your social media networks, the size of your email list, or the number of contacts in your CRM are all metrics you can use to measure your reach.

Revenue

Revenue goals measure raw dollars coming in the door. Total top line revenue may not be indicative of how well you're doing, or where you may be able to improve. You may want to dive deeper and look at such key metrics as:

- **Revenue by channel:** If you sell through different channels (distributors), you can see which bring in the most business. Your CRM tracks revenue by grouping or by campaign IDs, so you can measure which channels have the greatest impact on your business.

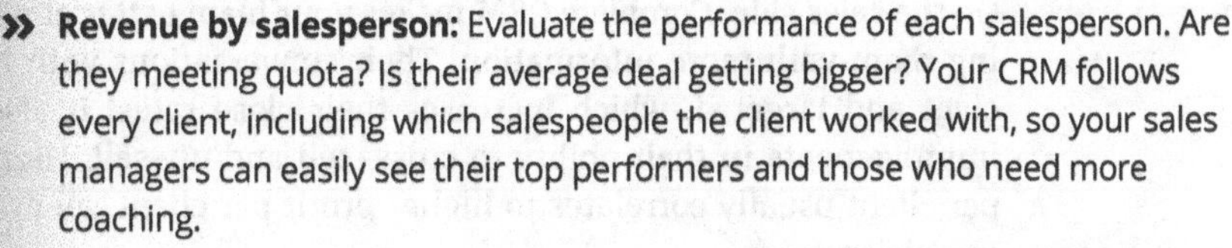

- **Revenue by salesperson:** Evaluate the performance of each salesperson. Are they meeting quota? Is their average deal getting bigger? Your CRM follows every client, including which salespeople the client worked with, so your sales managers can easily see their top performers and those who need more coaching.

REMEMBER

CRMs come with a leaderboard to keep track of your salespeople's statistics.

- **Average revenue per user:** Oftentimes, average revenue per client indicates the type of client you're closing. If this number goes up, it may indicate you're selling to larger clients, or you're selling at a high rate to your target market. If you have multiple clients within an organization, you may also measure how much each client within that organization is contributing to your top-line revenue. Your CRM gives you the ability to dive into details about clients, so you can extract metrics and valuable insights about them.
- **Revenue by region:** If you sell your product in different regions (local or international), you want to see how much is coming in through each area. Because your CRM stores regional information about each contact and company, this filter is easy to run.
- **Revenue by demographics:** Knowing whether certain demographics make up your revenue sources help you focus your marketing resources on the markets that demand your product or service. Look at gender, income, preferences, family status, homeowner status, and more for better insight. CRM platforms store an unlimited number of fields you can use to find which demographic characteristics impact your business. With included predictive analytics, an advanced user can apply this knowledge to help focus on leads most likely to convert and provide more revenue.

Profit

Profit is usually very closely related to efficiency, which is discussed in the next section. There are a few more variables related to financing and vendor costs, some of which may be impacted by effective use of your CRM.

Many people think CRM is for sales and marketing. But it can also track interactions with vendors and partners. By setting up your CRM and automation around all aspects of your business, you can measure and control variables that contribute to your costs.

TIP

If you have labor that contributes to your cost of goods sold, you can measure how long it takes your operations to complete a task. Deviations highlight inefficient procedures, vendor mistakes, or lack of training for employees.

On the sales side, Complete CRM makes your team better at what they do by arming them with more information. Their conversations with leads are more efficient and targeted, which increases their close rates. It also can contribute to improvements in their ability to cross-sell and up-sell. Higher average revenue per client usually correlates to higher profit per client, all driven by the increase in efficiency.

Efficiency

Efficiency is about being able to do more with less effort. Using machines (physical machines to save manual labor, or computers to save data entry or manipulation) to scale your business results in greater efficiency.

Some key ways that Complete CRM contributes to efficiency:

- **Alerts:** When measuring what leads and clients do across multiple channels (for example, websites, email, text, phone), your CRM can tell your sales team when a hot lead needs an immediate follow-up. Because your salespeople and their contacts are tied into your CRM, alerts are timely and contain the information they need to close more deals.
- **Auto-responders and drip campaigns:** When a lead or client fills out a form or activates some other trigger, you can set things in motion to automate what happens next, such as a series of emails or personalized printed material. Logs of these automated marketing functions are stored in the CRM, along with what your contacts did when they received these messages.
- **Overdue warnings:** When you set up workflows, or automated CRM activity schedules, you can set predefined to-dos for your team. If someone drops the ball on a regularly scheduled sequence, management can see it immediately.
- **Automatic CRM updates:** When software automatically updates your CRM, it saves manual data entry. For example, one-to-one emails are saved, phone calls are recorded and transcribed, chat sessions with customer service are added, videos are watched, and email newsletters are opened or clicked, as shown in Figure 1-10. Complete CRM automatically transfers this data to your contact records, saving you time and arming your staff with information to do their jobs more efficiently and effectively.

Costs associated with labor that could be automated often contribute to unnecessary overhead. These costs could be labor, but it could also affect your team's ability to respond to opportunities. If your salespeople don't know when a hot lead is showing interest, they aren't spending time effectively, which results in waste or missed chances to close deals.

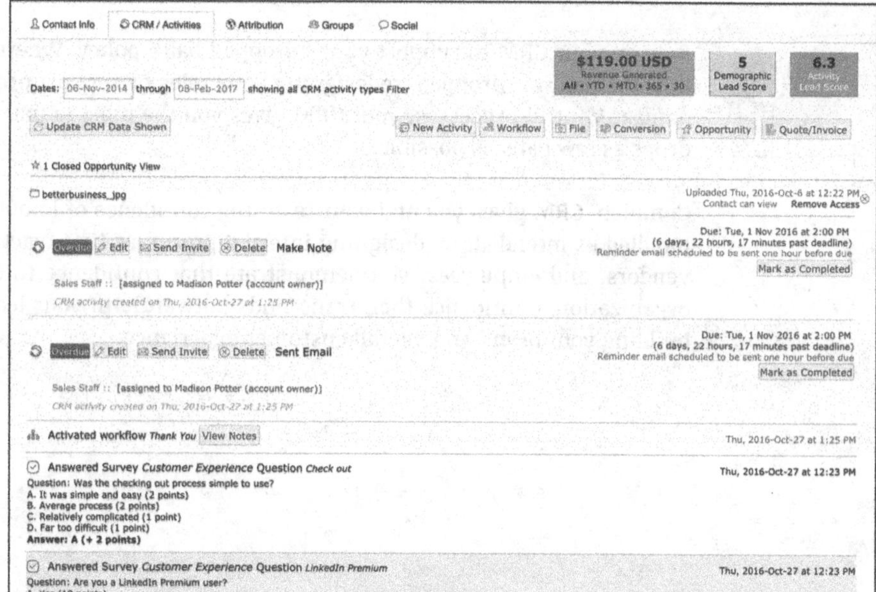

FIGURE 1-10: When a contact record includes all this information automatically, everyone wins.

Lifestyle

Wise men tell you that the true measure of one's wealth is in the amount of free time available. If you can take the morning, the afternoon, or the day off and not stress about it, you're making progress toward building a more free lifestyle.

Lifestyle isn't always just about free time. It's also about quality of life while at work. When stress levels are lower at work, people are happier. Ultimately, people are in search of more happiness, and Complete CRM brings you closer to that by giving you insight into how your business is doing and improving the customer experience. Better tools create efficiency and consistency for your team, improving morale and performance.

Workers and managers alike feel more stress when mistakes are made. Sometimes people forget things, and sometimes they weren't told anything about something that could have helped them do their job better. Complete CRM is your recipe to remove those mistakes by making relevant information available and automating reminders to complete tasks in a timely fashion.

When someone in your organization drops the ball, someone has to pick it up. Usually there is some amount of apologizing to a customer, coaching for the person who dropped the ball, and a reevaluation of internal processes. Every time this reevaluation happens, the team should think about how Complete CRM could help prevent it from happening in the future.

TIP

Rely on your CRM to support your "dropped ball" policy. Whether it's recording how the ball was dropped, redesigning your sales or support process, or tracking damage control processes, your CRM gives you the tools to make sure your team drops as few balls as possible.

Complete CRM gives you and your team the confidence of knowing everything is handled as intended. By designing internal processes that react to leads, clients, vendors, and employees, you demonstrate that confidence to everyone in your organization. Confidence then transcends outwardly to your leads and contacts, building your brand and overall customer experience.

IN THIS CHAPTER

» Recognizing and addressing the resistance to new strategies and processes

» Building a team that uses your CRM effectively

» Creating a singular vision for everyone in sales, marketing, and operations

» Teaming up with IT to build a data-driven culture

» Making CRM an integral part of your corporate culture

Chapter 2
Gearing Up Internally for CRM

CRM is more than a software package. It's a mindset and a collaborative effort that spans the entire organization and includes your leads, customers, vendors, and partners. Making CRM work requires a culture that supports it.

In this chapter, you discover how to gear up internally to implement an effective Complete CRM. You develop the knowledge and skills to anticipate common roadblocks and clear them with confidence. You build a creative, collaborative environment united behind the common purpose of improving customer satisfaction and developing customer relationships that drive profit and growth.

REMEMBER

To make Complete CRM work, you need your team on your side. You build a culture that involves everyone, forming a solid foundation for your CRM to grow from.

Overcoming Resistance to Change

Change requires effort and energy to overcome inertia — the reluctance to adopt new ideas or to change processes or procedures. Not everyone will be on board right away, but if you know the underlying reasons for the resistance, you can address whatever that's holding those individuals back.

REMEMBER

In any group of people, generally speaking, 80 percent will resist change. This 80 percent finds excuses to remain in the familiar patterns. To institute a change in your company culture, you need to anticipate this resistance and address concerns that may be standing in the way. In this section, I explain how.

Preparing for "not invented here" resistance

One main reason people don't like to adopt new ways is because they feel as though they're being forced to act in ways they didn't come up with or hadn't considered on their own. It's commonly known as "not invented here" resistance. Generally speaking, the more powerful a person's ego, the more likely that person is to resist change if he didn't come up with the idea and doesn't see a clear benefit to make the change.

TIP

Make the benefit of change clear to everyone in your organization. Start by showing how what's currently in place falls short of what the company needs. Then sell your vision of how the changes provide the benefit that matters to each person. That benefit may be doing their jobs better, making their lives easier, saving time, helping them innovate, earning more money, or a combination of these.

Confronting the ghosts of failed initiatives

Many organizations have launched initiatives that haven't turned out as planned. For example, someone in the company may have come up with the brilliant idea to switch to a new accounting system that's worse than what everyone in the organization was accustomed to using. Now, everyone is dealing with the fallout of that person's bad decision and is more reluctant to try something new.

CRM is one example in the world of failed initiatives. In fact, according to a study completed in 2014, over 60 percent of CRM implementations were perceived as "failures" by the company's employees. That number climbs to over 80 percent when any sales or marketing automation is involved. In the modern era, it doesn't have to be that way.

TIP

When dealing with employees who've been burned by failed initiatives, be prepared. Develop an integrated approach to CRM and clearly explain the benefits everyone will gain from it. Be honest about the learning curve and the fact that transitioning to a new system is never easy and always carries some risk. People are often willing to invest in a new initiative if you give them reason to believe that they'll realize significant benefits later and you acknowledge the difficulties in making the change.

REMEMBER

Be prepared to make tough decisions. For example, when confronted with resistance to new software, you may need to push through the difficulties or abandon the software to pursue a better solution. If your leadership team determines the current software and/or management team responsible for your CRM is unable to achieve the company's objectives, commit to finding a new, better way and give it a reasonable amount of time to succeed.

Overcoming the fear of accountability

At its core, CRM is about accountability — individually and collectively. Everyone throughout your organization is responsible for ensuring customer satisfaction and contributing to the health of your business. This level of accountability can be very scary, especially to people in the company who are unaccustomed to being held accountable. Sometimes negativity surfaces in the form of unsupportive questions and comments such as "Why don't they trust us?" and "I don't want someone looking over my shoulder."

Part of your role of CRM champion is to demonstrate how accountability actually is a good thing. Accountability encourages participation by everyone, fostering an environment of collaboration and growth.

Figure 2-1 shows a widget on a CRM dashboard that gives you insight into what people in your organization are doing. You can see at a glance how active your team members are. If, for example, you want to set a target for each salesperson to make 20 calls in a day, you could see whether your sales team is achieving that goal.

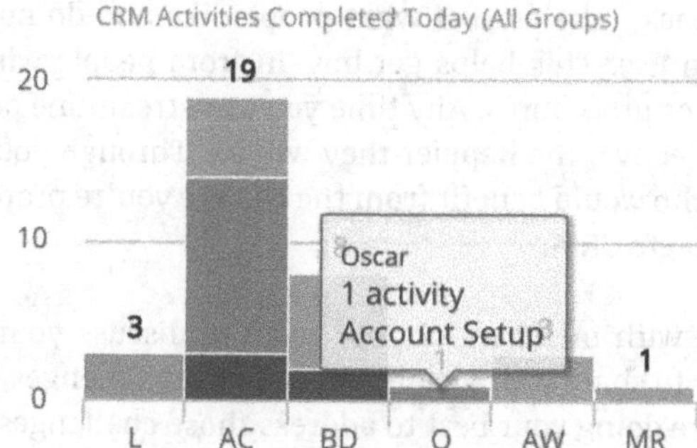

FIGURE 2-1: Activities can be monitored through a CRM dashboard.

When instituting organization-wide CRM, the organization's leadership team must communicate how crucial the company needs to succeed and its employees to reap the benefits of that success. For CRM to be effective, everyone needs to embrace it. Everyone plays a role in running the company efficiently, increasing income, and raising the level of customer satisfaction. Any negative attitudes toward CRM need to be addressed and corrected.

WARNING

Don't let negativity spread. People who are proud of their performance and know they're doing everything they can to benefit everyone around them will see CRM as a way to help them do their job better. Those who resist may be doing so because have something to hide. If you allow resistance to take hold, you condone lack of accountability as a culture. Ultimately, this lack will kill morale and result in the demise of the organization.

Conducting internal research

A first step to take toward understanding how your CRM will be used is to survey your team to see what they already use. Find out what software they have in place, how many people use it, and what it is used for. This information translates to requirements for your CRM.

In an ideal world, your new vision for your CRM includes all the existing processes your organization uses today. Processes may improve over time, but the end result of serving your customers should not be sacrificed. In a perfect world, that can all live in a single piece of software. While this may seem like a pipe dream, the more you understand how employees do their jobs, the more straightforward the transition to a new Complete CRM will be.

Before selling your CRM initiative to employees, identify potential sources of resistance and the reasons behind that resistance. If you work in a small organization, you may be able to sit down with people and ask them about their jobs. In a larger company, you may have to send a survey to everyone to gather feedback.

As you gather feedback, take note of what people like and do not like about the systems currently in use. This helps get buy-in from people who struggle with inefficient software or procedures. Any time you can streamline people's jobs and make them more effective, the happier they will be. Through your investigation, you can find allies who would benefit from the change you're proposing with your transition to a Complete CRM.

REMEMBER

When you sit down with members of your team to discuss your CRM, you also have an opportunity to share your vision. Listen to the challenges people face, and let them know you're doing your best to address those challenges and help them. When you share your vision and the benefits of your CRM, they're more likely to get behind you and what you're trying to accomplish.

At its core, this internal research is about developing a comprehensive list of requirements and "nice to haves" for your new CRM. Compile information from people who will use your CRM to build this requirements list. Here are common questions to ask in a survey, but you can ask for a deeper explanation if you have the resources.

- What is your job?
- What software do you use now? What do you like about it?
- What roadblocks or inefficiencies do you deal with?
- What do you need your software to do for you now that it currently doesn't do?
- What parts of your job directly impact revenue generation and/or customer satisfaction?
- In a perfect world, what would you like out of new software?

TIP

Compile your internal research information in a spreadsheet so you can see how many people work on each of the main functions in sales, marketing, and operations. This process helps you weigh the level of effort for transitioning these teams to your new CRM. Break out your spreadsheet into functional groups (for example, sales, marketing, events, account management, HR) for easier organization.

The more you know about what you have in place, the better you can ensure anything you move to (even if it's an enhancement of your existing CRM platform) won't sacrifice current capability. Communicate these requirements to your potential CRM vendors as early as you can, so you can focus on those who are best qualified to help you. Be sure to include access rights, so you can control who can see and influence what in your CRM universe.

Identifying formal and informal leaders

Every organization has formal and informal leaders. Formal leaders have a title, while informal leaders are those who are the most influential among their peers. Both are important when getting buy-in for your new CRM plans, but pay special attention to the informal leaders. Their influence will carry over into many aspects of your business.

Identifying the formal leaders is easy; these are people with titles, such as C-level executives, department heads, and managers. Informal leaders are more difficult to spot, but management usually knows who they are. Ask the managers of each department to point them out.

TIP

Take extra time to meet with the informal leaders and address their concerns. Make sure you incorporate their ideas and feedback into your requirements list, and make sure they understand your big vision. Listen carefully and with an open mind. The more you can get them to buy in, the smoother the implementation will go.

Selling Complete CRM to every level of your organization

User adoption is crucial for CRM success. When you're ready to get your team on board, treat user adoption like you would selling something outside your company. The key leaders and influencers, formal and informal, have to buy into your vision.

In selling your CRM program internally, develop your pitch like you would sell a lead. As with most sales, focus on the benefits and how you're meeting the requirements you learned about while doing your internal research.

The objectives and benefits you choose to highlight differ based on the role of the person you're pitching to, so be prepared to adjust your presentation to make it more convincing to the people you're addressing.

TIP

If one of these roles is yours, take the time to remind yourself why you're putting the energy into getting CRM working in your organization.

- **Owner/investor:** Owners and investors are most interested in sustainable, profitable growth. Building a business that is both sustainable and profitable requires discipline and planning. Sustainable growth requires a system in place that delivers excellent customer experience with trained personnel who care about what they do every day. A system that's efficient is an added bonus, because it boosts productivity. When pitching to owners and investors, focus on profit, growth, and productivity.
- **Manager:** Managers are looking for solutions that simplify their jobs and improve the performance and productivity of the people they manage. When pitching CRM to managers, consider focusing on the easy-to-access and easy-to-use tools you plan to provide them to help monitor and coach their subordinates. Your CRM software should increase visibility into subordinates' actions and provide insight into how those actions are impacting what the manager cares about (for example, sales, customer feedback, brand awareness).
- **Salesperson:** Information is power, something every salesperson wants more of. Insight into what leads are doing, what they're interested in, and how they are reacting to your marketing helps your sales team sell better. Better information

creates better conversions and focusing on leads that really matter. On one side, salespeople have the most to gain; on the other, poor performers will be most resistant to the insight their management will have, so focus on how this information will help them close more deals. One key mantra to remind your salespeople: "If it isn't in the CRM, it didn't happen."

- **Customer service representative:** With a good CRM in place, when helping a customer, more information about that customer and his history is instantly available. Having more information at each representative's fingertips makes it easier to help customers find what they're looking for. This resolves problems more quickly, reducing frustration, which in turn makes customers happier, which helps customer retention, and then increases revenue and helps the entire organization.
- **Account executive/Trainer:** When bringing on new clients or managing existing clients and projects, it's always easier to have defined processes in place. CRM defines and enforces those processes, so no one drops the ball at critical early stages of working with new customers. Automatically guided procedures for training new clients, managing projects, and resolving issues give account executives the structure and tools they need to effectively and efficiently provide an excellent customer experience.
- **Marketer:** With more visibility into what's working (and what isn't) and how leads and clients interact with sales, marketing is able to better segment your leads and clients. With segmentation comes improved capability to craft targeted messaging that appeals to your market. Marketers then measure what's happening across all channels and automate messaging. With better personalization of content, leads and customers will feel more connected to your brand, which makes them more likely to buy more from you and become advocates for your organization.

Encouraging and Facilitating Innovation and Collaboration

CRM thrives in an innovative, collaborative work environment, where every member of your organization shares a commitment to serving your clients' needs. Whether coming up with new ideas for products or services, or working together to resolve an issue, the positive environment supported by a good CRM makes the difference. In this section, I offer guidance on how to encourage and facilitate a more innovative and collaborative work environment to support your efforts to improve CRM.

Taking a balanced, structured approach to innovation

Everyone knows that innovation is important, if not critical to the long-term survival of any business. It enables a business to remain competitive in a continuously changing environment. Innovation is always talked about in the context of "more is better." Who doesn't want to be an innovator? Innovation by itself isn't enough, though. It must be guided toward making the right impact on the way you serve your customers and other people in your business.

Is it new technology that makes your product better? Is it a new way of servicing your clients? Is it a more efficient way of doing business? These ideas can be beneficial, but an organization needs structure around innovation to keep everyone focused on creating meaningful improvements. Without structure, you risk people coming up with a multitude of unactionable ideas and distracting others from their jobs.

WARNING

Innovation without direction can wreak havoc to your company's productivity. Be careful to encourage people to bring ideas, but not spend their days thinking of ways that ultimately disrupt normal business activities. It's important to put structure around the innovation process. Although some of the most innovative ideas can pop into people's heads when they're immersed in their normal work, it's best to channel those ideas through a defined process of evaluating and sharing. Define specific times and methods for brainstorming and sharing ideas before they spread across the company's desks and emails.

Development of innovation should be a managed process, not something randomly determined by people pushing their ideas. Establish criteria that set the bar for new ideas, so people can prescreen their own ideas before sharing them. A software company, for example, may use a combination of these factors:

- **Applicability:** How many clients would benefit from this innovation?
- **Weight:** Are the clients who could benefit paying us a lot of money?
- **Competition:** Do we have competitors who do this, and do they leverage it well?
- **Difficulty:** Will this require a lot of resources to implement?

Reevaluate your list of ideas regularly: monthly, quarterly, annually, or according to whatever schedule makes sense for your business and the competitive environment in which it operates. Markets and technologies change rapidly, so you want to be responsive and proactive whenever possible and reasonable to do so. Take advantage of shifting priorities from your customers and employees when it makes sense to change direction.

Identifying resources that contribute to innovation

The greatest resource you have for innovation comes from your own team and listening to feedback from customers. Your employees are vested in doing the right thing for you and the people they work with, so encourage that participation. Your employees are closest to your customers; they have insight into customer demand from first-person experiences. Similarly, your customers stand to gain from work you do that makes your products and services better.

Developing your plan for your new CRM require company-wide innovation around your business processes. When you have meetings where team members share their new ideas, be supportive of their efforts, no matter how small or misguided they might be. Make sure they understand that a framework is in place to approve new ideas and incorporate them into your organization. This framework provides a comprehensive way to prioritize innovative ideas, so the process doesn't become too political. To manage expectations, make it clear that only a relatively small percentage of all the ideas you gather will be implemented in the short term.

Going beyond having conversations with your employees and customers, you want to get a feel for how the culture of your organization feels about innovation. Find out how much your team is encouraged to share new ideas. If the culture resists change, talk to management and get support for the upcoming changes you're making to the business.

TIP

BE LIKE SKUNKWORKS

If you're a larger organization, consider having a part of your company act like Skunkworks, a division of Lockheed in the 1960s and 1970s when the company had a lean, no-nonsense, and bureaucracy-free aircraft design and development organization. It was able to rapidly prototype experimental aircraft and created the U-2 spy plane and the F-117 stealth fighter, both legends of their time. Skunkworks must be managed carefully, so as not to allow projects to be a total waste of time and money, but it can often turn risky, edgy ideas into competitive advantages for your organization. This same methodology applies to businesses innovating in how they use their CRM. New technologies can give your team a significant edge over your competition, but it may make sense to roll them out slowly to a small part of your business first.

Measuring the impact of innovation

Sometimes gauging the impact of a new idea on your business is difficult. To meet this challenge, put one person in charge of tracking innovations and set well-defined, quantitative criteria for measuring success. If you're trying to impact lead generation, for example, calculate the number of leads you can attribute to your initiative. If it's customer satisfaction, you may need to conduct before and after surveys to determine how the initiative has impacted customer satisfaction. Have the person in charge of tracking innovations produce formal reports to help identify what's working and what's not.

TIP

When implementing new ideas, be sure to clearly spell out criteria for success in quantitative means. If you're trying to impact lead generation, calculate the number of leads you can attribute to your innovation. If improving customer satisfaction is the goal, send surveys. Reporting, particularly when you can use your CRM to view the impact on different market segments, provides the feedback that guides future innovations.

BRAINSTORMING INNOVATIVE IDEAS

In the past few years, my company has come up with some interesting ideas; some were good, some not so good. The ones that tended to succeed could be measured in increments. Here are some examples:

- **Hire a vendor to redesign our user interface (UI).** We had always done our own internal design work, but we heard consistent feedback that our interface looked dated. No matter how hard we tried, our development team simply couldn't overcome this challenge. So we hired a company to help us with new wireframe designs. It was expensive, and took a lot of effort from our developers to integrate the new designs, but we no longer hear that complaint from our clients. When the occasional client leaves us, our exit surveys indicate 70 percent fewer issues related to the UI, with a corresponding increase in issues outside our control.
- **Write a collaborative e-book.** Because our software is designed to cover many aspects of a business, we wrote an e-book to help our customers harness the power of our software by integrating it into their sales, marketing, and operations. Several people from our company contribute their knowledge and insight based on their experience with helping customers. We see an average of 150 downloads of this book per month (all recorded in the CRM automatically), and the e-book has provided some additional positive qualitative feedback from customers in the training and on-boarding process.

Facilitating collaborative brainstorming for your CRM

To get buy in from your team on requirements for your CRM, you may want to engage some or all your team members in a collaborative brainstorming session. It opens the door for you to get a better understanding of requirements and nice-to-haves for your CRM.

Creating an environment that encourages and enables people to work together on sharing and developing new ideas may be harder than it sounds. A significant part of the challenge is often physical; for example, if people work in different parts of a building, telecommute, or work on teams that deal with different disciplines, communication and camaraderie can be difficult.

TIP

Fortunately, cloud-based computing offers numerous software solutions to facilitate collaboration, free and low-cost chat and screen-sharing tools such as Skype, GotoMeeting, join.me, or What's App. Other, more advanced software systems, including Slack and Yammer, are also worth a look. The best CRM platforms also have collaboration tools embedded into them as part of the platform you can use every day.

When you start the brainstorming process, you want to maximize the free flow of ideas as much as possible. If you have the resources to bring your team together in front of a whiteboard, that is a great way to facilitate creativity. Encourage everyone to pitch ideas; certainly some of them will be bad ideas, but suspend criticism during the creative phase. Operate on the premise that there are no bad ideas. You can winnow down ideas to the best of the bunch.

TIP

Limit the number of participants to no more than 25. Otherwise, it gets a little difficult to bring out ideas from everyone. Discussions tend to be run by a few strong personalities. If a few people monopolize the session, break out into teams. Depending on how you're set up, you can have them focus functionally (for example, customer service in one team, product development in another, and so on), or you can mix and match by assigning members from different departments to each team to provide a multi-disciplined perspective.

Collect the ideas and rank them to help identify which ideas to pursue. For example, you can use ease of implementation, impact on the customer, cost, risk to brand, and impact on revenue as factors in ranking ideas. A spreadsheet is often a good way to compile the data, but there are other brainstorming and decision-making tools.

Creating a Consistent and Effective Brand Communication Strategy

CRM provides you with an incredible opportunity to expand your brand reach and enhance your brand reputation. Your organization should already have some notion of what its brand is or what leadership wants it to be. Perhaps your brand is centered on innovation, trust, or quality. Whatever your brand is, you can use CRM to extend its reach and enhance brand reputation through consistent, data-driven messaging. In this section, you discover how to communicate that consistent brand messaging via electronic, print, and social media. (For details on how to adjust your brand message to appeal to different market segments, see Chapter 4.)

Sending electronic communication

Whenever someone in your organization sends a message, she represents your brand. Whether you intend it to or not, the most junior customer service representative impacts your brand. Interactions with your most loyal clients affect your brand's perception as much as those with new clients.

Because your brand is a living, breathing reflection of who you are and what you stand for, it's important to convey your culture to everyone in your organization. If you want to be seen as a professional organization, be sure your entire staff knows what is expected when they communicate via email, chat, or other means with anyone inside or outside the company. Being courteous, being professional, and using proper spelling and grammar are all important values everyone must adopt.

Use your CRM to create as many templates as possible, to eliminate the variability in human communication, language, and branding. Of course, where personalized, human-written messages are important, make the space for your employees to write those messages.

Remember that your brand is more than just your website and emails. You may have customer service people on chat, sales people following up with leads, or senior level executives networking at events. Everyone needs to know how to act and speak in ways that reinforce the desired brand image, especially when communicating with leads, vendors, or clients.

When you follow the principles of Complete CRM, all communication is tracked through it. Managers can monitor whether internal and outbound communication is adhering to your policies, and what impact it's having on revenue, lead conversion, and client retention.

Distributing printed material

The marketing team usually spearheads a company's branding initiatives, so you probably don't need to stress the importance of brand consistency to the people who spend their day broadcasting your brand to the world. However, if changes to the brand come from a source other than marketing, be sure the marketing team gets the memo. In addition, you may need to stress the importance of reflecting the company culture in any communication that marketing has with customers, outside vendors, or anyone else they come in contact with.

If they aren't already, responses to your printed material should be tracked in your CRM. Using a QR code (2D barcode) as shown in Figure 2-2, a special URL, or a discount code, you can see what works and what doesn't work. It's a good way to test your communication styles and media to see what resonates.

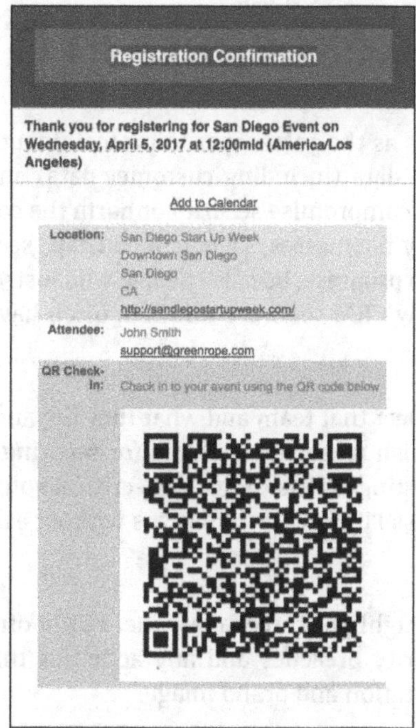

FIGURE 2-2: A typical QR code that can send people to a specific website.

One powerful tool for print is directing people to personalized URLs (*PULRs*), custom, database-driven webpages that create special pages for each individual. You can personalize the page with the recipient's name, or go deeper and put content on that page that you know is relevant to what that person is looking for.

Posting and engaging on social media

Social media is a dangerous tool in the wrong hands, particularly when it comes to your brand. You've heard stories of the wrong person (sometimes an intern) tweeting something inappropriate for a large brand. You want to avoid pitfalls made by other people and put policies and controls in place.

WARNING

Make sure anyone who has the power to post on your social media is trustworthy and conscious of your brand. Assign each user a separate ID and password, and be careful when assigning user privileges. Have a process in place to screen and approve posts for quality, grammar, and spelling before they go live. Anything posted on social media is there forever, and you want to keep your brand as consistent as possible. Have your team build a content calendar, so everyone knows who is posting what and when.

Working with the Gatekeepers in IT

Among other roles, IT serves as the gatekeeper to protect unauthorized access to the company's network and data (including customer data) and to prevent any internal activities that could compromise security or harm the company's reputation. Unfortunately, in many businesses, IT gets a bad rap; security experts are often perceived as barriers to progress, because people who just want to get things done, such as adopting a new CRM software solution, often have to wait for IT's approval.

REMEMBER

IT is there for a reason. Respect that team and what they do, and look for ways to team up with them to establish reasonable policies for securing data, controlling how data is used, and restricting access to mission-critical software. Reasonable policies are those that address IT's security concerns without excessively inhibiting progress.

In the following sections, I highlight three areas where CRM often needs to team up with IT to prevent security breaches and any activities that could possibly damage the company's reputation and brand image.

Securing your data

One of IT's main roles is to protect your data. This data may be internal, such as emails, shared files, customer data, or financial information. IT also protects your external brand from being compromised, such as preventing hackers from hijacking your website or social media.

With many stable cloud-based software providers available, it's easier than ever for your employees to open an account and upload your company data to a vendor's server. Your IT staff has fits, because it places the company's data on a system that IT has no power to protect. How secure is that vendor's network? What happens if that vendor gets hacked? Will it sell your data? All these questions must be answered before you choose a vendor, and they all need to be asked by someone who understands IT.

TIP

Work with IT to create a data security policy and make sure everyone in your organization understands and abides by that policy. As a business, you never want to lose control of your data, and that control starts with employees being responsible about how they store and share that data.

Your security policy should, at a minimum, include this information for your team to reference:

- Are team members allowed to install software on their computers?
- Can employees create and use accounts with Software as a Service (SaaS) providers?
- What data can be uploaded to any cloud-based services, such as Dropbox or Google Docs, and if it can, which services are employees permitted to use?
- Can personal portable digital devices (such as smartphones) be connected to company networks? If so, what software can they use?

Your CRM has to be included in all these discussions, and your IT staff should be aware of how CRM data is generated, controlled, and shared.

Controlling access to data

Your employees must understand that the data you collect is the lifeblood of your business. Unless everyone shares responsibility for stewardship of that data, it will get out. All employees need to understand how data is accessed and used throughout everything each employee and team member does. The more data you have and the better it's organized, the more powerful it is; be sure your team respects that power.

Figure 2-3 shows how everything is interconnected in your organization, and highlights the central role that IT plays in controlling the way the information is transferred between departments. Be sure someone is in this central role, even if your organization is too small to have an IT professional. While the goal of a CRM is to break down data silos and enable information sharing, from a security standpoint, you want to have control over that sharing.

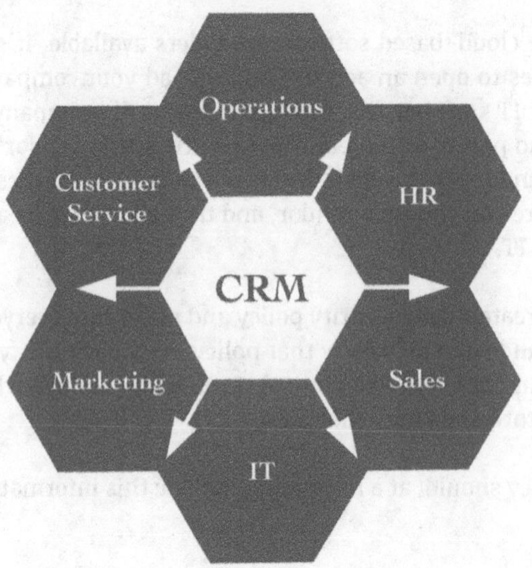

FIGURE 2-3: Your organization is connected.

Start with how and where data is accessed. If you have an IT department, it probably installed software on each device and computer to protect it. But that doesn't necessary protect everyone. Make sure that everyone connects to your network with a virtual private network (VPN) when connected outside your office with unsecured Wi-Fi. Make sure employees know to never plug in strange USB devices into their computers.

If people have access to data in the form of a portable file such as a spreadsheet or a word-processing document, make sure they only upload those files to systems that you approve. If they're using cloud-based software, be sure you understand how that software works and if your data can be shared.

Controlling access to your CRM software

Multi-user access to data is absolutely critical to your business. Not everyone in your company requires access to all the data that your company has and uses.

CRM software is a powerful tool with access to a great deal of sensitive data and the power to broadcast marketing content globally and almost instantly. Given its power, you must consider who really need access to which parts of your CRM. You don't want an intern with the ability to send an email broadcast to your client database without approval.

Fortunately, most CRM software platforms include features that enable you to restrict access to certain features or to certain activities, such as posting content or looking at customer data. You can create separate, password-protected user accounts and assign privileges to users individually, as shown in Figure 2-4.

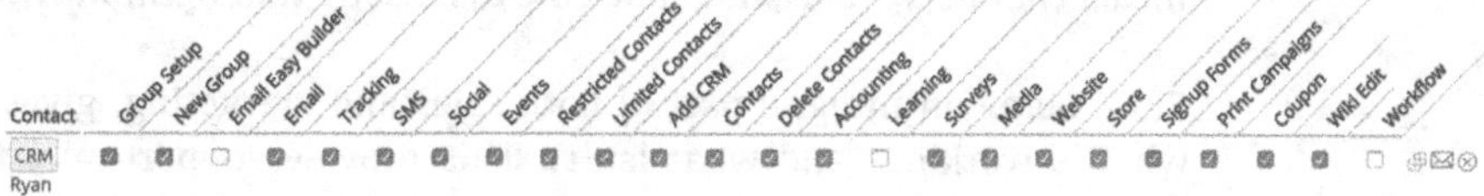

FIGURE 2-4: Shared access rights can be managed.

WARNING

Never permit users to share a login. If you do, you lose the ability to track individual user activities and hold each user accountable for what he does. If the CRM solution charges per user, then budget for separate user logins; don't try to save money by allowing users to share a login. You can also look for a CRM platform that doesn't charge per user.

Adopting a Data-Driven Mindset

I think it is an immutable law in business that words are words, explanations are explanations, promises are promises — but only performance is reality.

— HAROLD GENEEN

Many people become leaders by accident. Suddenly they're thrust into a position of having to make decisions, and they either bloom or crumble under the pressure. If they find early success from following their intuition (and some good luck), they may start to think they're smarter than everyone else in the room. But here's the secret: They're not.

For better, more consistent results, don't base business decisions solely on intuition and conjecture; operate with a data-driven mindset instead. In this section, I explain how.

Making decisions quantitatively versus qualitatively

When you make decisions, more and better data guides you to be more prudent, reducing your exposure to risk. That isn't to say that you should succumb to "analysis paralysis," waiting until you have a mountain of data before you make a decision. After all, one mark of a good leader is knowing when to say something is "good enough." Sometimes, the tip of the iceberg is enough to point you in the right direction.

Requiring people to back up claims with data should become a cultural norm that drives your organization to make better decisions more consistently. If someone comes to you and says, "We should invest more in advertising through social media channels," she should be able to back up that opinion with data.

CRM, being an integral part of both sales and marketing, gives you insight into what is working (and what isn't). This provides opportunity for making clear decisions based on data. Here are some questions your marketing team can answer with good data:

- How many impressions will you get for every dollar you spend?
- Of your various campaigns, how many impressions does it take to create a click to your website?
- How relevant to your product or service are the people who click those links?
- On average, how much does it cost to generate a sales qualified lead from pay-per-click advertising?
- On average, how much money does it take to generate a customer from social media?
- How long does it take a lead to become a customer? How does this vary between different marketing channels?
- Is the time and cost to obtain a client through social media better than pay-per-click advertising?
- Are you retargeting leads with ads on social media, and is it working?
- Are you generating leads through content syndication (writing blogs or stories and having other companies share them on other websites), and how much does it cost?

When the marketing team is able to answer these questions and report on them to the sales and management teams, you can see how to spend your money most effectively. With a good CRM, you can track different campaigns and see which salespeople are your best performers. Insight into sales and marketing successes helps you channel their efforts to maximize productivity and growth.

If you aren't able to get specific answers to these questions from your marketing team, they can improve how they're serving your organization. All these are well within the capabilities of software, with little to no technical experience required.

Figure 2-5 shows how these questions directly impact the flow of leads into your sales funnel. The better you can answer these questions, the clearer your understanding of how the sales process works.

By asking these questions, you make your sales and marketing teams more accountable. Money spent on advertising and marketing is an important part of the company's budget, and that budget has limits. The more you can hone in on what works and what doesn't, the more effective your advertising and marketing will be.

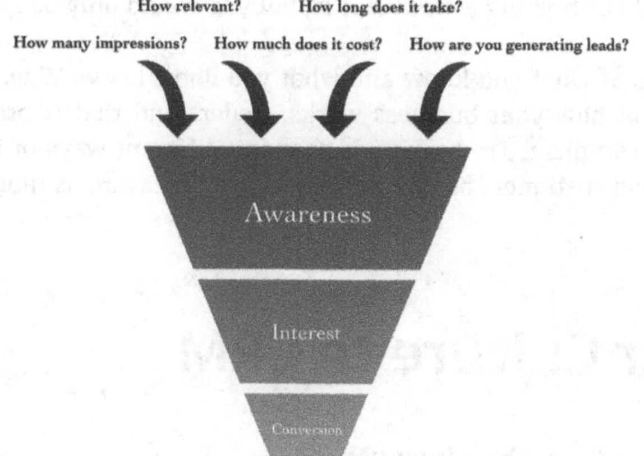

FIGURE 2-5: Know answers to questions that impact your marketing and sales.

REMEMBER

Your goal is to minimize the cost to bring in a client, while maximizing the amount of money each client pays you. Marketing and sales work together to achieve those goals. Break down the silos between these departments to maximize your conversion chances and minimize the cost to bring in a new client.

The same goes with anything you invest in, whether it is internal (for example, developing your product or service) or external (such as hiring another salesperson). The more you can rely on data to help you make decisions, the more confident you'll be in making those decisions. In the absence of data, you're at least cognizant of that increased risk, which probably encourages you to invest in those ideas more gradually.

Leveraging predictive analytics

Predictive analytics is a relatively new field that goes a long way toward helping you make data-driven decisions. By looking at what drives conversions (purchases or actions that are valuable to you), you can see what correlates to success. You see mathematical models that tell you how influential your social media ads are in driving customers to buy from you. You can see the influence of salespeople, email campaigns, webpages, and other channels, and you can allocate resources to where you have the strongest correlations to conversions.

TIP

The key to predictive analytics is getting the whole picture. If you're only measuring email and webpage traffic, you're missing many other channels that may be driving people to buy from you. Brand awareness and measuring how your leads begin their customer journeys are important factors that impact your business.

Imagine what would happen if you had a significant source of leads coming from people who called in to your company, but you didn't have a way to track those inbound calls. If you were to take money away from advertising your phone number, you could be hurting your business, but you would only be guessing.

REMEMBER

Be conscious of what you know and what you don't know. When you build your data model of how your business works, understand that it probably won't be 100 percent complete. Try to include as many different ways of interacting with your leads and customers as possible, so you can measure as much of the system as possible.

Applying Your Culture to CRM

Success depends on where intention is.

— GITA BELLIN

This chapter focuses on building a team and culture that connects your sales, marketing, and operations. Your CRM is the glue that binds everything together, but it's more than just software. It represents a culture focused on accountability, sharing, and efficiency. It creates transparency and puts the customer relation at your team's center of attention.

REMEMBER

CRM isn't just software. It's a well-coordinated, company-wide, data-driven system devoted to the high levels of customer engagement and satisfaction that drive growth and profit.

Thinking like CRM

CRM represents a way of thinking, a culture of accountability and teamwork in a company, where everyone contributes to the growth of the business. When done correctly, it revolutionizes the way the entire team works.

CRM sometimes has a negative connotation because it can be viewed as another way for management to drain productivity and look over the shoulders of people who would rather not have every minute of their day accounted for. That is CRM done wrong, and when it's done wrong, people hate it.

Beyond software, CRM is the centerpiece of your organization's culture. It's the glue that binds your team together, making it easy for people to get the information they need to do their jobs better. CRM is the environment of collaboration, tracked and managed by people contributing to the company's growth and success.

REMEMBER

CRM creates continuity in an organization. As the company evolves, the record of your interactions with leads and clients becomes an asset. The company becomes more valuable because that intellectual capital that you have worked so hard to build becomes permanent and integral. Information about those relationships and transactions provides the feedback the company needs to know in order to better serve clients.

Acting like CRM

There's an expression that resonates with organizational teams and helps them understand the value of having everyone on the same page:

> If it isn't in the CRM, it didn't happen.

This expression impresses upon everyone the need for documenting any and all interactions with leads and clients.

REMEMBER

As much as a leader can tell his or her team that they have to use their CRM, people resist change. They resist accountability. You need to understand how human psychology plays a role in getting your CRM adopted company-wide. People do things because they want to, so remember to remind your team of the benefits your Complete CRM will bring.

As people have relationships with each other, so do they have relationships with the software they use. You want to create a positive relationship between your team and your CRM right from the beginning.

Building two-way relationships

Like any relationship, treat your relationship with your CRM as a two-way street. If people are putting information *in*, make sure they get valuable information *out*. This concept is the crux of why most CRM implementations fail. When management doesn't commit to a CRM, it lets people work within the business without adding data into the system. Some people end up using it; others don't. When your team chooses to not use your CRM, they break the two-way relationship, which results in fragmented, inconsistent customer experiences.

For this two-way relationship to work, everyone must be able to get data out of the CRM — useful data that helps her do her job better. Here are a few examples:

- If you're a salesperson, you want to know if your leads are opening their emails, visiting your company's website, filling out forms, and/or talking to customer service.

» If you're in marketing, you want to know who your most interested leads are and why. Tracing your most effective marketing campaigns helps guide your future expenditures and forecasting.

» If you're in customer service, you want to know each client's history. If you're running an event, you want to know who's coming and why, and how you can follow up with the attendees and no-shows.

All these pieces are connected, and all of them require commitment by everyone else to find value in using the CRM.

Having a relationship with your relationship management software may seem like an odd concept, but it's absolutely true. Software by itself is just software. Software lies dormant until someone does something with it.

As the saying goes, "information is power." The more people work with CRM, the more powerful the CRM becomes. The more powerful the CRM, the more powerful the organization.

Adding a leaderboard to motivate your team

A big part of managing a sales team is encouraging a sense of competition between your salespeople. A leaderboard is a great way to integrate a CRM into your company culture.

Leaderboards work by setting certain quotas for members of your team. Salespeople are judged by their ability to meet and exceed their quotas, and if you publicly share their success (or struggle), they're motivated to work harder and sell better.

Consider using leaderboard software to show everyone in the organization who the best salespeople are (see Figure 2-6). They appreciate the recognition and people see the top performers, which is a motivator to increase sales.

FIGURE 2-6: A leaderboard can motivate and provide immediate feedback to your team.

IN THIS CHAPTER

» Deciding SaaS, building, or buying

» Deciding what you need in a vendor

» Picking software that's best for you

» Training users on the CRM

» Getting your security in place

Chapter 3
Choosing the Best Software

Picking the right CRM software is no small task. Because the CRM you choose will be a vital part of your sales, marketing, and operations, it's critical you make the best choice with all the information you can find. Every company has goals and challenges, and the better you understand exactly how you operate today and what your vision of the future is, the easier you can implement CRM into your business. There are many aspects to a CRM, so you need to define your requirements and find the best CRM vendor to match those requirements.

In this chapter, you develop CRM decision-making tools and get access to the resources available to help you make the best decision. It's important to remember that one size does not fit all. There's a reason the CRM software market has so many vendors; you get to benefit from that diversity and pick something that works for you.

REMEMBER

Implementing a CRM solution takes everyone in your company to be onboard. While you're considering solutions, it's a good time to get trusted employees' opinions on which features are important and even to help make a final decision.

Choosing between Software as a Service (SaaS) or On-Premise

The first choice you have to make in your CRM decision is whether you want your software to live in the cloud or reside on servers in your office.

For most businesses, choosing a cloud service, or Software as a Service (SaaS), makes the most sense for a number of reasons. If you really must go on-premise, be aware of the costs and risks of doing so *before* you head down that path.

Going with SaaS

There are a lot of good reasons why you want to go with a vendor that provides Software as a Service. It's what I (and most people in this industry) recommend for any business that doesn't have legal or security requirements to keep servers in an office.

The advantages are

- **Easy to start:** With SaaS, you can instantly provision your account. Vendors are set up so that the account creation process is just a matter of signing up online and paying for a subscription. The account creation process usually takes a few minutes.
- **Easy to upgrade:** Good SaaS providers design their networks so that upgrades are fast and painless. Most of the time, upgrades to your software happen automatically. If something significantly affects the way you see or use the system, the vendor may send you an alert or a newsletter, but the process should be fast and easy.
- **Easy to access:** When software natively resides in the cloud, it's available from anywhere. If your salespeople are on the road, they can update contact records and record meetings. If you have people working from home, they can still be productive. If your managers are traveling, they can still see what's happening with the business.

With SaaS, it's not all about the advantages. When you can access your data from anywhere, it's important you know exactly who can access what. You want to make sure your data can't be exported without your explicit consent. Any upgrades to your software are also likely to be on the vendor's schedule, and not yours.

BUILDING VERSUS BUYING

The world is littered with companies that believe they can build their own CRMs. Stop before you act on "I should have my own developers build our CRM, because they understand our business better than any third-party vendor can." It's a common misconception that CRM is an easy application to program; don't fall into that trap.

Building CRM is hard, and it's very different from what most companies do. Having your team develop something technical that is not your core competency is a recipe for disaster. This second decision should be easy, but if you insist on building your own CRM, be sure to expect it to cost ten times more than what your developers tell you, and take at least a few years before you have something you can use.

Why am I so biased against building your own CRM? Because you have to get a lot of elements exactly right, particularly if you attempt to build your own Complete CRM. Including the following:

- **Infrastructure demands:** You need enough bandwidth and server horsepower to make your software fast enough for your employees to use.
- **Upgrades:** Times change, your requirements will change, technology will change, and if you don't have a team dedicated to managing that change, you will be behind the moment you have a working prototype.
- **Support:** As you implement your CRM to your employees, you will have to train your staff on how to use it, which will be expensive. If you want to ease the burden on your developers, you'll need to hire people to document and produce educational content.
- **Channels:** Developing CRM may sound simple at first, but to make it useful, your developers need to have a deep understanding of sales processes, marketing, and operations. Developers are never taught these business principles and have to interpret your business requirements, which is a long, complicated process. They also need to link these channels together, which presents a spider web of knowledge connections they also have to learn.

In short, if you build your own CRM, plan for it to take years and millions of dollars of productivity. Enough CRM platforms are available now; it's a rare case where building your own makes sense.

Software development is a science in and of itself. There are methods of development, managing development, communicating requirements, and building architecture that are much deeper than most realize. Building a CRM software platform is no small feat,

(continued)

(continued)

and the number of moving parts required to make it work can take years. Given the speed that business moves, building a CRM solution is taking a huge gamble.

Buying software is not something to be taken lightly either. Sometimes companies have the attitude of "let's just try this and see if it works." This lackadaisical attitude almost certainly ends in failure. After your organization makes the decision to move to a Complete CRM implementation, do it right. Decide what you need, pick the software, and see it through.

Choosing on-premise

If your customers have security requirements (for example, government contractors) that prevent them from putting their data in the cloud, you need an on-premise solution. With data stored at your facility, you control who has physical access to the machines that house your CRM.

However, on-premise CRM requires a lot more effort to install and maintain than SaaS. Expect significantly higher costs and longer schedules to implement your CRM, because you need to host dedicated hardware and protect it with state of the art firewalls and data encryption.

Evaluating Software Vendors

Picking a CRM solution isn't just about finding a vendor and then closing your eyes and waiting until everything is done. The decision should be a measured, scientific process that brings you to a clear winner (or narrow the field to a few good choices).

It can be challenging to identify the best solution for you. Because CRM and marketing software is sold as Software as a Service (SaaS), you're using more than just a piece of software. You're buying into a complete solution for your business. Your CRM initiative serves your entire organization, including the design, implementation, and maintenance of the tools your team will be using. For the purpose of this book, I assume you're going with a SaaS solution for your CRM.

Analyzing vendor company culture

Not all vendors are cut from the same cloth. Just as your company is different from your competitors, you find a lot of variation between CRM software companies.

TIP

Look at the vendor's website. If it's easy to navigate and find the information you're looking for, most likely the software is also easy to use. If the website doesn't tell you a lot about the company and its software, ask yourself why. You should be able to see screenshots of the software, get a sense of the company's mission, and feel the cultural dedication to customer satisfaction.

TIP

You can learn a lot from your first interactions with the people you talk to. High pressure, boiler-room sales techniques turn a lot of people off, and if you feel uncomfortable talking to someone who is trying to force you to make a quick decision, listen to your instincts. Oftentimes, companies with high-pressure sales environments are driven more by revenue than customer satisfaction. Demand to be more than a number, and make sure the company's sales and customer service teams understand you and what you need.

You should be able to get a trial account as part of the sales process. Click around and get a feel for the user interface, its speed, educational resources, and reach out to customer service and see how quickly and accurately they respond. If you feel uncomfortable about anything in the trial phase, it's probably a sign of things to come if you sign up with that vendor. On the other hand, if you feel like the people at that company genuinely care about your experience, it's probably something that pervades the CRM vendor's culture.

Turn to Appendix A for a more complete list of criteria you can use to identify the best CRM for your business.

Finding reviews that matter

Reviews can be a tricky thing. Reading reviews about software companies can be similar to reading Yelp reviews about restaurants. Sometimes negative reviews are the result of unhappy customers who don't know what they're doing and are looking to blame the vendor. Sometimes reviews are written by people with unrealistic expectations. Sometimes reviews are totally bogus (both good and bad). A software vendor can only be expected to do so much, so take those reviews in context and place much higher value when the review calls out specific advantages, disadvantages, and experiences with that vendor.

REMEMBER

If you see a general positive trend from reviews, there's a good chance those reviews will reflect your experience with the vendor's sales process. If you see a disconnect between what you're experiencing and what others are experiencing, ask yourself why that might be happening. Are you setting unrealistic expectations? Have you done your homework so you know what questions to ask?

Check out a few review and information sites. Keep in mind that some of these sites are pay-to-play, meaning that vendors pay the review sites to have their software listed. In some cases, the more they pay, the higher they're listed, so there may be bias in almost every "independent" ranking website.

- **Gartner** (`www.gartner.com/reviews/home`): A site that caters to a large, enterprise business.
- **Expert Market** (`www.expertmarket.com`): A broad platform for evaluating all kinds of different business software.
- **GetApp** (`www.getapp.com`): A review site with a lot of content and easy comparing tools.
- **TrustRadius** (`www.trustradius.com`): This site contains indepth, detailed descriptions of different software platforms.
- **G2 Crowd** (`https://www.g2crowd.com`): A large review site with many reviews; categorizes and rates software companies.
- **Capterra** (`www.capterra.com`): A high-level, quick overview of major players in the software market.
- **Marketing Automation Club** (`www.marketing-automation.club`): Software review site focused on marketing automation software; provides detailed user stories of real-world examples.
- **Software Advice** (`www.softwareadvice.com`): A site that offers consultative help and can connect you directly with vendors.

Chapter 18 goes more indepth about these and other websites.

Evaluating pricing models

Just like all CRM companies are different in the software they offer, all of them also have different pricing models. You want to look at all the costs involved with getting your CRM up and running. This concept is called total cost of ownership (TCO).

TCO includes much more than the amount that you pay to the CRM vendor every month or year. Some additional costs to consider when deciding on the best CRM for you are

- **Per-user:** Some CRM platforms charge per user, as shown in Figure 3-1. You want to be absolutely sure to have one login per user for accountability reasons. If you need a lot of users, make sure you factor in those costs, as well as future costs as your company grows.

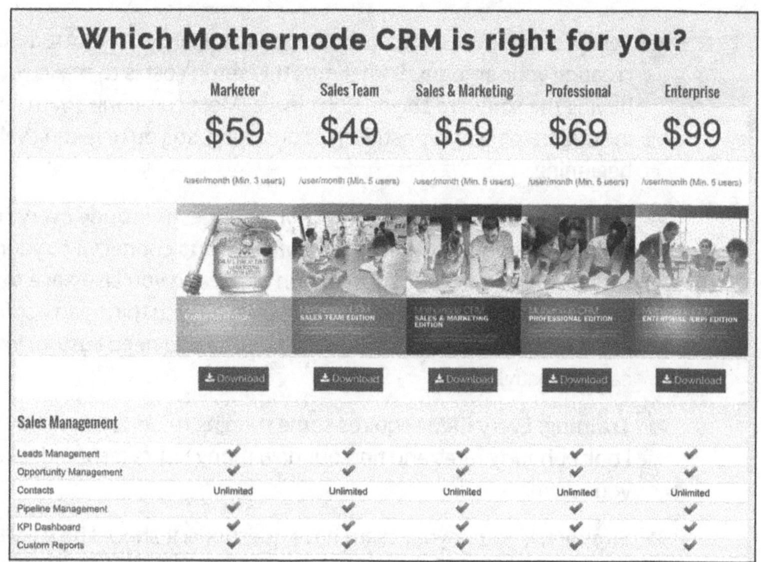

FIGURE 3-1: A CRM with per-user pricing.

» **Per-contact:** CRM platforms that include marketing tools sometimes charge per contact, as shown in Figure 3-2. This pricing structure may end up being more affordable, depending on the number of people in your company using the CRM. Be sure to find out whether there are costs or limitations for sending email, tracking websites, or other functions.

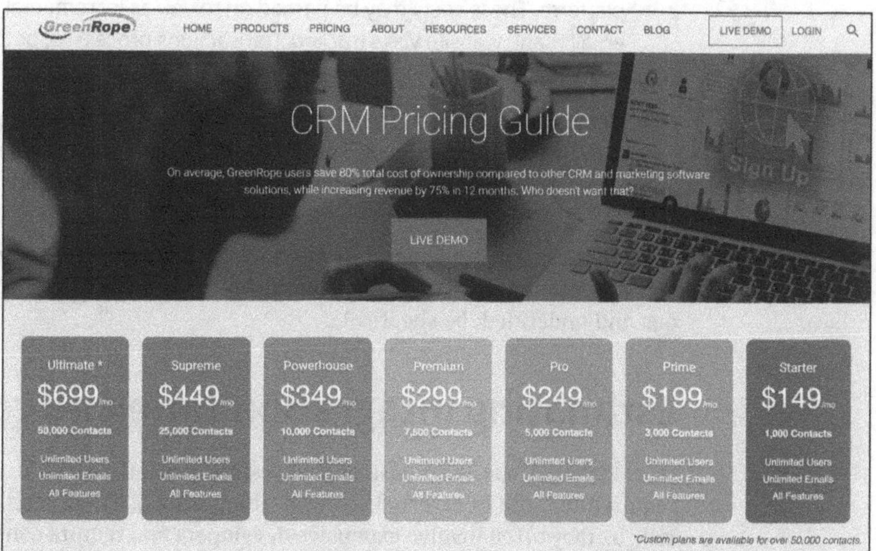

FIGURE 3-2: A CRM with per-contact pricing.

- **Setup:** Some CRM companies charge an initial upfront cost associated with creating your account. Sometimes this setup cost is to make you feel vested in buying the software so you don't leave. Most companies with setup costs include training and/or strategic consulting, so you're getting value from the beginning.
- **Integration:** If you're buying a CRM that doesn't include everything you need, you also need to buy third-party software and connect it to your CRM. That software likely also has subscription costs, and you also have to pay for integration. Automated integration, such as with third-party software providers like Zapier, is usually inexpensive, but if you need custom integration, it can be costly.
- **Training:** Every CRM requires some training to understand how to best use it. Look at hourly rates and find out how many hours it should take to onboard your team.
- **Support:** If you or your team have questions, it should be easy to get help. If you have to pay extra for email, phone, or live chat access to support, make sure you factor that in.
- **Custom setup:** If you want help setting up your CRM, there may be costs. Find out what is included in the definition of "support."
- **Creative:** If you need creative work done, such as designing an email template, building a landing page, or posting a lead capture form, there should be a given hourly rate, along with estimates for doing each.
- **Usage:** Most CRM platforms charge on a sliding scale with your usage of the platform. These costs may be passed on to you as incremental costs for emails sent, website visits tracked, transactions processed, or text messages sent and received.
- **Access:** If you want to use different parts of the CRM and its capabilities, there may be additional costs. Be sure to think through everything you want to use your CRM for and build in access to all the functions you need.

Take all these into consideration when you're looking at costs for your new CRM. If you're presented with an overly complicated cost schedule, or one that is ambiguous and undefined, be skeptical.

Estimating integration time and cost

In calculating the total cost of ownership, you also want to look at the effort required to build in external software integrations. These often carry the highest risk, as they often involve expensive developers and require considerable planning to manage interfaces that can be very costly to connect.

The high cost of integrating external software is one big reason to clearly define your CRM requirements before you look for a software vendor. The CRM has capability included in every account, but you might need specific functions outside the scope of the software.

TIP

If you need external software to plug into a CRM, hire a system integrator to help with making those connections. These companies come in all shapes and sizes, with vastly different recommendations and experiences. An integrator manages the entire process of piecing different software together to make all the software components of the CRM system work together. Remember that the more integration work you have to do, the more costly the system integration is, and the more high-priced expertise is required.

Any requirements that you have that are not included in the CRM require selecting and managing the integration process. If you aren't experienced with this process, you may find it to be a significant drain on your time and budget. Software developers and companies have a wide range of skills, both in development and management. A conservative rule for budgeting software development is to plan on it costing two to three times the original estimate, both in time and cost.

REMEMBER

Picking the right system integrator is just as important as picking the right CRM. Carefully evaluate how you intend to manage the integration between your CRM and any external software you need to connect it with. System integrators must have the same depth of understanding your requirements and how everyone in your team will use the other software systems. The system integrator has to know how your team uses the software, the data that is generated, and where that data must go.

Every successful CRM implementation requires understanding of what is needed and where the information flows. This understanding is needed regardless of whether you're integrating existing, legacy software or if you're purchasing new software that must plug into your CRM. Be sure to have these requirements and processes defined *before* you pick your CRM, as your system integrator must be comfortable working with all the software platforms involved.

Assessing service and support options

CRM, like your business, has a lot of moving parts. You don't want to go through it alone, and fortunately, good CRM companies have people who can help. The big question is, how easy and expensive is it to find that help?

Help from a CRM vendor should be available in a myriad of channels, so you want to know what is available to you, and what is included in your subscription. These are the most common methods of accessing help, along with questions you can ask the vendor:

- **Phone:** Can you call a number where someone answers? What are the hours of operation? If you leave a message, does someone get back to you? What is the expected response time?
- **Email:** How often are support emails checked? What kind of response time is expected?
- **Support ticketing system:** Does the vendor have a ticketing system in place? With support ticketing, you can easily reference a trail of responses and the issue remains open until it's resolved. Unlike email, which may be forgotten about if the notification gets deleted, a ticket stays open and the vendor's support staff can reference all their open tickets at any time.
- **Live chat:** You may want to initiate a chat via the vendor's website, rather than calling. Figure 3-3 shows a chat interface offered by one vendor. One advantage to chat is that the transcript should be emailed to you at the conclusion of the chat, so you have a record of it. If a similar problem arises in the future, you have a reference easily available.
- **Web conference:** Some problems are too complex to explain over the phone or through chat. In that case, you may need to get on a screen sharing session with someone to demonstrate where you're having issues.
- **Product-integrated resources:** To save time while you're working in the CRM, you want to be able to reference materials that can answer questions and show you how to do things. Some vendors include instructional videos, questions and answers, walk-through tutorials that lead you through using the platform, e-books, and whitepapers. Get familiar with what is available, how easy it is to find what you're looking for, how up to date the help files are, and how comprehensive the materials are.

Getting started with a CRM involves help and coaching from your CRM software vendor. Most CRM companies charge an upfront account setup fee that includes some measure of training and onboarding. Compare the different vendors you're evaluating to see the value you receive for this initial part of your relationship.

WARNING

Be wary of vendors who don't offer an onboarding or setup fee. If they believe you can figure things out on your own, there's a good chance you will be left trying to guess how to set up your CRM. Remember that CRM is as much software as it is business process management, so you want to work with a vendor who can help you connect all the dots in your business. Your CRM vendor must be able to help you get started and scale with you as you grow.

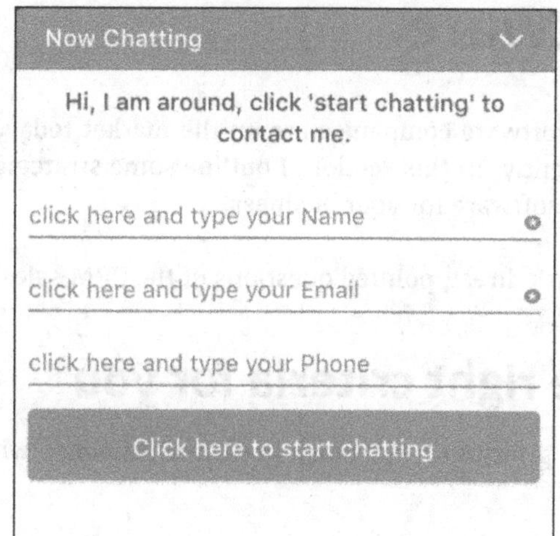

Now Chatting
Hi, I am around, click 'start chatting' to contact me.
click here and type your Name
click here and type your Email
click here and type your Phone
Click here to start chatting

FIGURE 3-3: Online chat is a great way to get support quickly.

Determining your need for outside assistance

If you don't have any experience designing, implementing, or even using a CRM, it may make sense to hire help. If your budget allows it, hiring an expert or two could save you thousands of dollars or hours in the future.

On the other hand, if you're reasonably business savvy and have the time set aside to work on your CRM, you may be able to do everything you need with only the help of the CRM vendor. The likelihood of requiring external help also depends on the CRM platform. A complex platform that requires a lot of external integration demands more expertise, both technical and strategic.

The first step in potentially hiring a consultant is to see whether you actually need one in the first place. Assess your team's experience and desire to work with the CRM vendor to implement your CRM.

The next step is to examine the onboarding process with the CRM software vendor. Depending on how complex your requirements are, how easy it is to set up the CRM, and how much external integration you need, you may not need a consultant. Your staff and the vendor's training team should have this meaningful conversation.

REMEMBER

If you determine you need someone to help you with your CRM, be rigorous about finding a good consultant. This person or team should be able to facilitate discussions with your staff, help you define your processes, and set up all the components of your CRM. You and your team must trust anyone helping you to have the experience and good intentions to guide you through a potentially big change in the way you do business.

Testing CRM Software

A lot of good CRM software companies are on the market today, but they all do things a little differently. In this section, I outline some strategies to use so that you choose the best software for your business.

REMEMBER

Do not be afraid to ask direct, pointed questions of the CRM sales team.

Finding the right criteria for you

Every business has priorities, and those priorities influence what you want in your CRM.

TIP

Create a matrix to weigh the contenders and pick the best one. Appendix A also includes a detailed list.

Use these criteria to judge the various CRM vendors on the market:

- **Capability:** Does the CRM do what you need it to do? What, if any third-party integrations do you need to meet your requirements? Are there any critical "must haves" that the CRM can't do?
  - *Sales:* Does the CRM manage opportunities easily? Can you set up funnels? Can you customize all the data fields you need? Can salespeople access and update information from a mobile app, if you need that functionality? Is it easy to see all the relevant data for selling and reporting? Is a leader-board available for motivating your team?
  - *Marketing:* Can you easily design and send emails? Is it easy to build automation like auto-responders and drip campaigns? Can you build behavioral logic into your communication? Does marketing data automatically become available to salespeople in real time? Can you send and receive text messages, and have those linked to contacts in the CRM?
  - *Events:* Can you set up internal meetings and public events and track registration and attendance? Can you automate follow-up appointments for those events?
  - *Support:* Can you easily set up a ticketing system with follow-up automation? Can you set up live chat and have that integrated into contact CRM records? Do inbound call recordings and transcripts automatically get attached to contacts?
  - *Operations:* Do emails sent and received from your inbox attach to the CRM automatically? Can you use a customizable dashboard to view your overall performance as a company?

* *Training:* Can you set up a learning management system (LMS) for tracking onboarding and HR-related progress? Does that data automatically sync up to the CRM?
* *Account management:* Does the CRM include project management with billing and invoicing? Can you track tasks and send invoices to clients?
* *Advanced analytics:* Does the CRM come with predictive analytics and the ability to set up custom lead scoring rules? Can you correlate campaigns to revenues and conversions?

» **Ease of use:** Is the CRM easy to learn? Can you accomplish important and frequent tasks easily, without an abundance of mouse clicks? Is the system fast?

» **Onboarding/help:** Are resources available to get you started? Does the vendor have a defined plan to help train you and your staff?

» **Support:** How accessible is support? What methods can you use to contact support? Is support onshore or offshore?

» **Price:** How much is the setup, and what is included? Is there a per-user cost? What other incremental costs are there to consider as you grow?

» **Contract:** Are you locked in for a long period of time? What are penalties for terminating your contract?

» **Reviews:** You can check out many websites for reviews of the vendor. What do other people say about the company? Are there significant strengths or glaring weaknesses that your sales contact can speak to?

» **Intangibles:** The vendor relationship always has a few undefined aspects to consider. Are the company's goals and culture in alignment with yours? Do you trust the people you talk to?

In each of these categories, break out specific details to rate each vendor. These details relate directly to your application, and can help you answer real-world problems with the CRM. Come up with a rating scale to go along with each detail, and total them for each category.

TIP

Each category also carries weight, or importance, to you. This weight determines the importance of a vendor excelling or failing at delivering something you want. Assign a weight to each of your criteria as a way to help you find the best vendor.

Eventually, you come to an answer for the best provider for your CRM software. This decision-making process can take some time, but a little extra time upfront helps avoid a costly mistake down the road.

Getting demos from vendors

Vendors should make it easy for you to see what their software looks like in real time. If a vendor won't show you its software platform at work with a lot of data in it, be wary.

REMEMBER

Request a demo of an account with a lot of data in it to see how the CRM looks and functions. If the demo shows convoluted steps and clicks to accomplish common tasks, take that as a warning.

Ask a lot of questions during your demo, but be sure to communicate to the salesperson what your business is about and what is most important to you. A good CRM company should be able to offer free tools (such as e-books, whitepapers, videos, or software) to help with your decision-making process.

TIP

My company, GreenRope, has created a free tool, JourneyFlow (`www.journeyflow.com`), to help you during the early stages of your CRM selection process. Fill out the easy-to-use, drag-and-drop application to design your processes before your get your demo, so you can ask the questions of the vendor to see whether it can accomplish the processes you need. Figure 3-4 shows a simple process flow diagram built with JourneyFlow.

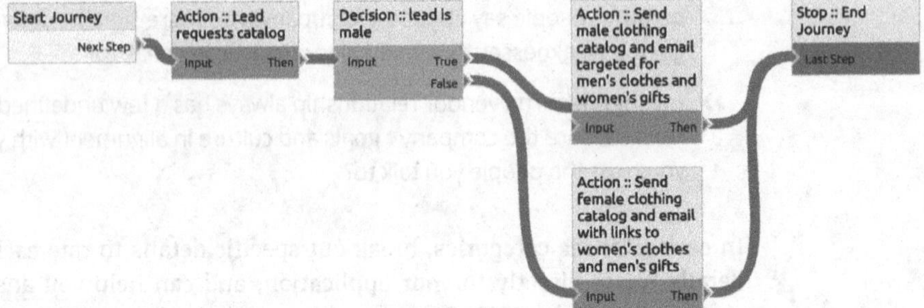

FIGURE 3-4: Start with a simple journey flow and build on it.

Playing around with trial accounts

A trial account is a good way to see what the software looks like when you use it every day. There are a few helpful things to look for when you're in your trial.

- **Welcome tools:** Do helpful tools show up while you're working in the CRM to show you how to do things? Are they easy to follow?
- **Help:** Is it easy to find help? What kind of resources are available? If you get stuck, are support people available? Is the help you get from human support reliable and courteous?

» **Limitations:** Most trial accounts limit what you can do, but is it so limited you can't get a feel for the software?

TIP

Spend a little time playing around the trial account, but don't go overboard. Remember that the vendor should have an onboarding team to help set up your account correctly, so if you dive into areas you aren't familiar with, you may need to undo what you build.

Making the Final Decision

After you've developed your requirements, collected all the decision-related information from CRM vendors that you need, and asked all the questions, it's time to make the big decision.

How to get buy in

Involving your key team members in the decision-making process is a good way to ensure buy in. A collaborative decision means people feel as though they have contributed to the decision, and take ownership in seeing your CRM come to fruition.

Chapter 2 discusses how to build a culture in your organization that sets up your CRM decision for success. Be sure you have addressed the cultural issues before you choose your CRM, or at least in parallel with this purchase process. Your leadership team is tasked with choosing the best software and getting the team behind it. The best CRM software in the world will fail if you and your management don't properly organize it.

Seeing things through to completion

After you've made the decision to use a particular CRM vendor, commit to it. Unless you see the vendor incapable of meeting a critical requirement, you're much better off working with your team and the CRM software.

You shouldn't stick with impossible software that doesn't work for you either; there may be a reason to pull the plug on a CRM vendor if you find it was deceptive about capabilities, radically changed its business model, or you suffer from exceedingly slow interfaces or significant downtimes. A number of vendors on the market offer good software, reliable support, and comprehensive training at a reasonable price.

Educating Users on Responsibility

After your CRM installation is complete, you need to make sure all who use your CRM understand the responsibility they hold when they have access to company data. Protection of your data must be on the forefront of everyone's mind, as accidental loss or theft can cause serious damage to your organization.

Adhere to a strong password policy. Gone are the days of "security through obscurity," where you hope no one knows where to log in to your private accounts. Make sure you and everyone in your company use passwords that mix letters, numbers, and characters and change them on a regular basis.

Installing the Right Data Security Tools

Your IT department no doubt has a lot of input on what software is installed on employees' computers and devices. Be sure any access to your CRM is over https (SSL), and if someone needs to access your CRM from a public, unsecured Wi-Fi, require a virtual private network (VPN) to connect to it.

TIP

Software companies like Avast (`www.avast.com`) offer VPN services to prevent hackers from intercepting your communications over unencrypted Wi-Fi. If you're at a coffee shop on a network that doesn't require a password, you need a VPN (see Figure 3-5) to prevent someone from reading the data you're accessing and potentially stealing your password.

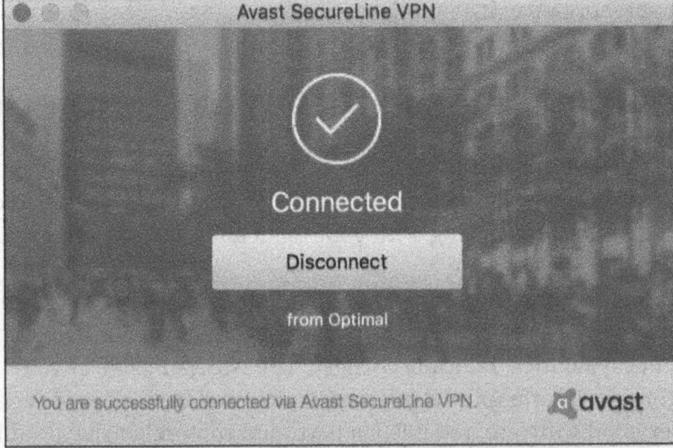

FIGURE 3-5: Avast VPN connects to the Internet securely, wherever you are.

PREPARING FOR SOCIAL ENGINEERING HUMINT ATTACKS

HUMINT, or Human Intelligence, is the gathering of information by tricking you into sharing information you shouldn't. You have probably seen or heard of callers impersonating someone to gather information such as a username, email address, or password. There are many news stories about how someone pretends to be the owner of a credit card and with just a couple pieces of public information about the person, the thief gets a new credit card issued and sent to a new address.

The best defense against HUMINT attacks is training and education. Be sure your team is prepared for these attacks and has a protocol to follow for every interaction with someone whose identity can't be verified by meeting that individual in person.

Your CRM should also support *two-factor authentication.* If someone accesses the CRM from a new computer, it should require a code that only the user has. The code, required on top of a username/password, is sent by text message or another authentication tool like Google Authenticator or Authy (`www.authy.com`) as a way to ensure access to the account is being given to the correct user.

A proven, up-to-date antivirus program is also very important. Be sure that all users run regular scans on their computers. If an anomaly is found, be sure everyone knows to take it to an IT professional immediately.

Training Your Staff

A good team knows how to use the tools they're given, and CRM is no exception. Your users should get comfortable using the CRM as quickly as possible. You must ensure everyone is on a training plan and has access to learning resources for self-study.

Every CRM vendor offers training to empower users to get the most out of the software. Too often, users try to power through the learning curve, spending far more hours than necessary. Rely on experts who can save you and your staff hours of searching for solutions to your more complex problems.

Sometimes experts are available to help you from within the CRM vendor's organization; other times the best experts are available as external consultants. Make sure that no matter whom you hire, the people who help you have experience setting up a CRM and understand your company's mission and marketing methods.

A reputable, established software vendor includes free educational resources for your team. Any good CRM vendor provides a wide array of helpful resources, such as recorded webinars, tutorial videos, and a searchable knowledge base, as shown in Figure 3-6. Your team should spend the time to learn from every method available.

Lesson 16 - Filters (Contacts & Emails)
Lesson 17 - Advanced Filters
Lesson 18 - Coupons
Lesson 19 - Website Tracking/Analytics
Lesson 20 - Conversion Tracking
Lesson 21 - Ticketing
Lesson 22 - SMS & Calling

Whiteboard Sessions

GreenRope Value Proposition
Groups, User Fields, and Tags
GreenRope CRM
Marketing Automation
Marketing Automation Tactics
Sales Automation
Email Marketing with GreenRope
GreenRope for Small Businesses
GreenRope for Legal Profession
GreenRope for Restaurants
GreenRope for Education (Schools)
GreenRope for Real Estate
GreenRope for Membership
GreenRope for Non-Profits
Overview Presentation

Recorded Webinars

Account Setup Best Practices
Before the Import
Customizing Email Templates
Calendaring
Signup Forms

Other Videos

Business Marketing Video
New GreenRope Account Welcome
GreenRope Animation
Who Is GreenRope

Your E-Books

High ROI Email Marketing
Effective CRM
CRM Buyer's Guide
Web Analytics & CRM
Marketing Automation Basics
Marketing Automation Planning Workbook
Campaign Marketing Basics
The Science of Growth

FIGURE 3-6: A good CRM vendor offers a plethora of resources for you.

Vendor-supplied support is another method of getting help. Be sure you're familiar with your CRM vendor's support policies. You should be able to access support via phone, email, and chat, as shown in Figure 3-7. If help is available, use it.

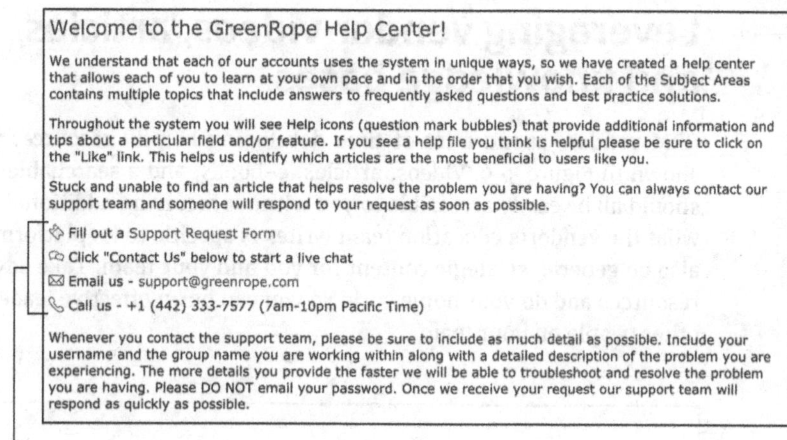

Welcome to the GreenRope Help Center!

We understand that each of our accounts uses the system in unique ways, so we have created a help center that allows each of you to learn at your own pace and in the order that you wish. Each of the Subject Areas contains multiple topics that include answers to frequently asked questions and best practice solutions.

Throughout the system you will see Help icons (question mark bubbles) that provide additional information and tips about a particular field and/or feature. If you see a help file you think is helpful please be sure to click on the "Like" link. This helps us identify which articles are the most beneficial to users like you.

Stuck and unable to find an article that helps resolve the problem you are having? You can always contact our support team and someone will respond to your request as soon as possible.

- Fill out a Support Request Form
- Click "Contact Us" below to start a live chat
- Email us - support@greenrope.com
- Call us - +1 (442) 333-7577 (7am-10pm Pacific Time)

Whenever you contact the support team, please be sure to include as much detail as possible. Include your username and the group name you are working within along with a detailed description of the problem you are experiencing. The more details you provide the faster we will be able to troubleshoot and resolve the problem you are having. Please DO NOT email your password. Once we receive your request our support team will respond as quickly as possible.

Vendors should offer a variety of support.

FIGURE 3-7: Multiple contact touchpoints for you to access.

Building muscle memory with walk-throughs

One of your primary goals is training all your new CRM users to be comfortable with working in the software every day. To that end, use the tools provided by the software vendor to educate your team.

Tools that walk users through their tasks step by step are powerful education resources and are an efficient way to get your team onboard. If the CRM has an integrated, interactive guide, it saves you a lot of explanation time and avoids repeating the same instructions over and over again. Take advantage of this kind of tool if one is built into your CRM.

Figure 3-8 shows a tool available on some CRM platforms. Leverage tools like that to get your team comfortable with using your CRM.

FIGURE 3-8: A walk-through initiated with the Guide Me button.

Leveraging vendor videos, articles, and knowledge bases

CRM vendors spend a lot of time developing helpful resources you can use, as shown in Figure 3-9. Videos, articles, e-books, and a searchable knowledge base should all be easily accessible to you without incurring additional charge. Some of what the vendor's education team writes is specific to its platform, but there may also be generic, strategic content for you and your team. Take advantage of these resources and do your homework, so you can be an effective leader and teacher to other people on your team.

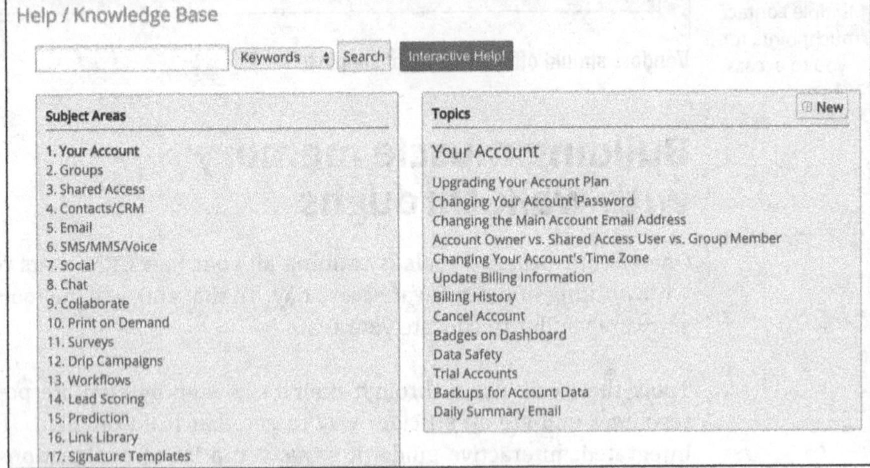

FIGURE 3-9: Searchable knowledge base with helpful topics.

Making dedicated resources available

Assign an internal champion, or team of champions, responsible for the implementation of your CRM. Champions ease the transition to your Complete CRM, answering questions and reminding team members of the benefits of change. Sending someone around to do individualized training is ideal, but may not be realistic.

You may want to teach a small class, invite the CRM vendor to host a web conference, or hold office hours. The more you can provide individualized help to your end-users, the more likely they adopt the new CRM into their everyday activities.

REMEMBER

Training, just like when interacting with your leads and customers, works best when it feels like a collaborative process. Your goals as the CRM manager are in alignment with your users' goals. You want them to work efficiently, leverage the power of software to help them be effective, and build a happy, productive work environment.

2

Setting Up Yourself for Success

IN THIS PART . . .

Apply proven marketing principles that feed your CRM.

Design buyer journeys so your CRM can capture and track leads through the sale.

Define the internal processes that you use with your CRM.

IN THIS CHAPTER

» Identifying who your buyers are and what they want

» Creating personas for each type of buyer

» Building a brand around what you communicate and your message

» Developing effective processes that convert leads into clients

» Avoiding key mistakes businesses often make in marketing

Chapter 4
Organizing Your CRM through Segments and Personas

Marketing and sales are inextricably linked. The people responsible for managing them must know what the other is doing, what is working, and why. A Complete CRM incorporates these two functions together into a single, connected platform. You can then break down silos in your organization, increasing collaboration and empowering your team to work more effectively.

Setting up your CRM to target and nurture different kinds of leads and clients is critical to grow your business. Deeper understanding of whom you're marketing and selling to helps you communicate and guide leads down their buyer journeys. Your business grows when you can serve your leads and clients better, which in turn builds stronger relationships and creates advocates for you and your brand.

In this chapter, you discover how to break your market into small segments so you can communicate to each of them differently. These segments translate directly into how you set up your CRM and the integrated marketing processes you design to convert the maximum number of leads into clients. The end result is messages optimized for each segment of your market, personalized and targeted to give the best chance for your leads to become clients, and for your clients to become advocates.

Segmenting Your Market

When marketing professionals use the word *segment*, they mean to break your total universe of potential customers into smaller pieces. Doing so gives you a greater understanding of who would become a customer and why. The more specific your message, the more people feel like you're speaking directly to them. Direct, personalized communication requires a CRM that allows you to collect and use the data about your market segments. Ultimately, you want to gain insight into understanding what motivates people to buy (or not buy) from you, so you can learn how to best serve the people who matter most to you.

REMEMBER

Knowing the "why" behind what people do gives you power. It gives you the power to analyze behavior, insight into influencing behavior, and ultimately, the ability to serve customers in the way they want to be served. Learning the "why" behind what motivates your target market helps you serve them better, which is the key to growing your business and staying competitive in the long run.

Choosing the right segmentation categories

You can segment your market in several ways. These all represent different data-driven aspects of people that set them apart. Generally speaking there are several main categories:

- **Geographic:** Knowing where someone lives can tell you a lot about that person. The language spoken, the weather experienced, and the political views of people in that area paint a broad generalization of a person's accessibility to and interest in your products and services.
- **Demographic:** Some of these characteristics, such as gender, birthplace, and height, are permanent. Some characteristics, such as interests, homeowner status, number of children, industry, or job title, change often.

- **Firmographic:** The company someone works for also determines what kind of products or services that person is interested in. If you sell a business-to-business product, this characteristic is especially important. Looking at the size of a company, the industry it's in, and who its customers are helps you identify whether that company is a likely candidate for you to sell to.
- **Situational:** When people partake in activities or find themselves in special situations, you have an opportunity to target them. Products or services related to holidays, travel, or specific situations where a product or service is needed fall into this category.
- **Behavioral:** Segmenting your market by behavior requires more of a fluid way to measure what people are doing. Different people engage with you differently, so the better you understand what your leads and contacts are doing, the more you can read into what they want and why. Tracking when someone reads one of your advertisements, visits your website, downloads your e-book, or watches your video are all examples of how you can segment your market by measuring behavior.
- **Psychographic:** Evaluating the personality traits of people can be challenging, but larger categories may be of use to you. Someone who is Type A versus being laidback may influence that person's purchasing behavior. If you can target people based on who they are as individuals, you can speak to fundamental needs.
- **Benefit:** Looking at how someone would benefit from using your product or service may be another way to segment your market. If you have a product or service that can be used in a variety of ways, you may want to communicate how your product can be used to different people. For example, if you are Apple, you might communicate the iPhone's camera features to people who travel a lot, but you might focus on business applications when marketing to professionals.

When you segment your market, look at all these categories. The more you use your CRM to group your leads and contacts into precise segments, the easier you can target those people with personalized messages.

You shouldn't rely purely on either demographic or activity-driven market segments. The measure of your target market is a combination of both. Review performance of your marketing and sales for each of the segments you're targeting, and see whether anything stands out as particularly high or low performing.

REMEMBER

Using a group-centric methodology to separate your significant market segments is a powerful way of organizing your CRM. By using groups, you build natural market segments into the way you look at your contacts.

Gathering data

One challenging aspect of running a business is organizing and compiling data about your contacts. People don't usually share details that allow you to segment them every way you want. Fortunately, there are ways to help you fill in information.

The first way is fairly obvious: Ask people to tell you. You can ask in a variety of ways, but like all exchanges, if you want information about someone, you need to give her a reason to offer it. Try these methods to fill in your current customer information database:

- **Put free content behind a form that captures data.** If you write a helpful e-book, whitepaper, or other educational piece, putting it behind a form that asks for basic information is a good way to start the conversation; see Figure 4-1. Don't ask for too much or people resist. And make sure the content is truly valuable. Access to statistics people can reuse for their own purposes, insights into how to do something better, or even simple how-to guides are all great ways to incentivize people to give you information you can use to target them more precisely.

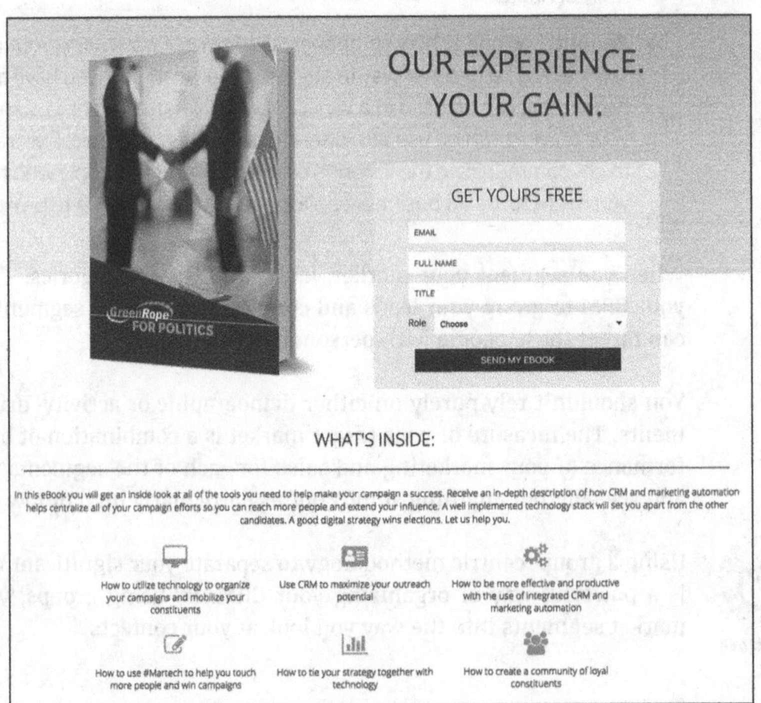

FIGURE 4-1: A landing page with useful content behind a form.

» **Send emails with "update profile" calls to action.** If you can remind your contacts to update their records and preferences with you, you can subtly and continuously create a stream of new data that you and your team can use. Usually calls to action for recipients to update their profile are not the primary call to action in a message, and you must be careful to not detract from the primary purpose. Figure 4-2 shows how you can include a link at the bottom of any email you send.

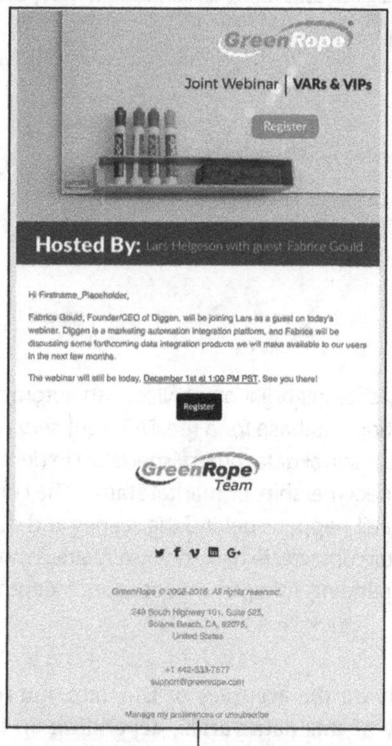

FIGURE 4-2: A link at the bottom of this page reminds subscribers to manage their preferences.

» **Send a survey to your database.** Asking people for information again usually requires an incentive, such as a discount. (See Figure 4-3.) The difference between a survey and a form is that you can send surveys to your existing client base. These surveys can be indepth and you can ask anything you want, storing the responses in your CRM and using scoring to activate automation around responses. (Turn to Chapter 11 to find out how to automate marketing around specific responses.)

REMEMBER

The more you ask, the more valuable the incentive needs to be to encourage people to complete your survey.

Hi Lars,

We want to hear from you! At GreenRope, we strive to be the best business partner and facilitator of your success we can be! Our platform was designed by entrepreneurs, sales professionals and marketers just like you to create the most integrated, user-friendly CRM and marketing automation system out there.

To help us keep our promise to you, please take a moment to fill out this short survey and let us know how we can improve! Once we receive your feedback, we will issue you a 10% discount off your next month's bill.

Click Here to Take our Survey

As always, if you have any questions, contact us! We are here to help!

Happy Holidays and thank you for being a part of the GreenRope family!

Sincerely,

Lars Helgeson & The GreenRope Team

FIGURE 4-3: An email that offers a discount to encourage users to take a survey.

» **Append data.** Third-party data aggregation services can automatically add relevant data to your existing database for a fee. Different services are available; some specialize in social data, others specialize in demographic data, such as income, homeownership, or marital status. The convenience with data appending is that it happens behind the scenes and doesn't require any participation from your contacts. Expect to pay a fee depending on the amount of data you're appending. (Chapter 8 goes more indepth on data appending.)

WARNING

Be careful to not rely entirely on the accuracy of the data you receive from data appending services. Accuracy of this data varies, depending on the data provider and the leads you're targeting. Social data and links tend to be accurate if you use an email address to find someone, but other methods may rely on out-of-date public information and may mislead you. Your own data collection from asking contacts or leads to update their own data is likely to be more accurate.

Ideally, your organization should be using all four methods to populate your database with current, relevant data. The more data you collect and store in your CRM, the easier it is for your team to target, measure, and convert leads to customers.

Organizing leads, contacts, accounts, and companies

Setting up your CRM to handle different kinds of data associated with people and businesses you work with requires considerable forethought. Do not jump into your CRM and set up fields, groups, campaigns, or any major structures without doing your homework first.

Leads and contacts are treated differently by different CRM software platforms. Traditional CRMs tend to separate these as separate objects. To these older CRMs, contacts usually apply to customers, while leads have yet to become customers. This terminology can cause confusion to users and often requires considerable workarounds, as people can be both.

Modern Complete CRM platforms combine leads and contacts, as they recognize the complexity of the buyer journey doesn't make sense for leads and contacts to be separated at such a fundamental level. Contacts are people, and those people can be customers of one product or service you sell, but leads for a cross-selling or up-selling opportunity. A single contact may be both lead and customer, at different stages of multiple buyer journeys. The better you understand those journeys, the better you understand the people and companies who buy from you.

Create a standardized language within your organization when referencing contacts at different stages of the buyer journey. Doing so ensures data is accurately entered into your CRM, and during strategic discussions, everyone is on the same page.

Accounts and companies are often used synonymously and represent collections of contacts. Everyone working for the same company is part of the same "account." Some CRM platforms use "company" to represent a company or organization as a way to simplify the jargon.

TIP

Go through your market segmentation analysis before you start organizing your CRM. Some CRMs refer to these groups of contacts as "campaigns" and others may tag contacts that share common traits, such as "All leads," or "Leads who have downloaded this e-book."

In addition to grouping by market segment, consider grouping your contacts according to who has access to them. For example, a salesperson should only be able to see contacts that he is working with. A sales manager should be able to see contacts associated with the salespeople who work under her, but not necessarily every contact in the CRM, as shown in Figure 4-4.

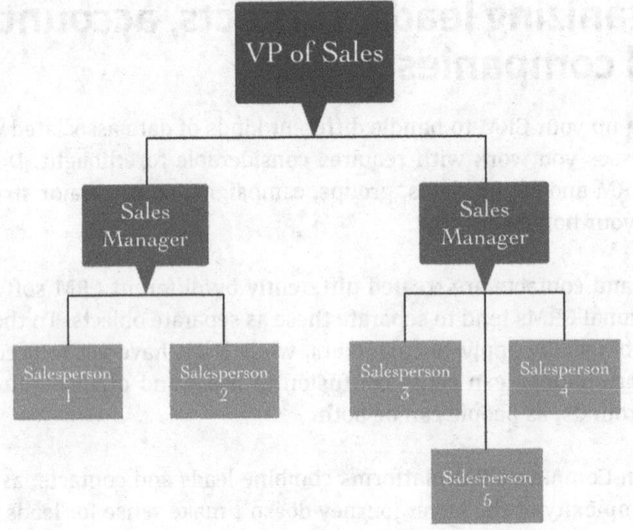

FIGURE 4-4: Typical sales manager group hierarchy.

Contacts, companies, and groups may also have other objects associated with them. Opportunities, or potential sales, may be attached to individual contacts or companies. You may want to start automated marketing campaigns to all members of a group (for example, drip campaigns for all new clients). If your CRM is combined with a project manager or support ticketing system, you want to see projects and tickets associated with companies as an easy way to view what's happening in your relationship with that company. Your CRM should help you identify which contacts within a company are doing what, and who the key players are in making the buying decision. Figure 4-5 shows how different objects can be attached to a single group of contacts.

TIP

Be cognizant of how you use your custom user-defined fields to segment your contacts and companies. (See Chapter 7 to set up user-designed fields.) You may not need a high-level group separation if you rely on those custom fields for minor customization, such as mail-merging your emails. Be sure to discuss this idea with your CRM vendor; it can become complex.

Every company organizes contacts and companies differently, as every company has unique segments and how to approach them. Take the time to draw out your market segments and processes, and then approach your grouping strategies.

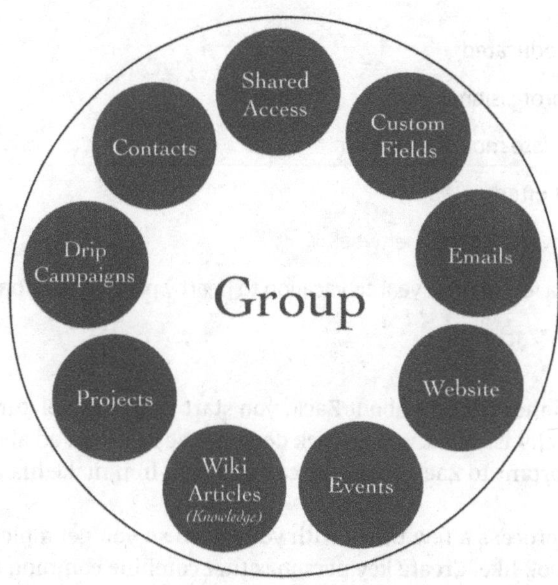

FIGURE 4-5: Attach objects to groups to give your CRM flexibility.

Identifying Buyer Personas

A buyer persona is a representation of someone in your market of potential buyers. These personas are estimates, stereotypes of people who are or will be clients. As you learn about your market and gather information about your clients and their habits, your personas evolve as well.

REMEMBER

You set up groups and processes in your CRM with your personas. Personas also drive your brand and the voice you use to communicate with people similar to your personas.

Brainstorming the persona

Start a persona by taking a few key segments and combine them together. For example, a 20-something male who lives in Los Angeles and likes baseball. From there, you can expand to include a few other items of interest to build a list of attributes:

- 25 years old
- Male
- Lives in urban Los Angeles
- Likes baseball (attends ten Dodgers games per year)

» College educated

» Young professional

» Drives a late model sports car

» Eats out often

» Works over 50 hours per week

» Travels a few times a year to vacation to nearby places in California and Mexico

» Call him "Zack"

As you fill in more details about Zack, you start to create a picture in your mind of who Zack really is. What would Zack do when he reads an ad about your product? What's important to Zack, and how can you help him make his life better?

Repeat this process a few times with your team so you get a picture of what your customers look like. Create key personas that combine common attributes of people who would buy your products or services.

REMEMBER

Buyer personas help create an image in your mind of your buyers. They connect emotion to data, which is important in creating messaging that resonate with your market. The more you understand your market and can communicate on an emotional level, the more you can sell to that market.

TIP

Don't limit personas to people. Create a persona for any company that is a client if you're selling B2B. You can draw a generalized company based on size, location, brand, and target market. If you can sell to XYZ Corporation, you can sell to its competitors.

Using personas to outline process

After you have a few personas drawn up, you can then examine how you want to sell to them. Chances are, someone in your company has sold to people or companies similar to your personas. If your organization has been in business for a while, you may have data that backs up what works.

Based on your experience and research, your next step is to design a process — a buyer journey — to sell to those personas, as shown in Figure 4-6. Start with how they find out about you, at the early awareness stage, and move along to the sale. Think how you want the personas to move in a single sequence.

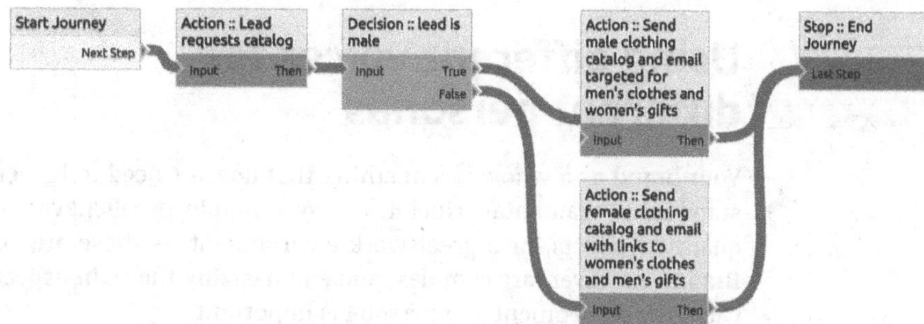

FIGURE 4-6: A simple buyer journey based on gender.

When you have a single sequence of actions, you can build a complete journey for each persona. It may be that there is little variation between different buyer personas going through their journeys, but it's still a useful exercise.

Connecting personas and journeys to your CRM

After you understand your buyers and how they buy from you, you can define requirements for your CRM.

Your buyers have characteristics that you can track in the CRM. Use these characteristics o build your *data model*, the fields that you use to track important information about your contacts. These fields could be demographic or activity data.

The process of buying from you should be modeled within your CRM. The CRM should give you the ability to graphically view your buyer journeys and track them as they progress toward becoming customers in real time.

Developing Your Best Brand

Your brand is a big deal. It encompasses the entire process of recognition of your organization, along with the emotional response when people see or hear of you. The point of personalization is as much communicating relevant information as it's conveying your brand in the way you want to everyone individually.

Your CRM manages your sales and marketing, and the impact of your brand is seen in how your leads and contacts interact with your business. Your brand is a constantly evolving thing. As your brand strengthens, weakens, and changes, you see an impact in buyer behavior. Use your CRM to measure how your brand impacts the effectiveness of your sales, marketing, and operations.

Using different voices for different personas

Your brand as a whole is something that doesn't need to be personalized. If you stand for fundamental principles — for example, excellent customer service, high quality products, or a great work environment — those are good for everyone. Brands, however, are complex, and emphasizing the right aspect of your brand to each market segment and persona is important.

REMEMBER

Different aspects of your brand resonate with your target market because people place value on different things. One persona you develop may be very sensitive to great customer service. Another persona may care about a specific feature of a product.

When you design your CRM and build processes for marketing and sales, your understanding of your market segments and buyer personas drives how you talk to them. Given how inundated people are with marketing messages, it's critical to use the little time you have with your target market to communicate what matters most to them. Your buyer personas should each be targeted with communication that showcases the benefits of why they should choose *you*. Figure 4-7 shows an email customized to the receiver.

The CRM fills in information to personalize this email.

Dynamic Data Rule #3

Rule Name: State is Oregon?

If State is Oregon

Replace placeholder with:

We have a special deal for residents of Oregon! Due to a tax incentive available to homeowners here, you have access to a rebate on your solar panels if you are a homeowner.

+ Add another "if" case

Otherwise, replace placeholder with:

Because you live in State_Placeholder, we can offer you a federal rebate on your solar panels.

FIGURE 4-7: Personalizing emails based on state changes your voice and message.

Changing your tone for different channels

Tone has a lot to do with how you reach your buyer personas. How you communicate your vision also can change, depending on which channel you use to communicate. When you segment your market by demographics or behavior, you can and should customize the way you communicate over different media.

Consider the way people use media. If you advertise with pay-per-click campaigns, you can test different pain points in short text snippets. If you post on social media, be cognizant of what your followers tend to do with the content you write. If you write long form, such as a blog or an e-book, you can take time to educate and explain details.

Testing Your Brand

The most important aspect of your marketing is the ability to learn and adapt. When you create a new campaign, you need to anticipate how well it will do without getting feedback. This feedback is critical to your future success.

Finding the right measurement criteria

Measuring exactly how well your marketing is doing can be difficult with some media. Radio, TV, and billboards are notoriously hard to attribute new business to. Press releases and other forms of PR are similarly difficult because there is no direct way to track how someone heard about your product or service.

Modern digital marketing changes all that. Online advertising, email marketing, and contributing content all provide ways for you to set up trackable links to your website. These links allow you to pinpoint exactly who is coming from where, and whether those people are buying from you.

TIP

Measuring attribution is usually done by tagging people with the source that drove them to you. Oftentimes, this is a campaign ID, which can then be attached to your leads and clients. Campaign IDs are another way you can segment people. A lot can be learned from tagging contacts with a campaign, often influencing how much and when you invest in marketing to those contacts.

Figure 4-8 shows how different campaigns can have different impacts on behavior.

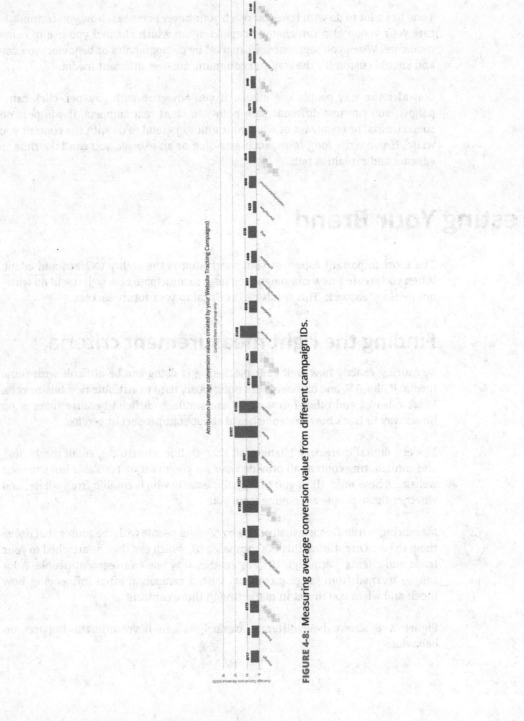

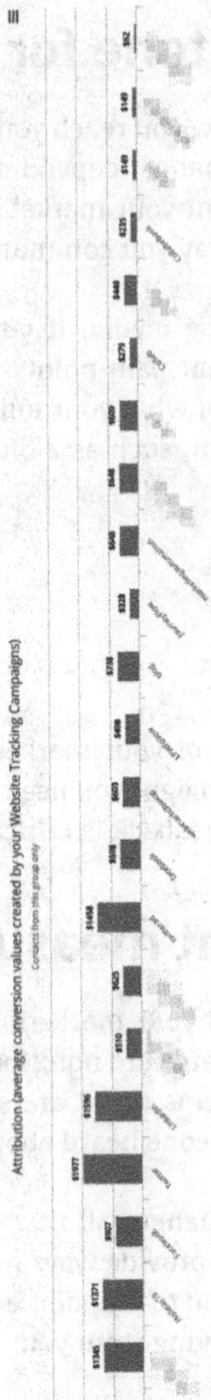

FIGURE 4-8: Measuring average conversion value from different campaign IDs.

In many ways, developing your brand is like designing your house. You want to have a theme, but you don't want to say the exact same thing over and over again. You can and should experiment with different imagery and headlines to see what resonates with your audience. With every message, be sure to check in with your brand and the voice you want people to hear.

One common method of testing your voice is an A/B test. With an A/B test, you set up two versions of a media piece (for example, two webpages or two different versions of an email newsletter) to see which one performs better. You must be careful to only change one element between the two (such as a color scheme). Otherwise, you could measure the wrong variable.

To be able to test anything, you must have a way to measure how people react to your brand testing. You can do so because your CRM tracks both marketing and sales performance. When you measure two different campaigns, track initial response and behavior all the way through the buyer journey, as shown in Figure 4-9. You see how and why different campaigns perform differently.

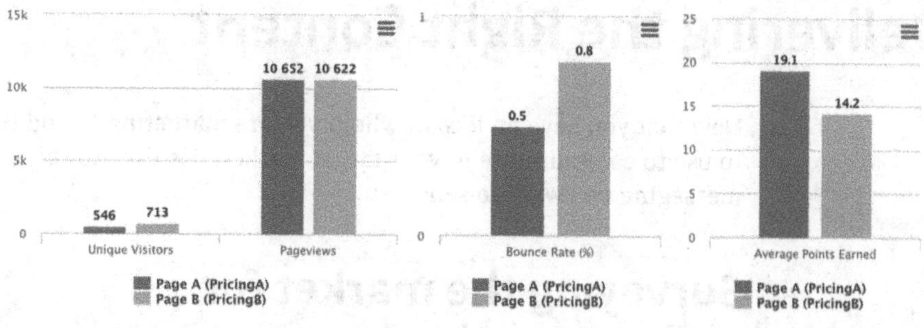

FIGURE 4-9: You can gather meaningful results from A/B split testing.

One practical example of A/B testing is to test your brand's voice by showing two different headlines, varying the headline text. If you keep the rest of the message the same (the content and design), you'll know for sure that the headline made the difference and not some other element.

Learning from test results

After you've accumulated data, you can use that information to adjust your marketing and sales to be more effective. Adjusting the delivery of your message based on what you know takes discipline and thought.

Testing is why the concept of Complete CRM is so critical. If you don't incorporate enough data, you come to the wrong conclusions. For example, if you don't measure the traffic you get from social media, you may think that your Twitter posts don't drive anyone to your website. Or worse, you might only measure the data that Twitter provides you, and not track people through to purchase. Twitter may report thousands of people visiting your website, but if they're not buyers, you may be losing opportunity by targeting the wrong people or even using Twitter at all.

REMEMBER

Learning from your testing is a multidisciplinary endeavor, and it's something you must do constantly. You must track how your leads and clients react to your marketing through the entire buyer journey, so you know what you should measure when you change parts of that journey.

If you change the way you target a market segment, your CRM should track how that is affecting your sales process. Does it impact the number of sales you make? The average amount of revenue generated per customer? The kinds of products or services offered? By encapsulating the entire buyer journey in a single system, it's easy to see the impact quantitatively.

Delivering the Right Content

Now that you have an idea of whom you are marketing to and the voice you want to use to communicate to your target market, it's time to think about the kind of messaging you want to send.

Surveying the market for delivery methods

Most marketers call the messaging they send to their target markets *content. Content marketing* is fast becoming a household term for anyone who does sales and marketing, but what does it really mean?

Everything you communicate has some amount of content in it. Your goal with CRM is to help store that content and track which content is best received. This data gives you insight into why, helping you continuously improve how you market and sell to your target market.

REMEMBER

When you write content for your audience, the more useful and helpful that content is, the better. People are tired of being sold to and don't respond well to repetitive "buy this now" messaging. They want to connect with the brands they buy from. Think about how you can make that connection.

Here are points to consider:

» **What kind of content you want to deliver:** Ask yourself how you can be of service to your target market. What are their pain points? Is there educational material that can help them to address those pain points in a generic way?

Many industries base their messaging on fear, uncertainty, and doubt, and many companies sell products based around that. Can you help dispel myths of those fears with tips and tricks anyone could benefit from? Would links to resources for more information provide confidence in the information you're providing?

Figure 4-10 shows how you can offer useful information to leads as a way to gather their information. After it's provided, you can start an automated marketing campaign or connect the lead with one of your salespeople.

What is Unified Marketing?

Mission Suite is the only online software that combines CRM, Email, Inbound and Automation into a single, easy to use platform that amplifies your efforts and saves you time.

Fill out the form below to see first hand how unified marketing works.

Name	Company
Phone	Email

Get Started Today

Are Your Current Sales and Marketing Solutions Not Giving You the Results You Want?

You already know marketing automation, email marketing, and CRM can help your company generate more revenue all while working less, BUT...

So far you're not seeing the results you'd hoped for.

You've got a skilled sales and marketing team. You've got all the best marketing tools and systems in place.

FIGURE 4-10: Create trust by making useful content available.

» **How to deliver your content:** Where does your target market go for information? Do they read blogs? Do they get their information from social media? Who are the influencers and can you reach them to become advocates of your products and services?

TIP

In the business-to-business arena, you may want to follow a generally accepted process of directing people to a landing page, where they provide their email address in exchange for a whitepaper or e-book, as shown in Figure 4-11. If that is a method you employ, how will you make it easy for someone to provide what you need to get into your sales funnel? Make your forms short and your calls-to-action clear.

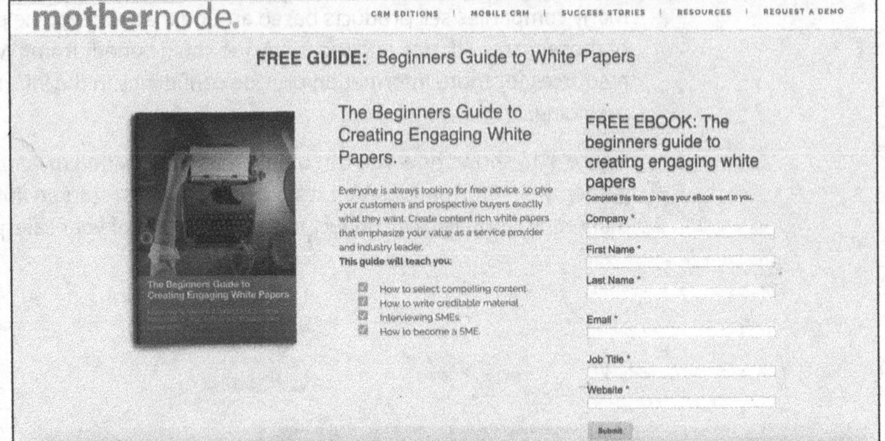

FIGURE 4-11: Collect contact information in exchange for useful tools.

Adapting content strategy for different channels

Apply the same personalization you do in your email marketing (see Chapter 10) to all your channels. Your content is different, depending on how that content is consumed. Someone reading a blog or an e-book has more time than someone on Facebook or Twitter, so you can go more indepth. If you're writing content for social media, it needs to be short, to the point, and more emotional with human interest.

TIP

You can also repurpose existing content into different channels. If you write a blog post or e-book, take excerpts and post them in social media as teasers for your longer content. If you have a long video, make a trailer that calls attention to some key points, driving interest in watching the longer film.

Figure 4-12 shows how you can use a blog to create compelling content for your target market. By becoming an expert in a field, you bring your target market to your website.

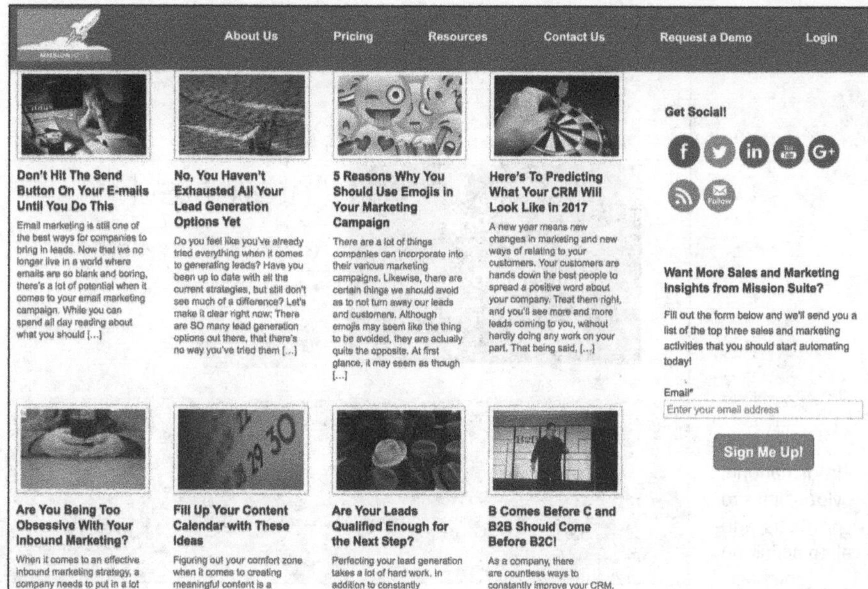

FIGURE 4-12: Use a blog to provide leads and clients with detailed information.

Examples of good content

You can generate content for your leads and clients in a number of different ways. Here are some examples:

- Webinars
- Instructional videos
- Videos interviewing your staff or thought leaders
- Whitepapers (short informational papers on a specific topic)
- E-books or printed books
- Landing pages
- Blogs
- Video blogs
- How-to guides
- Buyers' guides
- Email newsletters

Figure 4-13 shows how one company has embedded a video to tease customers with.

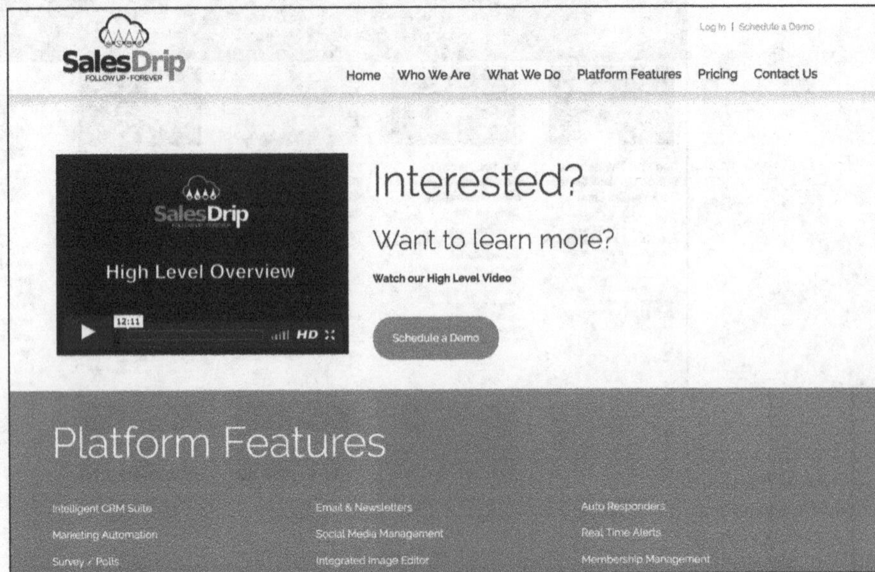

FIGURE 4-13: Informational video, links to products, and call to action on one page.

Avoiding Content Saturation

Writing a lot of content isn't enough. It has to be relevant and useful. Every day, people and companies are posting more content, and it's hard to stand out. To be successful, you must cut through the noise.

Sticking to relevant content

Remember a few important tips when writing content:

- **Be clear who you are writing your content for.** Remember to take the time to look at your market segments and understand what they want. If you're solving a problem that is specific to a market segment, it's much more likely to be read than something directed at all of humanity. For example, content you publish on LinkedIn would be different than content you publish on Facebook, as shown in Figure 4-14.
- **Solve one problem at a time.** People have short attention spans. If you can't summarize your content into a short paragraph, consider breaking it into different pieces. Your readers are more likely to absorb and remember the message you're sending if that message is simple and of singular purpose.
- **Be relevant.** Most important is being relevant. Because there is so much content available to everyone all the time, anything you create must have meaning for the recipient.

» **Before you publish, think carefully about the value you are providing.** There are a few questions that you can ask before you click Send or Post. Does it really help? Does it support your brand? Is it in the right voice? Will people care about this?

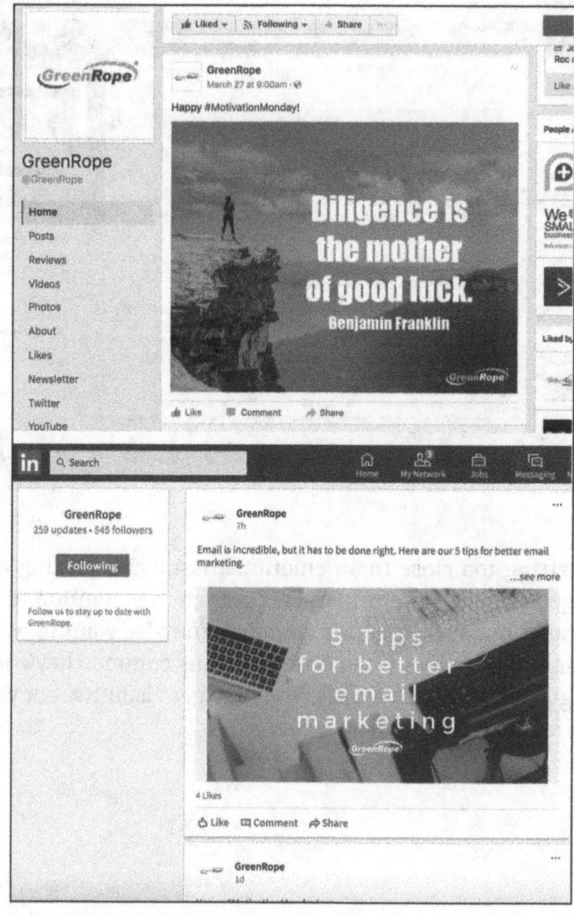

FIGURE 4-14: Content you publish on LinkedIn (bottom) has a different style and voice than the content on other social media (top).

Writing specialized content for your audience

Sometimes you have an opportunity to communicate with your market in extraordinary times. When you can capitalize on trends, recent news, or new developments, strike while the iron is hot. People respond to emotionally driven concepts, so if you can take advantage of current events, you can capitalize on those emotions and drive engagement.

Figure 4-15 shows one part of a multi-channel approach to marketing. The founder of the company was interviewed, and a blog was published about the interview afterward. Having timely content posted captures more mindshare when shared across channels.

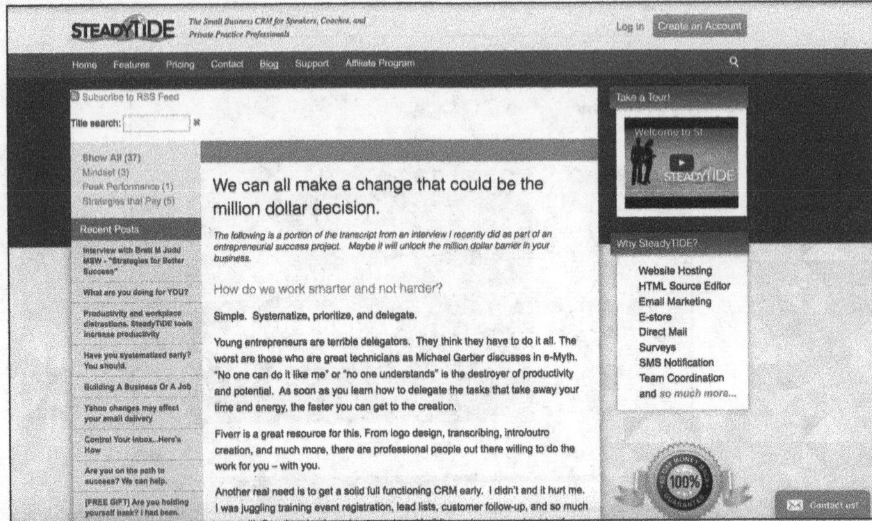

FIGURE 4-15: This post was written after the company founder was interviewed.

Be careful getting too close to an emotional issue and picking a side that could offend a large segment of your market. Leverage the emotion to get engagement with your brand, but avoid creating enemies. You also want to be careful of *news-jacking*, writing content about your business using common keywords and hashtags related to significant current events. You may get visibility, but you may also create negative sentiment around your brand.

IN THIS CHAPTER

» Maximizing exposure to you and your brand

» Making the first impression a good one

» Building process that converts leads to clients better than anyone else

» Turning customers into advocates

Chapter 5
Creating Story Arcs and Buyer Journeys with CRM

The journey that someone takes from first exposure to your brand to becoming a customer can be a long and complex one. In many ways, this journey is similar to a story, with twists and turns and unpredictable parts. That doesn't mean you have no control over a customer's journey. To the contrary, good process combined with solid understanding of your market gives *you* the power to write the story for your customers.

The story of a customer's journey may be long, and there may be many variations to it, but you can your CRM to measure the entire journey. When you combine all the steps in a customer's journey into a single, flexible platform, you can track and influence that journey.

REMEMBER

Keeping track of where customers come from and the journey they take with your company is why Complete CRM is so important.

In this chapter, you master how to design your business around the journey your customers take (called the buyer journey, but you also hear it called the customer journey). You measure how journeys start, how to track progress, where to automate reactions to deviations from your intended journeys, and how to convert a maximum number of leads into clients and clients into advocates. The ultimate goal is to use your CRM to create the best customer experience possible, personalized for each individual, to build your brand and grow your business.

Building Brand Awareness

If no one knows your company exists, there is a very small chance someone will buy from you. To generate leads and interest in your organization, you must first generate awareness. No matter how large or small your business, the awareness of your brand directly correlates to the number of leads that enter your sales funnel.

You have many tactics to generate awareness. Most methods have some amount of *attribution* built in, meaning you can identify the clients who found you through each marketing channel.

Offline advertising

The per-impression cost is often less than online advertising, but advertising offline is more difficult to track. You want to do everything you can to identify people by the campaign they came from. Special URLs, QR codes, or promotional codes that give people discounts are a great way to do so.

SEO

Search engine optimization (SEO) is all about driving organic traffic to your site. Digital marketers use the word "organic" to mean "not paid for." Organic searches happen when people search for something relevant to your product or service, and Google tells them that you have a relevant and helpful site.

Online advertising/pay-per-click (PPC)

When you advertise on the web, one huge advantage is that your efforts are trackable. After someone clicks or taps a link, you can capture all the resulting activity until sale. The problem is that those clicks tend to cost more money than other advertising efforts.

The goal for your PPC ads is to bring people to pages where they start their buyer journey. Figure 5-1 shows a typical landing page, with a video, call to action near the top of the page, and supporting information below.

FIGURE 5-1: Landing page with educational video and call to action.

Retargeting

Retargeting is the practice of displaying ads to people who have visited your website. You can get very specific with retargeting and show ads that are particular to certain pages, products, or services. When you know a lead has looked at a particular page on your website, you can customize the ad to remind that visitor what was on that webpage.

Social media

Each social media network works differently. You want to be careful sharing too much business-related content to your Facebook friends. You want to limit how much you share personally on LinkedIn. The larger your network, the more awareness you generate.

Take a look at the general usage pattern for people on various social networking sites. For example, Digg and Pinterest both share content, but Digg is focused on news and business, while Pinterest is for consumer-facing brands and sharing design and creative ideas.

Social media sites also have their own advertising, which may prove to be useful for you. Displaying retargeting ads on social media is a great way to remind people about you after they leave your website.

Retargeting on social media is a very effective way to follow and target people after they have visited your website. Because people spend so much time on social media, it's a great opportunity to stay top of mind.

Figure 5-2 shows how a retargeting ad showed up on my Facebook feed.

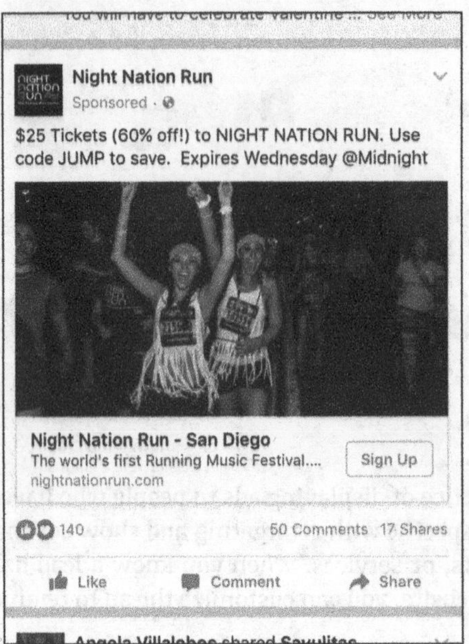

FIGURE 5-2: A retargeting ad on my Facebook feed.

Improving Brand Perception

Before a story can begin, there has to be a main character. The story that your lead hears starts with the first impression of your company. With the majority of the buyer journey being completed before someone ever talks to you, it's important you're aware of what your brand looks like to an outsider. Take the position of your buyer as the protagonist in your story and help that protagonist find the happy ending with your organization.

People won't go on journeys or engage with your story if you have a negative brand perception. Your brand is critical in reducing what marketers call "risk of purchase." A strong brand that communicates that you sell a product of value encourages people to engage with your marketing. This positive perception of your company drives revenue and interactions with your sales and marketing content, which in turn gives you more information about your target market, helping you sell better to them. This feedback is good for business.

Building your reputation

Because your reputation is so important to give your leads the confidence that your organization is one to work with, you should conduct some background research on your brand. If your target market finds negative information about you online, your leads' journeys could stop before they start. Your goal is to minimize any fear or risk associated with visiting your website, interacting with you on social media, or sharing any information about you.

Type your company name into Google's search bar and see what you find. It gives you a good idea of what other people find when they do the same thing.

Most industries have review-driven websites. For example, G2 Crowd and TrustRadius cover the software industry. Find the review sites where your company is listed, and encourage your clients to visit those sites and leave reviews for you.

Reviews represent an investment in time. You can offer an incentive for a review — for example, 10 percent off the next purchase — but make sure you're clear that it's not an incentive to leave a positive review, only a review.

Software as a Service providers provide *social listening* services, which may be of use to your marketing team. They give you insight into your brand presence and sentiment around your brand on social networks. Listening to what people say about you and why points you in the direction of happy and dissatisfied customers, while also showing what you can do to prevent and resolve problems with your customers' experiences.

Figure 5-3 is a review of my company, GreenRope, on Google. Notice how the basic information is there, along with some review data. Google attempts a fair and balanced summary in the area, including both positive and negative.

TIP

If a reviewer has a genuine problem, try to fix it. But if the reviewer left a review only to complain or unnecessarily criticize, it's best to leave the review alone and let it sink to the background. Review sites don't generally remove reviews, and if you respond or try to get it removed, you call undue attention to it.

Making it easy to support your customers

The customer experience is vital to how you're perceived in the market, particularly when you have a complex product or are a service-based organization. If customers have issues with you and can't get those problems resolved, they often find places online to vent.

REMEMBER

It is a generally accepted phenomenon that when you have any presence on the web, the negative experiences written about your company outnumber the positives 20 to 1. You also hear about only 5 percent of the complaints. For every happy customer, you have to work extra hard to get that person to share his positive experience. It also means that if you hear something negative, chances are good a lot of other people are experiencing the same thing.

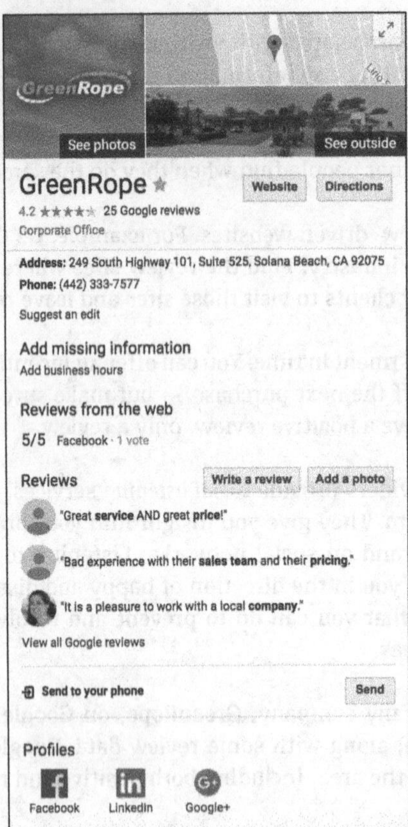

FIGURE 5-3: A typical review on Google.

The best way to offer outstanding support to your clients is to make it easy for them to talk to someone in your company, or at least get answers to their questions. If you're on social media, have someone monitor it. If you have a website and have the personnel to manage it, offer a live chat widget, as shown in Figure 5-4 (see Chapter 9). If you have more complex cases, set up a ticketing system (see Chapter 8). These should be linked to your CRM automatically, so you can track who is having issues and why.

When you manage the way customers get help, you can also set up automation to improve their overall experience. Ask for feedback about their experience. While you don't want to engage in outright pandering, if you know a lead or a client is a heavy influencer in your market, you may want to pay special attention to what that influencer says. A positive or negative customer experience may impact a great number of leads, so be cognizant of how someone's interaction with your company could inspire her to share her story.

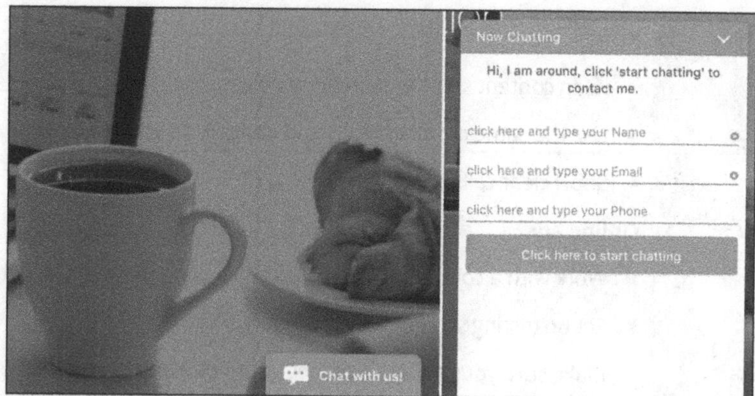

FIGURE 5-4: Use a live chat widget to engage with leads and customers.

Making the Best Contact the First Time

First impressions are everything. You want to put your best foot forward wherever your potential clients can see your brand. As the saying goes, you never get a second chance at a first impression, so do what you can do to make that first impression a good one. Common places to put your energy are:

- **Social media**
  - Be active, not letting any social media site go more than a week between updates, and respond to comments on your posts within a couple hours.
  - Make sure your profiles are complete, attractive, and professional.
  - Check spelling and grammar.
  - Add content that fits with your voice and matches your personality.
  - Direct people to your website so you can track them.
- **Website**
  - Design your website for SEO.
  - Make sure it is responsive (it looks good on all devices).
  - Don't write in long text blocks.
  - Use flat graphics, with limited or no use of gradient shading.
  - Make it clear where the user can click to learn more information about products and services.

» **Print**
  - Keep content short in marketing pieces.
  - Use the same design, colors, and imagery as your website.
  - Show clear calls to action.
» **Online ads**
  - Work with a company to help you place your ads with the right keywords.
  - Set up testing so you can see what works.
  - Make sure your ad text matches your voice and brand.

Your website analytics — and by extension your CRM — can track the sources of all inbound clicks. Measure how many people find you by assigning campaign IDs to each link that brings people to your website. Once at your site, you can measure how active they are, how many engage with you, and ultimately, who ends up becoming a client.

You can measure engagement by looking at how contacts from different campaigns act on your website. If you break this up by day, as shown in Figure 5-5, you can see daily variations in traffic behavior, which can illuminate different strategies that may or may not work.

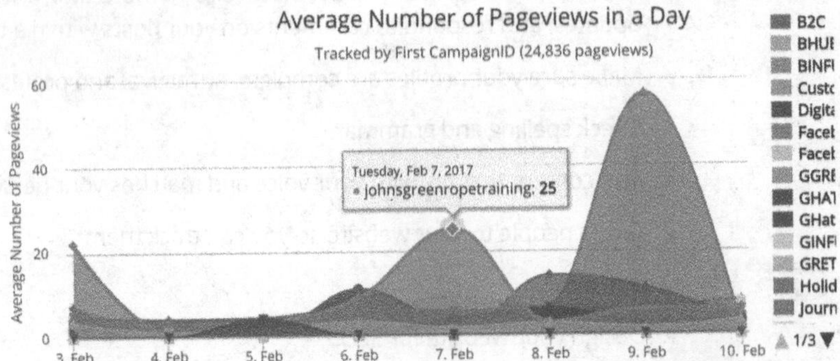

FIGURE 5-5: Average daily page views by campaign ID.

By tracking traffic to your company from each of these sources, you learn which lead source generates the highest quality leads. Combine the data with the amount of money spent on each channel, and you can calculate your return on investment (ROI) for each channel.

Figure 5-6 is a useful chart from Google AdWords (analytics software). It compares campaign IDs and summarizes the interaction by campaign ID over a specified date range. Higher numbers represent more page views per visitor, usually indicating more interest in the website and therefore the business.

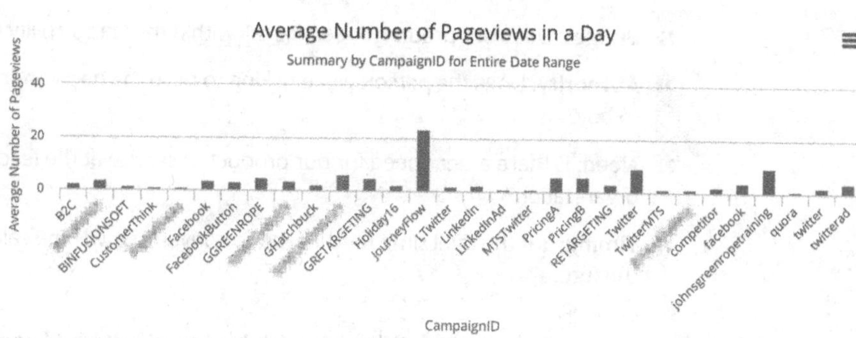

FIGURE 5-6: Summary of average page views over a date range by campaign ID.

Qualifying Leads

One important part of making the closing process work is to categorize leads into different qualities. There are two levels of lead qualification:

- **Marketing qualified lead (MQL):** This lead has expressed interest through a channel. Generally speaking, you know this lead has self-selected eligibility for whatever you're selling.

  Examples of a marketing qualified lead are people who fill out a form to download a whitepaper, or people who have spent a considerable amount of time on your website. Lead scoring is a useful tool to qualify someone's interest in your product; you could set a minimum number of points that qualifies that lead as someone your sales team should reach out to.

- **Sales qualified lead (SQL):** After someone passes the minimum requirements to be eligible to buy from you, she becomes sales qualified. Usually the lead has had a conversation with a salesperson who has confirmed that person or business is a good candidate to become your client. The purpose of the sales qualification step is to eliminate browsers and anyone who isn't really serious or qualified to become your customer.

TIP

Through this qualification process, you want your team to categorize leads into quality levels. Oftentimes, salespeople qualify leads as A, B, C, or D. This ranking helps focus each salesperson's energy on the leads most likely to convert.

Done manually, a salesperson can apply any number of rubrics to determining how lead ratings should be applied. Intel developed the Budget, Authority, Need, and Timing (BANT) method. A salesperson could look at a lead and apply these questions to determine the quality of that lead:

- **Budget:** Does our product or service fall within the lead's ability to pay for it?
- **Authority:** Does the person we're talking to have the decision-making power to buy?
- **Need:** Is there a clear need for our product or service at the lead's organization?
- **Timing:** Is it the right time for the lead to convert? Or will the sale happen in the future?

You can automate lead qualification with lead scoring (see Chapter 6) and predictive analytics (see Chapter 17), taking some of the guesswork out of the determination of A/B/C/D status, saving time, and increasing each salesperson's close rate.

Getting Your Leads into Your Funnel

After people see your brand for the first time, your primary objective is to get them into your sales funnel. A sales funnel is a depiction of how your leads (people who haven't become clients yet) move through various stages to become paying customers. The better you can categorize this journey, the better you understand how and why people buy (or don't buy) from you.

Figure 5-7 shows an example of how a CRM software company traces the journey of a lead from initial contact to becoming a customer. In this case, each phase of the journey can be seen, from landing on the demo request page, to getting a demo, to getting a trail, and becoming a client. (Chapter 15 talks more about measuring the buyer experience through a funnel.)

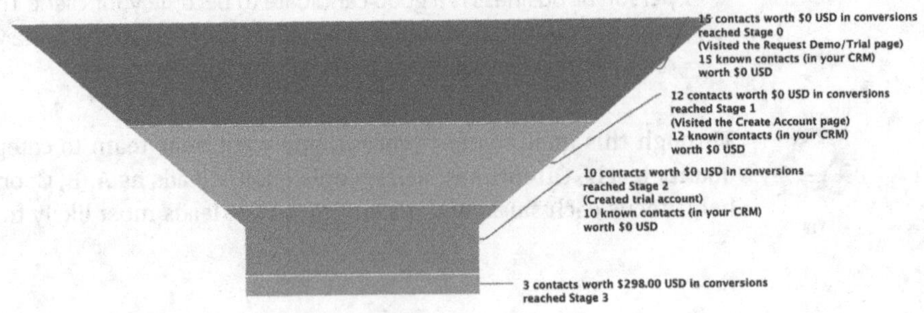

FIGURE 5-7: A funnel tracing the acquisition of a software customer.

When you think about the story arc of bringing your leads toward becoming clients, start with a reason, a purpose. Getting people interested in whatever you're selling (even if you aren't selling a physical product or a defined service) requires you to step into their minds and see things from their points of view.

Put yourself in your leads' shoes. Think about your buyers and imagine them clicking an ad, finding you in search results, hearing about you from someone they know, or reading about you in an informational article. The person ends up on your website, and then . . . what?

Maybe they land on your homepage, maybe they land on an inner page, or maybe they land on a dedicated landing page (a page you built to address a specific market or a campaign). Think about what that person is there for. Usually the first inquiry is about gathering information, but he wants to know more. Your ability to create the desire for more information is what will convince that potential client to progress on your buyer journey.

Most of the pages where you control content need a call to action (CTA). This call to action is usually in the form of a button that clearly tells the visitor what to do. Common CTAs are "click here to learn more," "click here to get a free whitepaper," "email us to get demo," or other action-related phrases. Figure 5-8 shows a call to action; the contact info leads give goes into the CRM and the lead starts through the funnel.

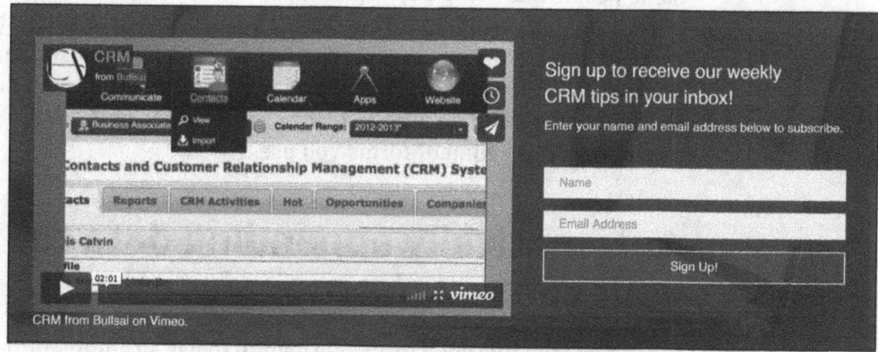

FIGURE 5-8: This call to action gets leads in a funnel.

Capturing data with effective forms

With digital marketing, the use of forms is the key to capturing information and filling your funnel with qualified leads. Use these forms to gather information in exchange for offering the lead some tangible incentive (for example, a discount, a downloadable whitepaper, or access to more information).

As your leads progress through your funnel, your relationship with them changes. New leads are looking for high-level information, so they can make the decision to investigate your products or services further. As they learn more about you and what you offer, the relationship becomes one of building trust and confidence that you can deliver on what you promise. Accordingly, your messaging needs to change.

If you have a complex product, it may make sense to provide long-form educational content to leads. Detailed e-books or blogs may be more relevant, particularly if you sell something technical, where product performance is important to your leads.

TIP

When you build forms, be mindful of who your webpage visitor is and what that visitor is looking for. Always ask for the minimum amount of information, to make it as easy as possible for someone to fill out the form.

REMEMBER

Make sure that when you have a landing page, the landing page's content matches the corresponding ad. If someone clicks an ad because you offer a special product, information about that product should be on your landing page. Coordinate the ad and landing page with your website manager and the people who manage your ad campaigns.

Some people like using pop-up ads, pop-under ads, and other intrusive methods of encouraging people to fill out forms. While some data suggests a higher rate of people filling out forms, there is a corresponding increase in the annoyance factor of your webpage visitors. This risk may be acceptable to you, depending on your overall strategy, but be sure to test to see whether lead quality goes up or down, depending on the kind of forms you use.

Automatically appending data to your contacts/companies

When someone fills out a form, one helpful tool is an automatic data appending and validation. You can then fill in extra data that the user didn't explicitly enter into the form. Your CRM platform should offer lead capture tools that augment form data with data appending, validate the email as a valid email, and do a reputation assessment based on the email and the network that is filling out the form.

Using Workflows to Engage with Your Customers

When someone fills out a form on your website, that information is immensely useful. The lead leaves tracking information: how she got to your site. The marketing system also tags each visitor with a unique cookie to follow that lead as that person clicks around your website. Your forms can also initiate other kinds of automated tasks, such as send emails and schedule follow-ups for your sales staff.

Figure 5-9 shows a form connected to an automated follow-up campaign. The user requests information to learn about automated sales, and receives a series of emails about automation.

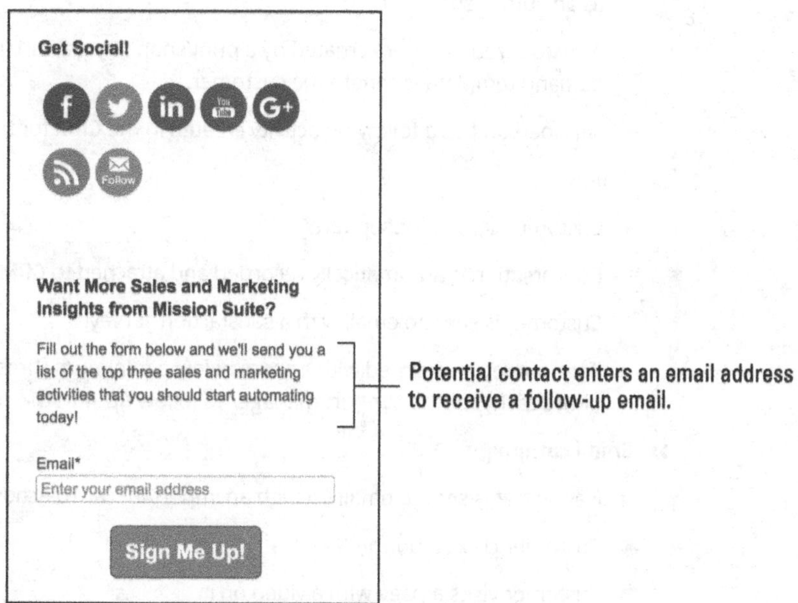

FIGURE 5-9: A business that relies on workflows benefits from automation.

The important part of this engagement, particularly at these early stages, is consistency. Your message to leads and clients must reflect your brand and what you stand for at every stage. To this end, you must understand what all those touchpoints are, so leads and customers get the information they need when they need it.

Knowing when and how to communicate with leads and clients requires you to build a model of your customer journey. This journey begins at the first mention of your brand to a potential customer. Whenever possible, automate those communication methods so your team can focus on the critical personal touch when and where it matters most.

This reason is why the use of workflows is critical for the business. A *workflow* is a predefined method for taking an action. These methods call upon the software connected to your CRM to take action. It's up to you to define these workflows; here are a few workflows:

- **Landing page**
  - Customer fills out lead capture form.
  - Automatic sequence of emails is sent every day for three days (also known as an auto-responder).
  - A customized brochure created by a print shop using a variable print-on-demand template is sent to the customer.
  - Salesperson has a follow-up activity created in the CRM for the following day.
- **Call-in**
  - Customer calls in for support.
  - Conversation is automatically recorded and attached to CRM record.
  - Customer is sent an email with a satisfaction survey.
  - If the survey is returned with a score below a minimum threshold, create a CRM activity for the support manager to follow up with the customer.
- **Email campaign**
  - Newsletter is sent to email list with an important call to action.
  - Customer clicks a button.
  - Customer visits a page with a video on it.
  - If the customer watches more than 120 seconds of the video, an email is sent to the customer, and a follow-up activity is created in the CRM.

Workflows can take many forms and are limited only by your imagination and the capabilities of the CRM and marketing automation software platform you're working with. Workflows are why it's important to create your story arcs and understand how managing process can and should work within your organization. The more you can automate workflows with software, the better you can control the customer's experience and measure the effectiveness of your methods.

Sending automated and transactional messages

When people take actions that you can use as a reason for sending automated messages, you open the door to increased customer engagement, satisfaction, and promotion of your brand. In the world of marketing automation, you must identify as many triggers as possible that could justify sending an automated email. (Chapter 11 goes into more detail about marketing automation.)

A trigger can be an obvious action, such as when someone makes a purchase or requests information from you, but it also can also be when someone visits a high-value page, such as a webpage explaining details for your flagship product. Figure 5-10 shows a flowchart of what happens after someone buys a product from your website.

Each message you send to a customer after a purchase is an opportunity to confirm someone's actions (such as a transaction receipt), educate the consumer (why she's getting this email and tips to help her), and learn more about what you do. Even if it's subtle, links in an automated or transactional email to your website open the door for you to sell consumers on more products and services. If you provide an incentive for doing so, such as a discount code, you greatly increase your chances of converting a lead to a contact, which in turn improves conversion rates, driving revenues.

Scheduling the right CRM activities

Workflows can be used to set up CRM activities for your sales team. When you need to ensure a human does something, setting up CRM activities is the best way to do it. These activities can be to make a follow-up call, write a personalized email, or accomplish another offline task.

WARNING

It can be tempting to set up activities for every possible scenario, but be careful to not overwhelm your staff. Be sure that when creating a CRM activity, the person you're assigning the activity to won't be given meaningless or too many tasks.

When you schedule CRM activities for opportunities (high-value sales), don't forget to include activities for ensuring every aspect of the opportunity is closed when the deal is won. Include activities related to quality assurance, so the customer has the best experience possible.

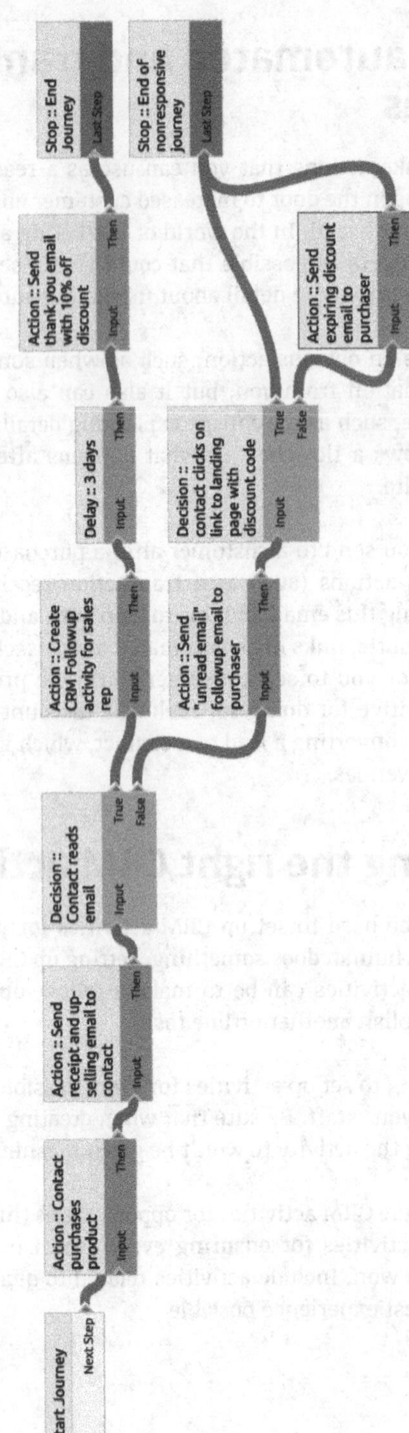

FIGURE 5-10: This journey maps how a purchase can trigger automated actions.

Designing Workflows

Workflows are the lynchpin that makes your sales and marketing automation turn your business into the efficient, growing system you want it to be. Figure 5-11 shows a visual description of what a workflow could do when it's activated. This automation saves your team time, so they don't have to manually send emails or make entries in the CRM.

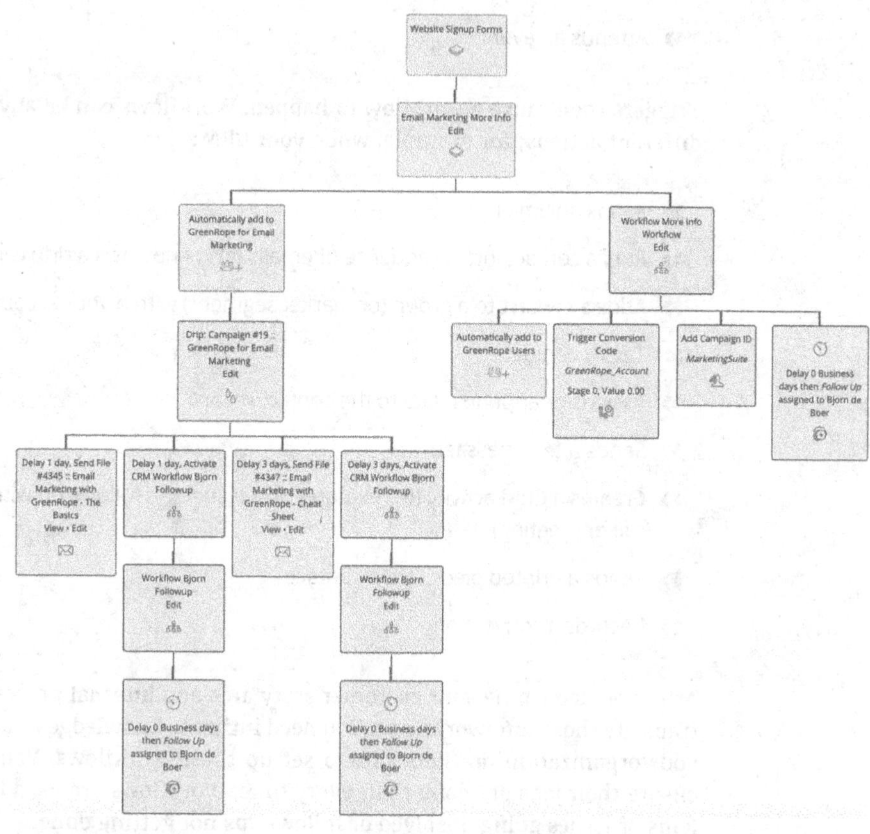

FIGURE 5-11: Complex, cascading workflows can automate any part of your business.

Workflows are built using two components: triggers and actions. Triggers are things that someone does to initiate the workflow; for example, when a lead:

- Clicks a link in an email
- Watches a video
- Visits a webpage
- Interacts with you on social media

- Updates contact data
- Fills out a form
- Sends a text message
- Opens a chat session
- Calls a salesperson
- Requests an appointment
- Attends an event

Triggers then cause a workflow to happen. Workflows can be any combination of different actions; for example, when your CRM:

- Sends an email
- Puts a contact into a sequence of emails (also known as a drip campaign)
- Adds a contact to a group (or market segment) within your account
- Tags a contact
- Assigns or appends data to the contact record
- Sends a text message
- Creates a CRM activity (for example, a salesperson follows up with a phone call or meeting)
- Sends a printed piece to the contact
- Records a conversion

After you determine your customer story arcs and internal processes, it's time to translate those into workflows. You need intimate knowledge of how the people in your organization do their jobs to set up these workflows. Your objective is to ensure their jobs get done right every time. Workflows are used to prevent problems or issues going unsolved or follow-ups not getting done.

Figure 5-12 is a useful management report, showing you the number of workflows that have been activated in a given day. These reports that your CRM provides give you an idea of how much effort the workflows are saving your team, as well as the kinds of interactions your leads and customers are having with your organization.

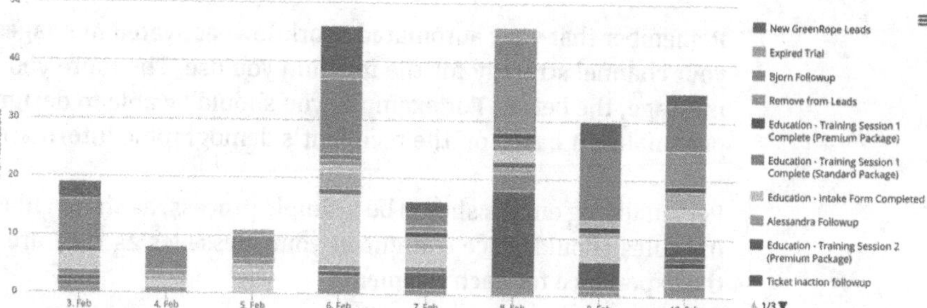

FIGURE 5-12: Keeping track of all the workflows activated on a daily basis.

Considering limitations of your workflows

Workflows can only be triggered by actions you can measure. The principles of Complete CRM — where the CRM is measuring every channel possible — give you the power to automate virtually every step of engagement with your leads and clients. If you don't measure an action a contact makes, you can't take action on it to help steer that contact down a path.

On the other side of the workflow, the more you connect to the "action" side of a workflow, the more you can make happen. If workflows can schedule CRM activities, send emails, send text messages, trigger campaigns, and/or update contact records, you can cover the more common actions in your workflow.

REMEMBER

Some limitations are useful by design. One of these is a workflow activation limit. An activation limit prevents a workflow from getting activated too often. For example, you don't want to trigger a workflow a second time when a recipient clicks a link in an email multiple times. By setting a maximum of one activation per day, you prevent too many actions being taken automatically.

Communicating across multiple channels

Omnichannel marketing describes a consistent customer experience across different channels; similar language and design are used for email, brochures, and social media sites. The same idea applies to your workflows — when you send emails, drive people to webpages, and send printed collateral with your workflows, make sure your leads see consistent content and language.

Workflows activated by your Complete CRM should allow you to communicate across any number of channels, but you want to be careful. Be sure you think through your overall strategy and buyer journey before you decide to overwhelm your leads and clients with too many messages.

Remember that your automated, workflow-activated messages should conform to your channel strategy for the medium you use. The more you can personalize the message, the better. For example, you should be able to design a single email and personalize it based on the recipient's demographic information.

Personalizing emails should be a simple process, as shown in Figure 5-13. Cascading rules should place content in your messages as they are sent, personalizing the experience for each recipient.

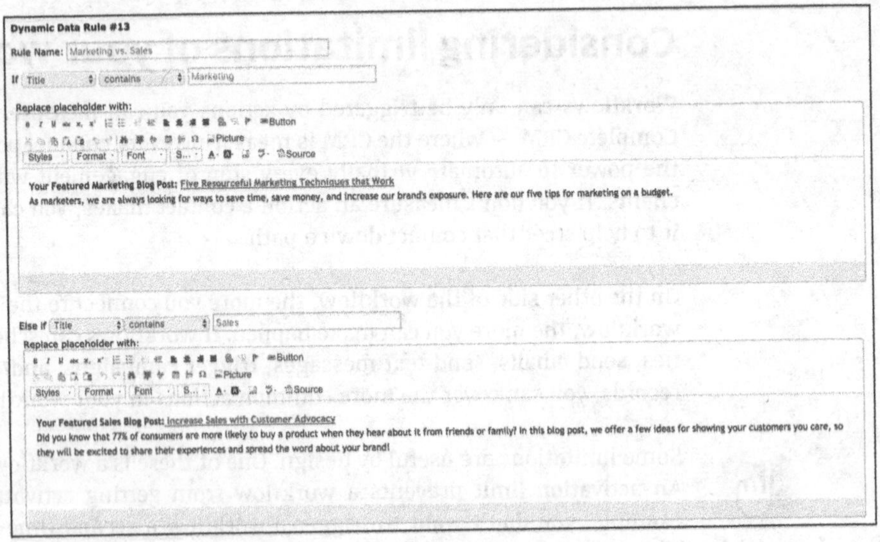

FIGURE 5-13: Personalizing content based on recipient title.

You also should be careful to not inundate your leads and clients. Keep your messages focused and don't flood them with too many emails or text messages. Workflow activation limits should prevent too many messages, but be cognizant of each workflow, so you don't annoy the people you're trying to sell to.

Building different workflow actions for opportunities

Opportunities are objects that track larger sales deals. If a workflow gets activated and connected to an opportunity, you should be able to specify different behavior based on the opportunity characteristics.

Opportunities have creation dates and close dates, representing when the opportunity was realized and when the sale is expected to be completed. As such, you should be able to define CRM activities based on those dates, allowing your team to schedule predefined sales and onboarding activities that must be accomplished.

Figure 5-14 shows how you can define workflows to have special activity creation rules when they're activated for an opportunity.

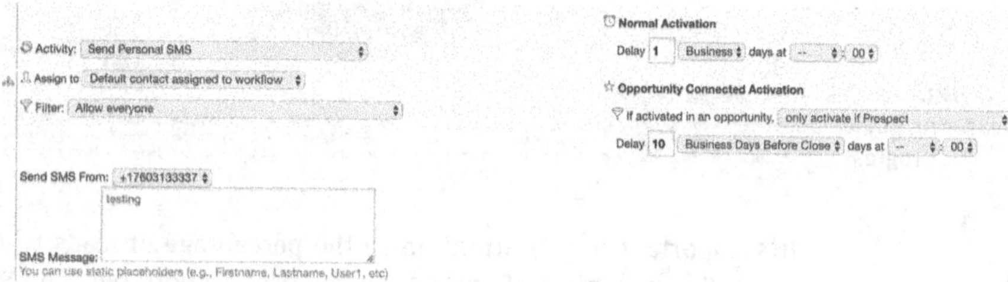

FIGURE 5-14: A custom activity created when activated within an opportunity.

TIP

Opportunities generally represent more valuable, complex sales, so make sure you define processes that ensure nothing slips through the cracks. Setting CRM activities for specific delays after the opportunity closes ensures a smooth welcome to each new client you bring onboard.

Closing Leads with Effective Process

Your leads convert to customers at some point along your story arc. At this point maximizing the chance of that conversion is important. You need to measure how long a lead takes to get through the funnel, and how often leads fall out of the funnel. You can then refine the way you do business, a term some refer to as *conversion rate optimization.*

Figure 5-15 shows an interactive four-stage funnel (stages zero through three). Some key metrics are the amount of time spent in each stage and the percentages of leads progressing through their buyer journeys.

A certain percentage of people fall out during every stage of your funnel and don't progress to the next stage. As a business owner, you want to be prepared for this inevitability and try to recapture as many of those people as possible. Sometimes it's an automated action (such as an email is sent); sometimes it's a manual process (such as a salesperson calls the potential lead to find out whether he'd be interested later).

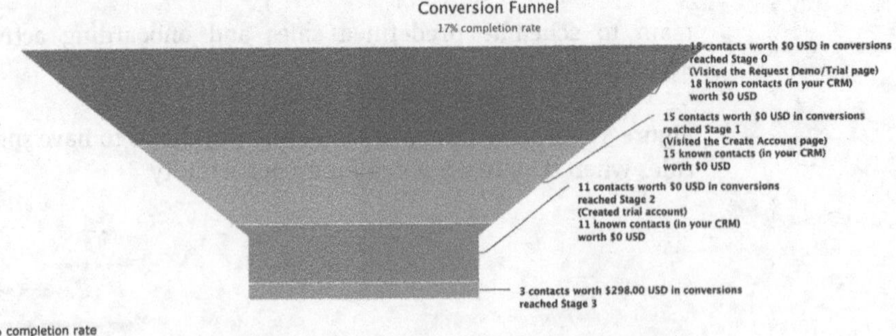

FIGURE 5-15: Measuring funnel progress.

It's important to pay attention to the percentage of leads who drop out of each stage. For example, in Figure 5-16, the first dropoff, between Stage 0 and Stage 1, keeps only 54% of leads, which tells you nearly half the leads entering the funnel during this week didn't qualify to get a demo. The success rate between Stage 2 and Stage 3 is the most important statistic, as it tells you how many qualified leads become clients. Watch that number conversion between Stages 2 and 4 to see whether there are significant variations and why those variations occurred.

Determining what is automated versus manual

Some communication should be personal. Automatically setting up a CRM activity for your salesperson to call a lead may be appropriate if you're selling a high-value product or service.

Some CRM activities are activated when the lead or client completes a task. For example, signing a contract, providing you with an asset you need to build something, or coordinating something with another vendor. You then want to create CRM activities that build on each other, so that when one activity is completed, it triggers a workflow, which can then set more activities.

Testing different methods of closing

You can set campaign IDs or tag contacts with workflows, which makes for an easy way to test different methods of closing deals. If you can separate different populations of your clients by these campaigns, tags, or groups, you can compare close rates.

Looking at different sales techniques and strategies is important in identifying the skill and dedication of your sales staff, as well as the effectiveness of different strategies. Different campaigns may drive different quality traffic, or different demographics that close better with different tactics.

Figure 5-16 shows different campaigns and the revenue generated by each during a specific time period. This data can help you identify which campaigns provide the best return on investment (ROI) for you.

FIGURE 5-16: Track revenues generated by campaign to measure effectiveness.

The ability to measure your success and identify why you're successful (or not) is the beauty of Complete CRM. Learn from your mistakes, adapt your marketing strategies and sales processes, and improve.

Measuring real success of closing

Success with different workflows may seem obvious. Higher close rate percentages usually mean your sales processes are improving. There is more to it, though.

When comparing different sales processes, be sure to account for factors that could cause you to come to the wrong conclusion. These factors could be seasonal, dependent on the salesperson, or the quality of incoming leads. It's wise to react slowly.

You may also want to consider the amount of time it takes to close a lead. If different sales processes are dragging out the sales process, it may be affecting the efficiency of your sales staff.

CONVERTING BETTER LEADS

My company decided to modify our sales process to require people who wanted to test-drive software to get a live demo first. We then compared what our funnels looked like with each method and found the demo weeded out the non-serious leads and reduced the number of workflows activated.

Using Opportunities versus Consumer Sales Funnels

When a sale is closed, you want to record that sale within your CRM. Generally speaking, sales are tracked in one of two methods: as an opportunity (used for tracking fewer, higher-value items) or as an automated funnel (used for tracking large numbers of conversions).

Selling to the business (B2B) with opportunities

Opportunities are a way to track complex sales, usually business-to-business sales. Consumer sales funnels can track similar progressions without the details typically found with opportunities.

Because opportunities are separate objects attached to contacts or companies, you can store more information about the sale. Usually this information takes the form of these data fields:

- **Title and description:** General descriptor fields for easy recall.
- **Products and/or services:** What you're selling in this opportunity.
- **Proposal due date:** The date when the potential customer requires a proposal due for the effort you will perform.
- **Close date:** The date when you will find out if you won or lost the deal.
- **Phase:** Many opportunities go through various phases from initial conversation to requirements review to proposal submission and review to final disposition (winning or losing the deal).
- **Source:** How you found out about the opportunity.
- **Quality:** A subjective assessment for the quality of the opportunity. Usually this assessment is correlated to the size of the opportunity, relationship with the potential client, and ability to meet the requirement.
- **Chance to close:** The percentage chance you will win the deal. Use this number in forecasting.
- **Fulfillment dates:** The dates you will be working on the opportunity.

You can build automation around opportunities, so when leads move from phase to phase, a workflow can be activated, which helps you streamline your sales process.

When tracking opportunities, a salesperson sells fewer high-value items. Opportunities are designed for a more detailed look at every individual sale. Oftentimes, they involve multiple components, with multiple products and services bundled together. There are often a series of defined phases the opportunity moves through, such as:

- Prospect
- Qualified lead
- Proposal
- Negotiation
- Deal won/lost

In this way, a salesperson can keep a detailed record of everything associated with that opportunity. And, because the opportunity is tied to a contact (or multiple contacts) and/or a company, every interaction with the contacts related to the opportunity is tracked.

Opportunities, like the one shown in Figure 5-17, store a lot of information with them to keep a record of the ongoing relationship of the sale.

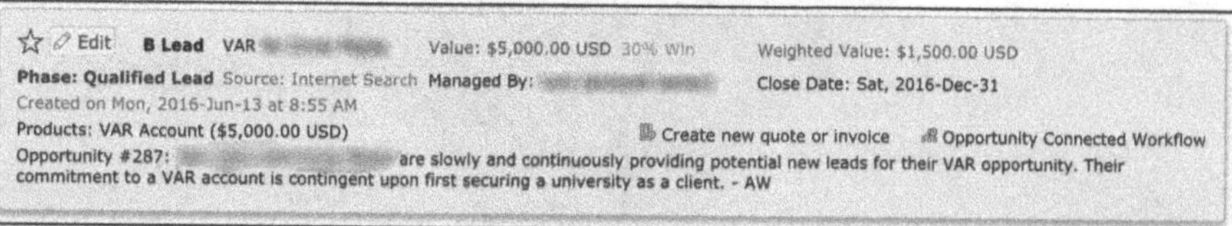

FIGURE 5-17: Data you can attach to an opportunity.

Opportunities are where the synergy of Complete CRM and integrated marketing and operations starts to show its power. If you're a salesperson working on an opportunity, and you can see when your lead opens emails, clicks through your website, and watches videos, you can take immediate, targeted action. This knowledge is power and opens doors that your sales team never thought possible.

You can also forecast what will happen in the future when your sales team enters in predicted close dates and chances to close those deals. Figure 5-18 is a simple chart that shows the value of deals closed and some deals predicted to close.

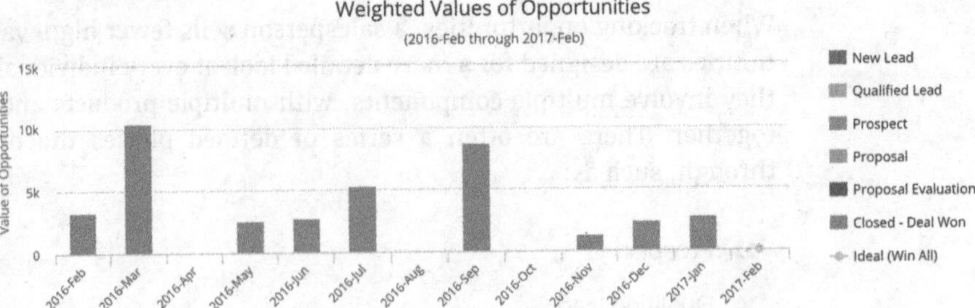

FIGURE 5-18: History and future of closing deals with opportunities.

Selling to consumers with funnels

Funnels are an easy way to visualize the sales process you want to manage. At each step, fewer people remain, with the bottom of the funnel representing the people who have purchased your product or service. It's up to you to determine when someone moves to a new phase in the buying process.

Figure 5-19 shows a funnel for opportunities. Opportunity funnels look similar to consumer sales funnels (refer to Figure 5-15).

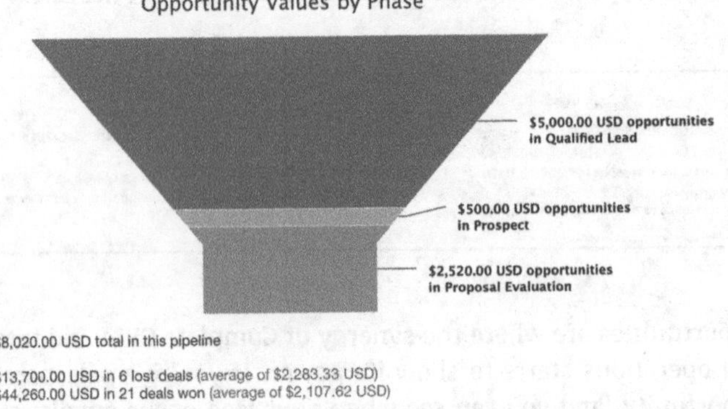

FIGURE 5-19: Opportunities fall into B2B funnels.

Sales funnels are a great way to track the progress of many people through your buying process. When you track a greater number of people in your marketing and sales process, it can be a useful tool for managing the business-to-consumer (B2C) buying model. Instead of salespeople manually moving an opportunity through phases, you can automate this process, moving people through your funnel as they hit certain milestones. These milestones can be:

- Visiting a webpage
- Filling out a form
- Hitting a thank-you page after the form

» Buying a product

» Reviewing your product

Be cognizant of how you want to track your sales and marketing processes to determine whether your salespeople are using opportunities to track individual sales or using automated sales funnels to automate people moving through the buying process.

Figure 5-20 shows how a lead capture form starts the B2B funnel. After someone fills out and submits the form, he is entered into the first stage of the funnel.

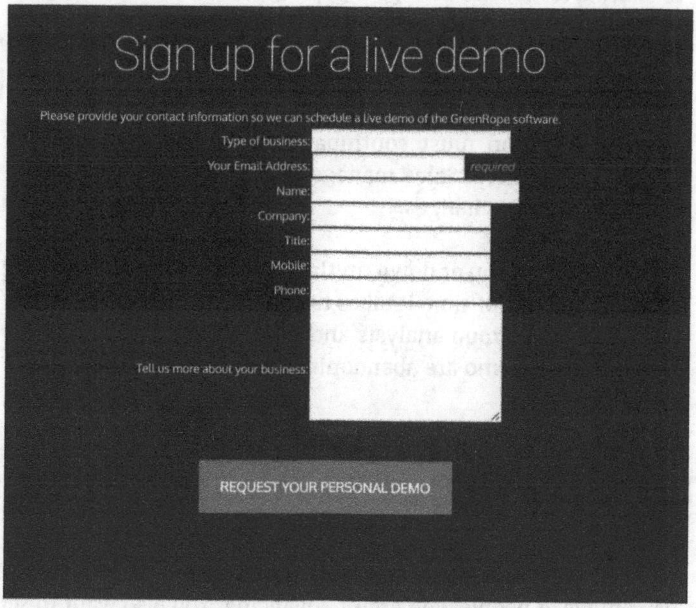

FIGURE 5-20: Starting the consumer purchase process with a lead capture form.

Measuring key metrics

Conversion rates through each stage are important metrics to watch. It's important to look at what is affecting those conversion rates, as leads look for different things as they progress through their buyer journeys.

Every B2B sales process has metrics you can measure to help you understand how your business is performing. Some examples are

» **Time in each stage:** Are your leads taking too much time to advance? Can you do something to push them along?

- **Percentage of leads dropping:** Are you finding a large number of leads leaving the buyer journey at a particular point? Find out why and address those pain points.
- **Number of CRM activities:** Are your salespeople spending an inordinate amount of time with each lead to get them through a part of the buyer journey? Can automated communication streamline the way you do business?

Separate the individual accounts from higher-value leads with opportunities. With opportunities, you can track which leads show interest, when they get a demo, when they get a trial account, and when they convert. You can watch percentages of close rates for each of these, as they represent lead quality, the ability to educate leads, and salesperson performance.

Evolving your sales and conversion processes

Your organization must continually refine and improve your sales process to remain competitive. Sales management must monitor funnels continuously and watch for sudden changes.

If changes occur, up or down, in the rate of conversion from one stage to the next, or in the amount of time it takes to convert someone, there may be other forces at work. Use your group analysis and related CRM data to identify common threads between people who are abandoning their buyer journeys.

Implementing Process Abandonment

At each stage of the funnel, you need to measure the time between stages and the percentage of people who aren't advancing. You also want to set up process abandonment, so that workflows can be activated when a potential lead doesn't advance to the next step after a certain amount of time.

Process abandonment is in place in many buyer journeys already. The most common is shopping cart abandonment. If a buyer places a product in a shopping cart, but doesn't actually complete the process, an email is sent to remind the buyer. This process is usually automatic, and studies have shown it to close almost 30% of those abandoned carts.

Figure 5-21 depicts a straightforward way to set up automated process around leads not converting. You see two main catch points — the decision to put something in a shopping cart, and the decision to purchase something. In case of failing to do either of these, you can use your CRM and marketing automation software to encourage buyers to continue on their journeys.

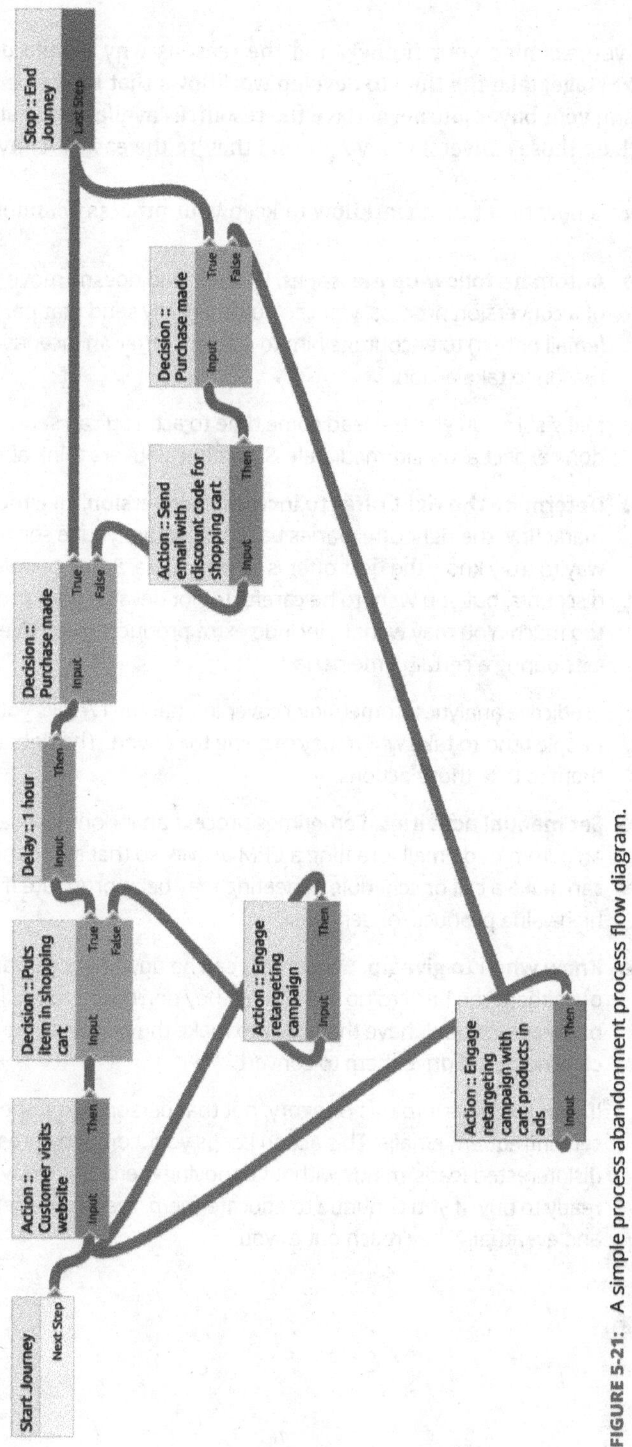

FIGURE 5-21: A simple process abandonment process flow diagram.

As you examine your funnels and the reasons why people don't advance to the next stage, take the time to develop workflows that target people who aren't fulfilling your buyer journeys. Have the resources available to catch those people and pick up those conversions; you'll find they're the easiest conversions to get.

Here's how to set up a workflow to keep your process abandonment low:

- **Automate follow-up messages.** When a lead doesn't move to the next stage of a conversion process, you can automatically send that person a message (email or text) to encourage him to convert. Offer an incentive for another reason to take action.

  Make sure you give the lead some time to act. You can send an email, but don't expect action immediately. Sometimes buyers think about their options.

- **Determine the right offer to increase conversion.** Like most things in marketing, the right offer varies based on whom you're selling to. The only way to truly know the best offer is to test offers. Some people respond best to discounts, but you want to be careful to not devalue your product or service too much. You may want to include extra products or services when the lead acts during a certain time period.

  Predictive analytics, something I cover in Chapter 17, tells you what actions people tend to take when they're going to convert. The right offer encourages them to take those actions.

- **Set manual activities.** Sometimes process abandonment requires more than an automated email. Creating a CRM activity so that someone on your staff can make a call or schedule a meeting may be appropriate if you're selling high-value products or services.

- **Know when to give up.** Consumers can be downright cantankerous if you push them too hard to do something they don't want to do. If they're simply bad leads, or don't have the ability to make the purchase, no amount of convincing will drive them to convert.

TIP

If your lead falls into this category, put that person into a special group that is sent infrequent emails. This action keeps your company present in your disinterested leads' minds without annoying them. Someday they might be ready to buy. If you continue to educate them, they appreciate what you send and eventually they reach out to you.

Following Up after the Sale

Your relationship with your customer doesn't end with the sale. This part of the relationship is something that many businesses neglect, leaving a shocking amount of money on the table. After buyers make a purchase from your company, they have intimate knowledge of your buyer journey and are the best people in the world to talk about your product.

Surveying customer satisfaction

After a sale, you want to ensure the customer experience remains positive. Find out whether customers are satisfied by surveying your new and existing customers. Surveys are easy to send by email and can be stored in your CRM, scored, and activate workflows.

TIP

Set up a workflow to respond to negative responses.

One common question asked that serves as a metric for your brand is the Net Promoter Score (NPS). NPS is a simple question: How likely is it that you would recommend our company/product/service to a friend or colleague? Include the NPS as a follow-up to a purchase to give you an indication of how well you're doing in providing a good customer experience.

The NPS is rated on a scale of 1 to 10, but you can define your follow-ups however you feel best fits your market. You can use multiple-choice questions with answers like "excellent" or "good" as a way to provide context to the person answering the question. Figure 5-22 shows an average score from the respondents to a customer satisfaction survey.

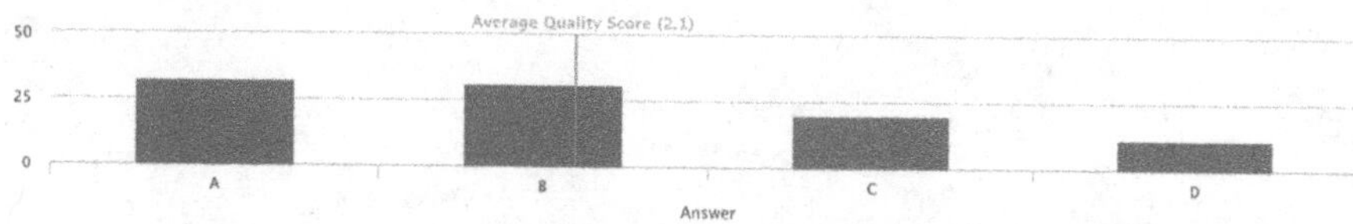

FIGURE 5-22: Asking quality of service questions to new clients gives valuable insight.

Converting clients into advocates

Your objective after the sale is complete is to convert as many people as possible into advocates for your products and services. There are a variety of ways to do so, most of which can be automated:

- **Send a thank-you message.** Sometimes an email is sufficient, but for high-value conversions, you may want to take another step and include a discount for other products and services, access to a special part of your website, a phone call from someone in the C-suite of your organization, or a simple gift. The effort required to say "thank you" goes a long way.

- **Create an affiliate program.** Affiliate programs are a great way to involve your customers in the growth of your company. You can give your customers a discount code, or a special campaign ID that tags any inbound leads to that customer. With that referral comes a form of financial reward, either one time or recurring.
- **Engage with customers on social media.** Follow your customers on Twitter, connect with them on LinkedIn, like their companies' Facebook pages. These steps serve to better connect you to them, which opens the door for sharing content with them, which in turn opens the door to cross-selling and up-selling more products and services.

TIP

Whenever a new client comes onboard, set up a workflow for that client's salesperson and marketing manager to connect with that person and his company on LinkedIn. This workflow encourages participation in the client's social media community, while also making it clear you're available to help him for the long term.

Revitalizing existing clients

Your quiet clients can be a huge source of referral, reviews, and social proof that you are a great business offering excellent products or services. Oftentimes these clients can be awakened with the right email, thanking them or incentivizing them to share information about you.

IN THIS CHAPTER

» **Assessing how your business works and talking to influencers in your company**

» **Translating business process to CRM**

» **Customizing record fields**

» **Ranking your leads and clients**

Chapter 6

Defining Process and Your Data Model

Every organization is unique, and setting up Complete CRM is different for every business. Figuring out how your company operates can be a tricky thing sometimes. Even the word "process" has different meanings to different people.

When it comes to CRM and managing your business, understanding and defining process is about triggers and actions. Someone does something, which then causes something else to happen. Process isn't always about formalized procedures. Some business processes are informal, not written anywhere. Effectively implementing CRM requires you to get in your employees' minds and find out what really happens every day.

In this chapter, you discover how to set up your CRM around process that matches the way you do business. You first set up your data model, which captures the information you need about your leads, clients, vendors, and their companies. Then, you set up lead scoring and automation around that scoring, as a way to segment and target your best leads.

Applying Management by Walking Around

If you aren't intimately familiar with how your business operates on a minute-by-minute level, you need to spend some time with your employees. Leave your office and observe how business is done. The better you listen, the greater your understanding.

Gathering cultural information informally

Go to your customer service department and listen to the phone calls that are made. Notice how your support team interacts with customers. How do your employees answer the phone? What happens when they have a problem they can't resolve there? How is their quality measured? Can customers give feedback to the company about their experience?

Go to marketing and sit through a marketing strategy meeting. Are their strategies consistent with your vision? Is their voice consistent with your brand? How do they hand off their leads to sales? Are they tracking which campaigns are working, and which are not?

Go to your sales department and listen to them talk about the leads that are coming in. Are they happy with them? Are there frustrations with the product? Why are clients happy or unhappy? Do they have marketing-related information to help them close deals? What happens when a new lead shows up? How often are they following up with leads?

Answering these questions help you learn more about how your organization runs on a daily basis. In turn you gain direction in how to design your CRM.

Looking beyond the obvious answers

Sometimes when you sit in on a meeting, you may miss verbal and visual communication. Look beyond what people say and what is on the PowerPoint presentations. Pay close attention to the informal leaders, the people in those meetings who are looked to for guidance and approval. Sometimes that person is not the one with the formal job title.

When information is presented about operations, look behind the numbers you see. Examine how those numbers were collected and look for subjective bias. If people are filling in the gaps with assumptions, question those assumptions.

When you apply the concepts of Complete CRM to your business, the data is there to show you what you want to know. As your organization transitions to becoming data-driven, you rely on what the numbers tell you, but it's important to make sure you have the *right* data. Break down the silos of information so that information from sales, marketing, and operations all contributes to the big picture.

Collecting company feedback through surveys

Surveys are a powerful intelligence-gathering tool. When directed internally, you can ask questions about what your employees feel is working and not working. This can guide you toward making strategic decisions that benefit everyone.

Surveys are not only useful for getting feedback from clients. Employee feedback can easily be collected through surveys, too. When you write your survey questions, be as specific as possible to get the feedback you can use. The more detailed information about how people do their jobs, the easier it is to establish requirements for your CRM.

Outlining Key Areas

A big part of understanding who the important players are in an organization is by looking at how your business works. Set up a process diagram to see how your leads move through their buyer journeys. Draw another diagram for how your organization manages customer services.

After you have a clear picture of how things work within your organization, you see the key players who influence critical steps in that process. Those key players are the ones you must win over in the implementation of your CRM. See Chapter 2 to find out how to sell them your CRM vision.

Moving from Whiteboard to CRM

The final step is figuring out how to go from your ideal process model to your CRM. This step is tricky because you have to work within the limitations of the software you're using. If you are still in the vendor selection phase, share your process diagrams with your CRM vendor to understand where challenges lie. If you already have a vendor chosen, work with the staff to translate your ideal model into its software.

If you find the vendor is unable to accomplish your goals, you have three options:

- **»** Live with it, accepting that some processes have to be done outside the CRM.
- **»** Develop custom software.
- **»** Find a new vendor.

Looking at the complete picture

Using a flowchart builder such as JourneyFlow (`http://www.journeyflow.com`) helps you visualize what processes you need to support with your CRM. Build multiple flows, as you follow the purchase process for different market segments and different products and services that you offer.

Process flowcharts are also valuable in modeling and designing your marketing campaigns. These flows determine how you guide your leads toward the process of buying from you and encompass all the channels you wish to use.

Building flowcharts of business processes

Flowcharts that you use for documenting your business processes generally have four main components:

- **»** **Decisions:** A decision point looks at whether the person in the journey takes an action or possesses certain characteristics. Based on the contact's behavior or demographics, different actions are triggered. For example, when a lead who reads an email is sent a different follow-up email than a lead who didn't read the initial email.
- **»** **Delays:** A delay is a pause in the process flow, waiting for someone to take an action. For example, you want to incorporate a delay to give a lead a reasonable amount of time to read an email and reach a decision point.
- **»** **Actions:** An action can be either one the contact takes or your organization takes. For example, scheduling or completing a CRM activity, sending an email, updating a contact record in the CRM, or anything a workflow can do. The possibilities are endless.
- **»** **Stop:** A stop represents the end of the journey. When someone has completed a process flow, or disqualified herself from the rest of the journey, her journey ends. For example, if a lead says she's not interested in what you have to offer in spite of your best efforts.

Figure 6-1 shows a buyer journey. In this journey, the lead starts with a web lead capture form and progresses to the next stage of lead nurturing.

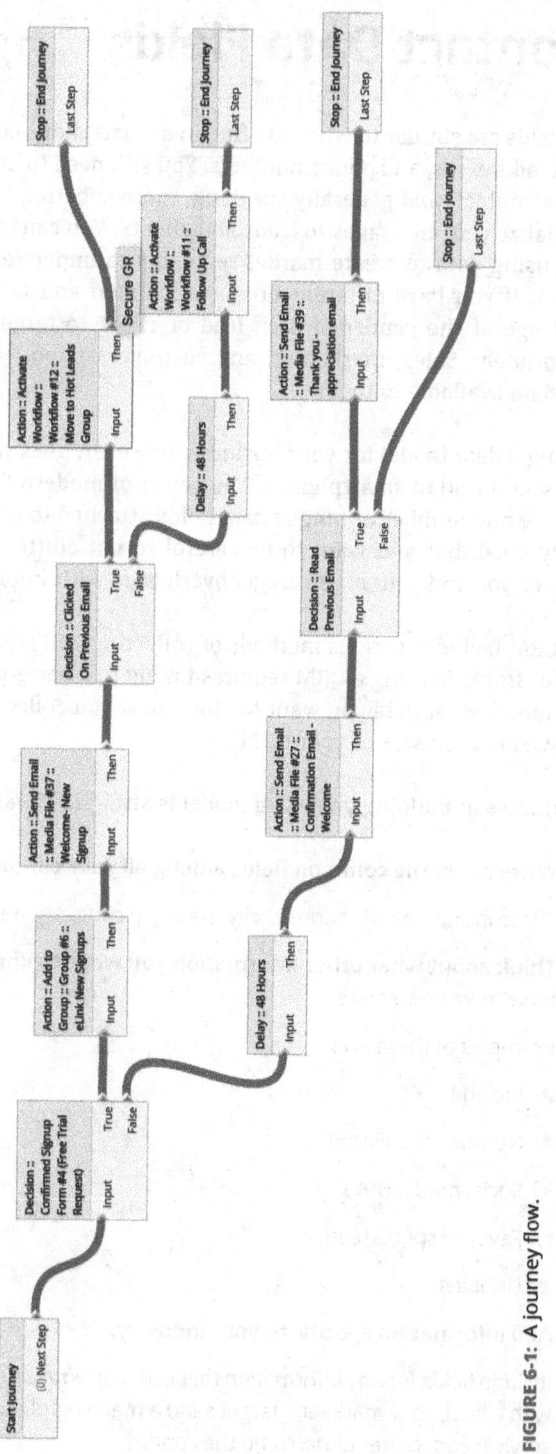

FIGURE 6-1: A journey flow.

Defining Contact Data Fields

CRM fields are similar to what you find in a smartphone contact list: names, companies, addresses, and phone numbers. You still need to know all that information about a contact, and generally speaking, more is better. With more data, you can personalize your messages to leads and clients. You can measure behavior differently, using data to create market segments to understand why people do what they do. If you have different products for men and women, you can use your knowledge of the gender of each lead or client to target each market segment appropriately. Sales, marketing, and customer support all benefit from having more data available to them.

Building a data model for your business, however, goes way beyond the standard fields you'll find in smartphones. The power of modern CRM software is that you can store any number of unique data fields attached to each contact. More data is usually good, but you want to be careful to not clutter your database with too much, or you and your staff can get overloaded with information.

Your CRM includes various methods of collecting and organizing your data. Every plan for implementing a CRM requires taking this variety into consideration. You must model what data you want to store, how you collect your data, and how it's displayed to the users of your CRM.

The process of building your data model is straightforward:

1. **Write down the common fields among all your contacts.**

   These include name, address, city, state, zip code, phone, website.

2. **Think about what other information you want to know by going through your buyer personas.**

   Examples of these are:

   - Income
   - Number of children
   - Social media URLs
   - Favorite sports teams
   - Hobbies

3. **Add information specific to your industry.**

   TIP

   Include fields for any information that can help your sales team better connect with a lead, your marketing target send a meaningful message, or your customer service team better understand the contact.

A good CRM offers many configuration possibilities for your user defined fields. Customize where and how these fields are displayed, and who can see them. Set up triggers so that if you want a workflow to activate when data changes, those activations happen automatically. Equations are also useful if you combine numerical data into calculations automatically.

TIP

When you design your data model, certain fields are more important than others. A good CRM allows you to customize the way those fields are displayed, so think about how your data will be used by different people in your organization.

Building automation into data field values

Your CRM data fields themselves can be used as triggers for workflows. Triggers give you flexibility to set up automation around the raw data in your CRM. For example, you might have a workflow take affect when someone changes a contact's status from an "active" to "declined" credit card status. Use the change in the data field to drive action. Chapter 11 goes more indepth about setting up automation around your marketing efforts.

Another example is to automate action centers on lead scoring, which places greater value on your better leads and clients (see the upcoming section). If you connect your data fields to lead scoring (Figure 6-2 shows an example), you can set up lead scoring gates. A workflow could be something like "if a contact goes from having less than 100 activity lead scoring points to more than 100 activity lead scoring points, activate the Very Interested Client workflow." More complex rules such as this one can help you identify subsets of interested clients.

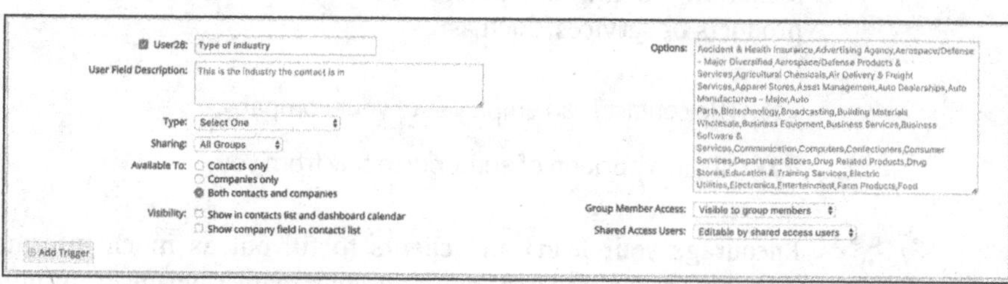

FIGURE 6-2: Configuring a custom data field.

Scoring Your Leads and Clients

Lead scoring assigns points to people based on attributes that make them a better lead. Higher scores help your sales team determine quality and interest, focusing their efforts, and becoming more efficient. Scoring identifies when individuals show a lot of interest by interacting with your brand.

Lead scoring comes in two basic types: demographic and activity-based.

Building demographic lead scoring rules

Demographic lead scoring is derived from rules you set up around certain demographic characteristics of a lead. If you're selling to specific kinds of people, you can increase a contact's score because they exhibit traits that make them better targets for your products or services. Examples that result in positive demographic lead scores would be:

- Gender
- Title
- Age
- Position/role
- Decision-making authority or influence over buying from you

Conversely, you could assign someone a negative lead score if you knew there was something about that person that would not make her a candidate for your products or services, such as:

- The contact is an employee of your company.
- Not in a position of authority to buy from you.

TIP

Encourage your leads and clients to fill out as much information as possible through profile updates. You and your team then need minimal effort to enter additional data.

You also want to work with a CRM that automatically researches a contact and fills in the data you don't know (see Chapter 8). This information is extremely beneficial, as you can add relevant data that helps your sales team understand more about all your contacts. FullContact (`www.fullcontact.com`) and TowerData (`www.towerdata.com`) are two data providers that can provide this service.

Figure 6-3 show how you might set up rules for your business. The top rule removes someone with a company email address from automation and from the "hot contacts" reporting.

Demographic Lead Scoring

New Lead Score

If Email	contains	greenrope	then contribute	-50	points	Delete
If Title	contains	VP	then contribute	5	points	Delete
If Title	contains	President	then contribute	10	points	Delete
If Title	contains	sales	then contribute	9	points	Delete
If Title	contains	marketing	then contribute	8	points	Delete
If Title	contains	Director	then contribute	5	points	Delete
If Title	contains	account	then contribute	5	points	Delete
If Title	contains	manager	then contribute	4	points	Delete
If Title	contains	Vice President	then contribute	5	points	Delete
If Title	contains	senior	then contribute	5	points	Delete

FIGURE 6-3: Setting up demographic lead scoring rules.

Building activity lead scoring rules

Activity lead scores are based on people taking action. You can give a lead points for interacting with your brand in any number of ways. Examples would be:

- Reading or clicking an email
- Visiting a webpage
- Watching a video
- Filling out a form
- Chatting with your support team
- Meeting with a salesperson

REMEMBER

One important characteristic about activity lead scoring to consider is that the value of actions decays over time. Recent actions are more important than past actions. For example, someone reading an email six months ago is not nearly as valuable to you as someone reading an email today. If a lead watched a video about one of your products an hour ago, it's more relevant to a salesperson than if that video was watched last week.

With activity lead score decay, you determine how fast those points decrease over time. One common method is using the same math as radioactive half-life calculations. Don't be scared by this math, but it looks like this:

Current Points = Original Points * $e^{-\text{Time Elapsed/Half-Life}}$

The end result looks something like Figure 6-4.

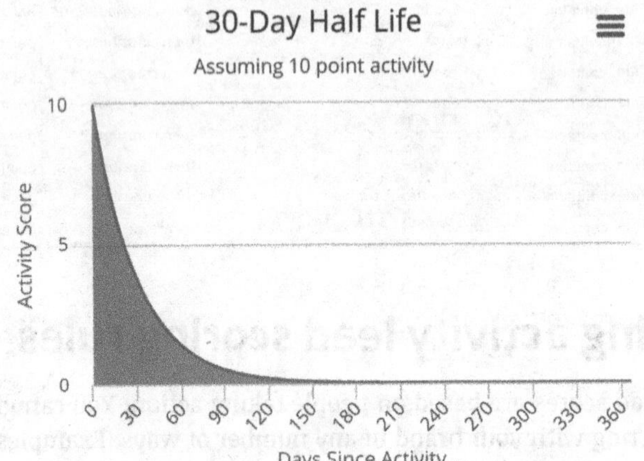

FIGURE 6-4: Decay rate of an activity score with a half-life of 30 days.

Generally speaking, you want to set your half-life to two or three times your average sales cycle. Unless you have a very short "churn and burn" approach to your business, keep your half-life more than 30 days.

Activity lead scoring decay is absolutely critical to have in your CRM. Without it, your data becomes cluttered and you're unable to differentiate between high quality recent leads and leads that were important a long time ago but are no longer relevant.

3 Implementing Your CRM

IN THIS PART . . .

Set up your CRM for success and tie the components together efficiently.

Create effective lead capture with follow-up techniques that work.

Use chat, phone, and social channels to capture and market to leads.

Market to leads and clients with email in a way that generates response.

Automate communication and follow up with the right marketing automation tools and techniques.

Store corporate knowledge in a searchable knowledge base connected to your CRM.

Manage projects and billing with your CRM.

Host events, collect registration, and track attendance with tools that tie back to your CRM and marketing.

IN THIS CHAPTER

» Establishing roles and responsibilities for your users

» Defining groups and data fields

» Storing your data effectively

» Automating interfaces with accounting

» Connecting other software to your CRM

Chapter 7
Setting Up Your CRM Elements

Your CRM is the heart of your business. Your CRM database stores detailed and relational information about the relationships you have with your leads, clients, and vendors. The information stored and transferred between members of your organization is connected like branches in a tree. Data collected and the conclusions drawn from your analysis must travel to the right branches to keep the tree alive.

In this chapter, you discover the first steps in setting up your CRM. Your users must have access to the relevant data they need to accomplish their goals. Users need access to information that helps them do their jobs better. They need rights to view and edit data in the CRM that is relevant to them, but not change data they shouldn't be able to change.

Contact versus Account-Based CRM

Good CRM platforms are flexible enough to support interactions with both individual contacts and "accounts," which are often synonymous with "companies."

Contacts are individual people, and they are usually treated as unique entities based on email address or a combination of name and company or name and phone number. Your CRM assigns a unique ID to each individual contact.

Accounts represent clusters of contacts all bound together by the same entity. They're often a company, but sometimes can represent another binding organization.

Account-based CRM allows you to aggregate the activity of contacts within a company or an account together. It allows you to attach custom fields to both individual contacts and companies.

If you sell to businesses, you want the flexibility to work directly with contacts, as well as the companies they belong to. It's an important distinction when you are evaluating CRM solutions.

If you sell to individuals or consumers, you likely will not have much use for a account-based CRM. You track individual buyers through your sales funnel. On the other hand, if you sell to businesses, it's helpful to see how all the contacts in a company interact with you and your team. Looking at CRM activities, email interaction, webpage visits, and more at a company level (see Figure 7-1) likely indicates who your champion at that company is. Evaluating key decision makers helps you sell better.

Even with account-based CRM, you're still selling and communicating with individuals.

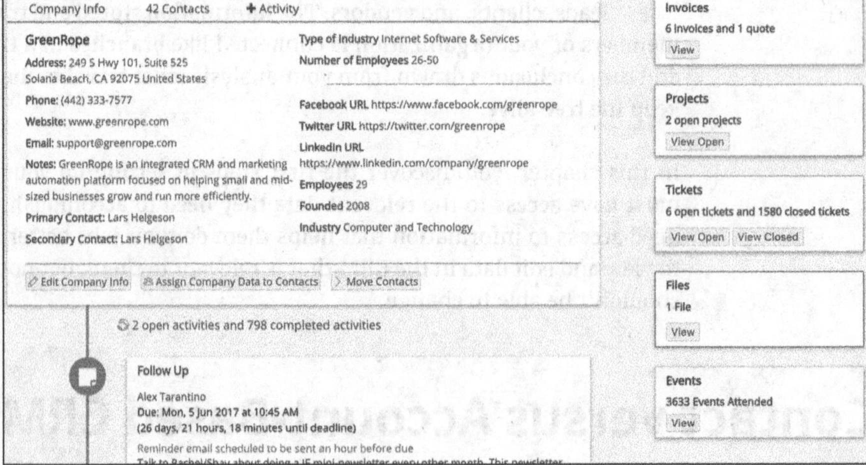

FIGURE 7-1: Looking at account-level information gives insight into how to sell to a company effectively.

Defining Users and Their Roles

An important part of designing and managing your CRM is understanding who uses the software and how. Ideally, everyone in your organization who is involved in sales, marketing, and operations has access to the parts of the CRM he needs. The contributions each team member makes flows into the system, helping others do their jobs. This workflow creates a culture of collaboration, efficiency, and consistent customer experience.

Controlling access to information

Not everyone on your team should have access to everything in the CRM. For example, an IT tech has no reason to look at product development data, and vice versa. You must determine who should see what and set a policy for everyone in those roles by job title.

Groups in a CRM create divisions of access. You can restrict access by groups of contacts. Give each group separate permissions, and each user in that group can access those functions associated with the group. (See Figure 7-2 for an example of shared rights.) With groups, you can set up contact-related access for salespeople, but not give them the ability to send a newsletter to everyone.

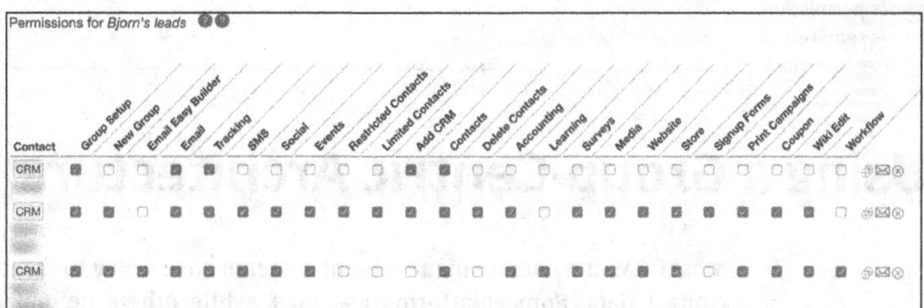

FIGURE 7-2: A shared access controls screen.

WARNING

One common trap that many companies fall into is sharing logins. Many CRM platforms charge per user, so in an effort to save money, companies allow users to share the same login. This practice is extremely dangerous and should never be done. Not only does it confuse the accountability trail, but it also opens the CRM for exploitation by people who shouldn't have the same access. If one of your users shares a login and someone else accesses data he shouldn't have, downloads data, or enters erroneous data, there is no way to track that activity to the individual who did it.

REMEMBER

Marketers who are responsible for designing and tracking automation likely need broad access to the CRM. The data required for personalization and designing automation is a multi-channel activity that spans your different market segments.

Every CRM should have an internal manager (or two) to ensure shared access rights are granted appropriately. When someone leaves the organization, that access manager revokes permissions. Keeping your permissions up to date is important for long-term security.

Limiting data export

One issue that many companies face is controlling the ability to export data from your CRM. It's of upmost importance that you take every possible measure to prevent critical client data from falling into the wrong hands. Requiring special permission to export data is a good way to lock down your data. Look for a setting in your CRM that allows you to alert users about exporting data, as shown in Figure 7-3.

Export Contacts

To export contacts, you must first unlock this account for exporting. Clicking the button below will send the export request to lars@myteamcaptain.com. Once the link in that email has been clicked to confirm it's ok to export contacts, click the Refresh button to activate your export.

Request Export Ability | Refresh

FIGURE 7-3: Warning users that account owner permission is required to export.

Using a Group-Centric Architecture

Most CRM and contact management systems have a way to create subsets of your contact data. Some platforms use tags, while others define campaigns, but I believe groups are the best way to segment your contacts. However you decide to segment your contacts, it's easier to plan this grouping and tagging before your team starts using your CRM.

Define your groups around how you and your team use your CRM. Think about who needs access to which contacts and why. A few examples of how you can segment your CRM with group-centric architecture are:

- Salespeople, so they can manage their leads and clients (and not other contacts belonging to other salespeople). Sometimes multiple groups for each salesperson are created to help them segment their contacts (for example, leads, converted clients, and lost clients).

- » Contacts entering different phases of an opportunity. For example, if an opportunity entering the proposal evaluation phase always triggers the same action on your side, you may want to add someone to a group that triggers a workflow or a drip campaign.
- » Significant market segments, so your marketing team can focus their efforts if messaging usually doesn't cross over between those segments.
- » Market segments for those speaking different languages.
- » Different business operating units. If different staff accesses the CRM, you want to ensure a virtual wall is between those contacts.
- » Recurring events with the same attendees. Create a separate group for those events and their attendees.

Figure 7-4 shows group architecture built into the navigation of a CRM. A user can dive into a specific group easily. This particular user is a salesperson, with different groups of leads, as well as some groups for a booking calendar, remarketing, and testing.

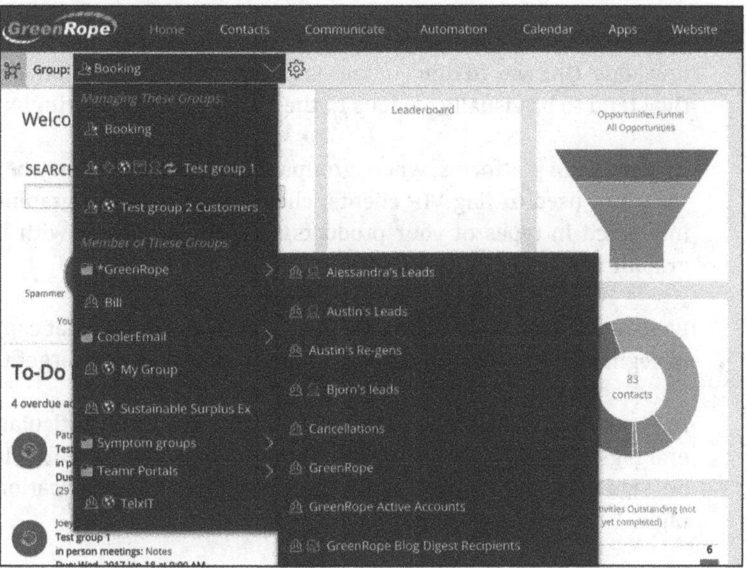

FIGURE 7-4: Group management in a salesperson's account.

Differentiating between tags, custom data fields, and groups

Different CRMs use these terms to mean different things, but some have agreed on a few standard definitions.

- **Groups:** These are groups of contacts or companies. Usually they're associated by having the same interests in your products or services, or they may be grouped by who has access to them. Any contacts or companies can be in multiple groups, so be aware of any overlap that may occur.
- **Custom data fields:** These are attached to the contacts or companies themselves. These represent data fields that describe the contact or company.
- **Tags:** Tags are high-level ways to segment your contacts and companies. You should be able to easily pick out contacts and companies that are tagged with the same tag.

Keep in mind that you also want to be mindful of using custom fields or tags to segment your data. There are nuances to the implications of the different tactics, so be sure to talk to the vendor or your consultant if you need direction.

TIP

Tags are a useful method to segment your contact list, but too many tags can get unwieldy. One way to think of tags is as very important custom data fields. Because they tend to be visually obvious to the user, use them sparingly.

In some CRM platforms, where groups are not used, tags may be your only option. They can used to flag VIP clients, clients in specific geographic regions, clients interested in types of your products/services, or clients with important demographic characteristics.

Be sure you work with your CRM vendor to understand what capabilities you have in segmenting your contacts so you can limit access and target those contacts.

In Figure 7-5, tags flag a contact visually in a list. This particular contact has several tags (CW, CSS, HTML5, USA). You should be able to search for contacts based on tags assigned to them and target outbound communication based on those tags.

Any data you want to store about a contact or a company should fall into a custom data field. Your CRM should allow you to have as many of these as you like, but you want to be prudent with storing and displaying information you never use.

FIGURE 7-5: Displaying tags on a contact record for easy identification.

Setting attributes for groups

Grouping your contacts is a foundational element of your CRM. These groups are also useful for performing other tasks and giving you insight into your business. As such, contacts are a part of groups, but you should also be able to attach other objects to your groups. A useful list of these objects are

- **Custom data fields:** Data should only be accessible to people who have access to a group. Custom data fields give you the ability to limit access to private data.
- **Campaigns:** Target campaigns to existing or new members of a group to address specific market segments.
- **Email attributes:** You may want to default emails that are sent to a group to be from a particular name or email address. You may also want to specify a default physical address or language to be used.
- **Email syncing:** If you want to synchronize emails from your staff with your CRM, using groups to do so is a convenient way to maintain security and privacy.
- **Events:** Manage recurring events with invitations and driving registration from all members of a group. Set reminder frequency for events, languages, locations, and more.

Limiting access by group

If you have salespeople who only need to access a subset of the total contacts in your account, or if you have business units that you want to keep separate, groups are a great way to separate access rights. CRM platforms give you the ability to set specific permission levels into different subsets of your account, and using groups is a very easy way to accomplish it.

REMEMBER

In designing your groups, take into consideration if you want to have only a few people able to access part of your account. Create a separate group for those people. A good CRM platform allows you to have contacts in as many groups as you like, so you can maintain flexibility in your access controls. Figure 7-6 shows three users who have access to the group "Austin's Leads." These users have permissions defined by the checked boxes.

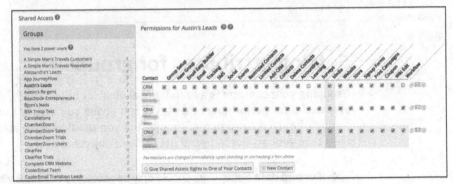

FIGURE 7-6: Three shared access users can affect this group.

Setting Up Custom Data Fields

You also want to refer to the needs of your sales, marketing, and operations people to ensure you're capturing and storing the data you need. These custom fields are attached to contacts and companies (also known as "accounts" in some CRM systems).

REMEMBER

Some custom fields are restricted to a particular group. Some are universal. Be cognizant of which are applicable.

For example, you can set up a custom field for a specific segment of your market. If you decide to create a group for people who are interested in buying one of your widgets, and that widget comes in blue, green, or red, you could store what color your leads prefer. Then you could send an email to them with a custom image of the widget in the color they're interested in, personalizing the message they receive.

You should be able to assign workflows to changing values in the CRM (see Chapter 11). You can easily trigger actions based on someone updating data in the CRM.

TIP

You can trigger a workflow to activate when someone enters values into a form for lead capture. If someone indicates an interest in a product, that could be stored in a custom data field. After that's set, it can alert a product sales team to follow up in a scheduled series of CRM activities.

Defining custom data fields by type

Most CRM platforms allow you to specify the kind of data that goes into a field. If you want to limit typing mistakes in data entry, use field types that constrain what can be entered into a field. Usually data entry is in the form of a drop-down list or check boxes. If you want a number entered in a field, you can force the data entry to be a number. Data entry is then accurate and consistent.

Figure 7-7 shows how you can configure a custom data field. The editing area includes the type of field and certain permission and visibility settings. You can also set a trigger setting, which automates a workflow if a value is set.

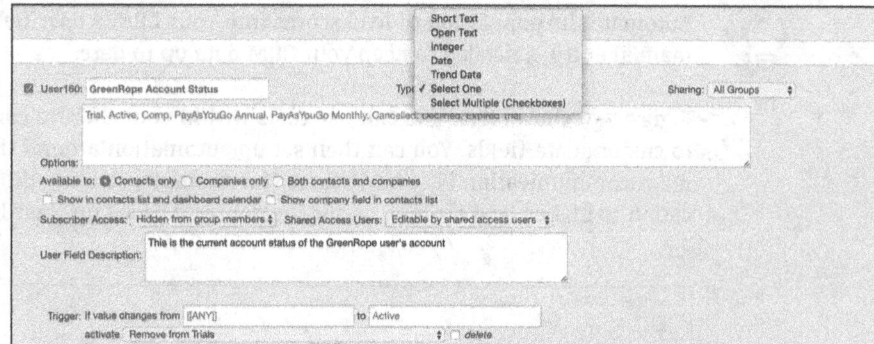

FIGURE 7-7: A data field configuration screen.

Using equations to draw conclusions

Equations are a powerful way to show combinations of data in a single field. If you know that several factors contribute to an overall score, equations built into your CRM can make your life easy. With the user field for combined lead scores in Figure 7-8, a single combined score represents the addition of demographic and activity lead scores. Chapter 6 talks about lead scoring.

User373: Combined Lead Score Type: Short Text Sharing: All Groups
Available to: Contacts only Companies only Both contacts and companies
Show in contacts list and dashboard calendar Show company field in contacts list
Subscriber Access: Hidden from group members Shared Access Users: Editable by shared access users
User Field Description:
Equation: User370 + User371 Set Data
Add Trigger

FIGURE 7-8: An equation user field that combines demographic and activity lead scores.

Linking lead scoring to user fields

One perfect example of how to use equations with your user fields is to set up a simple rule that combines your activity and demographic lead scores. You want to assign these lead scores to user fields, which makes it easy to use an equation — for example, User3 + User4 = User5. User3 is the activity lead score, User4 is the demographic lead score, and User5 is the calculated total lead score. You can use the total lead score for reference, or trigger an automated workflow.

TIP

Automate the population of lead scores into your CRM's user fields. That way, no manual entry is needed to keep your CRM data up to date.

Figure 7-9 shows how you can use tools within your CRM to connect lead scores to custom data fields. You can then set up automation around those scores, segment communication based on scores (for example, sending different communication to higher lead scores), or sorting contacts based on their lead scores.

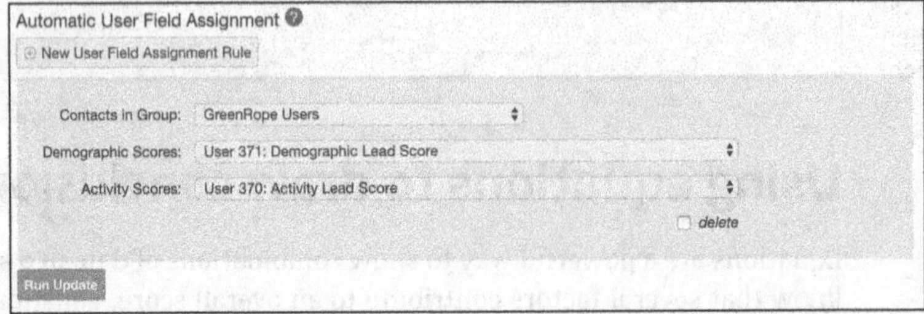

FIGURE 7-9: Set up automatic lead scoring syncing to user fields.

Storing Files

One useful part of a good CRM is centralized file storage. These files can be used for storing assets that can easily be called up by your sales, marketing, or operations staff.

Saving files and snippets for easy access by users

Integrated file storage (see Figure 7-10) has many uses in your CRM, including these examples:

- **HTML emails:** Either as templates for your salespeople to send one-to-one messages from the CRM, or as templates for your marketing team to design newsletters, email files are important to form a standardized basis for communication.
- **Images:** When building emails or webpages, it's helpful to have access to imagery you're likely to use on a regular basis. Your company logo, photos of key personnel, or screenshots are all useful to have available to your entire team.
- **Informational PDFs:** If you want your leads, clients, and/or staff to access data sheets or other useful documents, storing those files in a library can save the time to find where those critical files are.

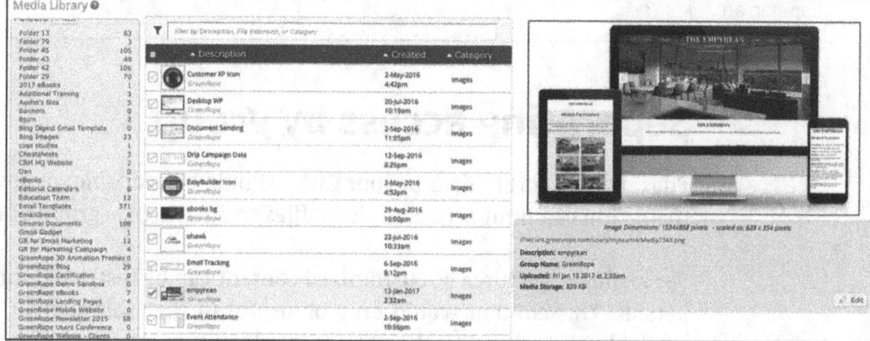

FIGURE 7-10: A centralized repository of assets makes retrieving what users need easy.

TIP

Make all your files accessible through a trackable link shortener (for example, bit.ly), so you can keep track of by whom and how often your files are downloaded.

Storing snippets or articles

You may want to store more than complete files in your library. It may make sense to save HTML snippets or fragments of content for use in other applications. You can then easily reuse reviews, articles, or blogs in different marketing channels. Or your support team can use them to answer tickets.

TIP

Storing snippets is useful when you have multiple people generating documents or parts of documents to use by your team. If you give certain contributors or editors the ability to write articles that your marketing team can use for blogs or emails, storing snippets allows them to reuse that content. This storage may be available through Dropbox, Google Drive, or even embedded directly within your CRM.

Figure 7-11 shows how members of your team can contribute content to be used and reused again, which is sometimes referred to as *evergreen content*.

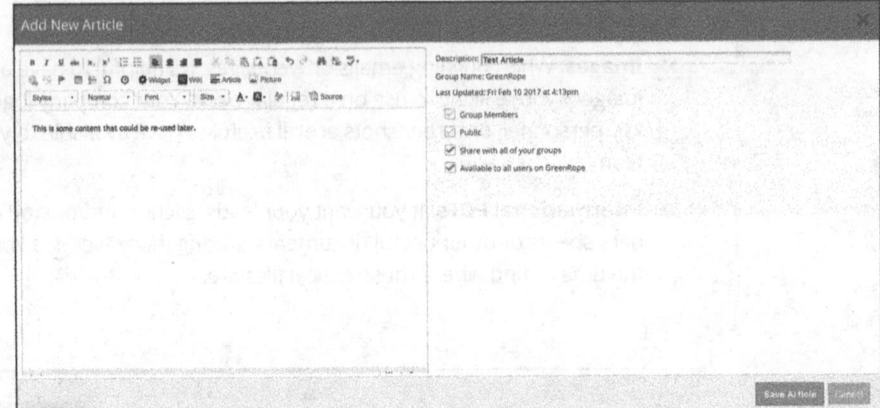

FIGURE 7-11: Using a stored snippet in an article.

Separating access by group

Files, just like other data in your CRM, should be available to only users who need them. You can limit access to those files to a particular group of users.

For example, pictures or customized content can be restricted for a specific salesperson. This content would only be useful to that salesperson, so by making it available exclusively to the salesperson's group, that data doesn't clutter other salespeople's libraries.

Signing Documents Automatically

A Complete CRM includes the ability to streamline your document signing process. If someone needs a document or contract signed, you can auto-populate parts of the form, track when the document is sent and opened, and record its signing through your CRM.

CHOOSING A GOOD E-SIGNATURE PLATFORM

Any e-signature platform you choose should integrate with your CRM. Be sure you can easily send personalized versions of documents and automatically attach them to the contact record of the person you sent them to.

Because workflows are such a critical part of your CRM, you want to make sure a workflow can trigger a document to be sent to someone. Ideally, you want to be able to personalize that document as well, filling in relevant information such as the contact's name, company, and any contractual specifics you can embed in user fields.

Figure 7-12 shows how document signing can be used for automating an internal process of employees signing their handbooks. With your CRM integrated with a document signing system, you can automate the process and store the digital signatures electronically — making a process that can be cumbersome simple.

Template: GreenRope Handbook

Account: @greenrope.com
Subject: GreenRope Handbook
Message: Please sign this document
Upon Completion: Activate Workflow :: Bjorn Followup

FIGURE 7-12: Automating employee handbook signing.

Bridging Your Online Store and Your CRM

Many businesses sell products or raise funds online. E-commerce has been around for many years, but now with advances in CRM and marketing automation technology, you can connect your e-commerce with the rest of your business processes.

Picking a good storefront

A wide variety of storefront options are available to you, most providing at least basic functionality to display products and categories, and place items into a shopping cart for purchase. Beyond that, you can look at higher-end solutions like Magento or Shopify, or simpler solutions that plug into a WordPress or Wix website.

REMEMBER

Like the rest of your CRM process, you want to ensure the storefront meets your requirements for displaying your products or donation options, gives you the tracking you need, and integrates well with the rest of your system. Data transfer is important here, so you can record purchases in your CRM automatically. Most good e-commerce storefronts and shopping carts have Zapier zaps available to push the transaction data to your CRM.

Picking a good merchant provider

You have many options when it comes to finding a processor for taking credit card payments. On the surface, it's an easy task. Accept a credit card and have the funds deposited into your checking account. There is room for negotiation, though, so you want to be savvy about how the credit card industry works before you settle on a company to help you take online payments.

There are two components to taking credit cards: the processor and underlying software it uses. The software that hosts forms and has services available to automatically charge customers is, generally speaking, a commodity. I have worked a lot with Authorize.net, but there are others like Card Services International. Make sure that the software you choose is compatible with your CRM.

The processor is an intermediary company, bridging the gap between the charging software and your bank. They negotiate the agreement with the credit card companies, including the rate you pay when someone gives you his credit card to charge.

The rate that you pay has profit built into it by the processor. As a merchant, it is your job to find the best rate, as most processors don't provide any service other than as a middleman, collecting a part of every transaction you run. Interview at least two or three processors to find out what they charge for each kind of transaction. This gives you insight into how much of every transaction will be lost due to processing fees.

One important aspect of getting the best rate is to understand how processors quote their *discount rates*. A discount rate is a percentage of the total charge amount that goes to the processor. You want to insist on getting a rate that is based on a fixed margin over the *interchange rate*. The interchange rate is the wholesale charge that the credit card company charges for every transaction processed. This depends on the quality of the transaction (lower quality means higher risk and therefore higher fees) and is something you can't influence. What you can influence is the margin above the interchange rate. Processors will tell you that the margin depends on your processing volume (how much you charge every month) and the average charge amount.

Be wary of processors who quote you a single rate, as often this is indicative of the rate they charge for an ideal transaction (such as when a card is physically present for the transaction). If you run a charge through that is not ideal (like an e-commerce transaction), they are not required to charge you that amount. Make sure you ask the right questions and read the fine print.

Processors will also charge you a monthly access fee, which should be fixed. They will also likely charge a fixed per-transaction fee. When you are running your numbers, take all of this into consideration so you make the most informed decision and pay as little as possible to the processor.

Automating purchase actions

With your CRM connected to your e-commerce engine, you can have transactions trigger workflows. These workflows may automatically send a thank-you message, a product quality survey, or a discount for other purchases. They may also schedule a follow-up CRM activity for a salesperson to check in on the new client. You're only limited by your imagination on what you would like to have happen after the purchase is made.

Integrating Billing, Quotes, and Invoices

Building accounting and money management into your CRM closes the loop between your marketing and the execution side of the sales process. One important factor in designing your CRM is making sure the financials tie into your sales, marketing, and operations.

Sending quotes and invoices from your CRM makes setting up reporting and automation easier. Your sales and financial systems should be in sync with each other, and people in your organization want to know relevant information such as how much a client has paid, whether a client is delinquent on any invoices, or whether any quotes are already in the hands of a lead.

Accepting credit cards for payment

Accepting credit cards for payment gives your CRM an easy way to gather purchase data and automatically trigger workflows when purchases are made. This automation streamlines your interaction with customers, allowing you to operate more efficiently while gathering vital data in real time.

The decision to accept credit or debit cards for payment has implications on several parts of your CRM. You need a *merchant account*, where payments you receive by credit card are deposited into your organization's checking account. The primary advantage, of course, is immediate payment. There are some issues to be aware of.

- **Fraud:** Be sure you consider that some transactions will be fraudulent, so you will want to minimize what you can upfront. Require some form of identification that comes with the purchase process.

- **Chargebacks:** Sometimes unhappy clients will ask their credit card company to reverse charges. Most of the time, the credit card company will side with the consumer, so be sure you have clear documentation about the terms of the purchase. Be prepared to manage chargebacks and send records to your credit card processor.
- **Discount rates:** Your merchant account provider, the company that facilitates the transfer of money between your buyer and your bank, will charge a fee for that service. They usually work with a credit card processor, such as Authorize.net or Card Services International. These rates are negotiable and will vary depending on the fraud risk of your company, average value of your transactions, and total number of transactions you run per month.
- **Fees:** There are often other fees to consider in setting up your credit card processing. Setup fees are usually charge by your bank or process, but should never be over $100. Transaction fees are usually fixed per-transaction charges, and should never exceed $.25. Statement fees are charged by your processor and should never exceed $20 per month.
- **Recurring charges:** You may want to have the ability to charge someone several times, something that not all merchant account providers support. Be sure to have the ability to do this when you do your research.

With discount rates, you can usually negotiate a rate as a margin over interchange. The "interchange rate" is a rate that the credit card company charges to your processor for every transaction. This rate varies on the kind of card and quality of transaction (card-present transactions are considered lower risk and therefore have a lower discount rate). Negotiate an interchange-plus-margin payment model with your processor. Depending on your volume and average ticket total, you should expect to pay between 0.05% and 0.50% above interchange. Shop around and look for a reputable merchant processor. Sometimes your bank provides competitive services and pricing.

Building and sending quotes and invoices

When using your CRM, you should be able to choose a contact within your database and send a quote or an invoice directly to that person. You should also look for these features:

- Give the recipient the ability to accept the quote and immediately turn it into an invoice.
- Force quotes to expire on a certain date.
- Track when the quote or invoice is opened and read, so that you and your accounts receivable team can confirm the customer has received your invoice.

When you send an invoice, make it easy for your contact to pay that invoice. Payment updates your CRM and your accounting system. A merchant account for your business also allows you to paid by credit card.

Connecting Legacy and Related Software

Your CRM may not be able to do everything that your company does with sales, marketing, and operations. When you have to connect external software, you need a way for that software to talk to your CRM.

Software can be connected in several ways. When using a cloud-based CRM, everything must function over the Internet. The slowest way to transfer files and data is by exporting data from one system and importing it into another. Importing and exporting can be a tedious process, more susceptible to human error, time-consuming, and an inefficient use of resources.

REMEMBER

You also want to limit export/import permission to specific groups of users to keep control of your data. Permission should be set up through your IT department.

The other way software can be connected is through an automated programming interface (API). APIs allow two services to talk to each other in an automated fashion, so you don't need any people involved in systems keeping each other up to date.

Building API bridges to your CRM

An API is only as good as the capabilities built into it. When you're connecting two different software systems, you must look at the four sides of the connections (see Figure 7-13):

- **Export from the other software.** The other software you're using must be able to pull data out and format it in a way that your CRM accepts. If you're importing contact data, you need to make sure that data maps to your CRM data. Some data seems easy, such as someone's name, but the process can be complicated because you need to set up rules on how to format that name. Are first name and last name separate fields? Do you care about the middle name, title, or suffixes such as PhD?

» **Import into your CRM.** The data then must be transferred to your CRM. Make sure the data transfer is secure and encrypted, and verify formatting. Do a test to ensure the data transfers to the correct fields.

» **Export out of your CRM.** Talk to your CRM vendor to see what kind of data you can export. Be sure to get an understanding of what kind of format the export uses.

» **Import into other software.** You need to translate the CRM-exported data into a format that your other software accepts. Just as with importing into your CRM, you need to map the fields and test your API before you turn it loose on your entire database.

An API requires the skills of a developer or system integrator with a team of developers. The developer needs to know what your requirements are for integration, and translate those requirements into software that connects all these pieces together.

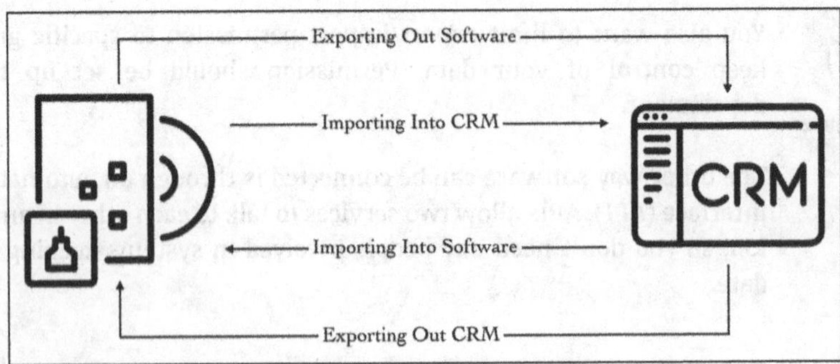

FIGURE 7-13: The four sides of an API.

Choosing master-slave versus master-master

One decision you need to make is how to handle conflicts in data. If one system says one thing but the other system says another, you must have rules in place to make sure your API connections know what to do. You can follow two types of rules:

» **Master-slave:** One system is always correct. If the other gets out of sync, the master always overrides the slave. In this scenario, good data can be overwritten, so make sure you fully understand what it means for your data management. The weakness of this system is that when the master fails, a new system must become the master before any updates to the data can occur.

» **Master-master:** This approach relies on which data set is most up to date. The most recently updated data becomes the master. Setting up master-master control is more difficult. If any system can update any part of your data, you must have strict rules that govern what happens in case of a conflict. You have to account for *latency*, where a delay in updating could cause issues with overwriting good data.

Understanding server and network limitations

Whenever you have two computers talking to each other, data is transferring and computer CPUs is processing data. Sometimes the people who manage those servers and networks place limitations or charge you for using the tools you need for those connectors.

Some CRM platforms charge extra to connect to their API, so when you're looking at pricing for different solutions, be sure to account for that. If either side of the connection charges for bandwidth, get an estimate for transferring that data. You may be surprised by the increase in cost that some companies charge to access their networks.

Importing Leads by File

When you load contacts and companies into your CRM for the first time, you likely are transferring that data from a system you already have in place. Your current system may be an existing CRM, or it may simply be an Excel file.

Usually data from your current system is exported into a CSV (comma separated values) file delimited by tabs or commas. These simple text files are a convenient way to import and export data from different platforms. A typical line from a CSV file looks like:

"Joe","Smith","ACME Widget Co","123 Main Street","Sometown","CA"

It may be helpful to set up a header row that defines what each of the columns means first. Be sure as you import new data or fields into the CRM that the CRM is set up to receive and store that new data with custom data fields (see the earlier section "Setting Up Custom Data Fields").

You then need to import this data into your CRM. If you follow the instructions provided by your CRM platform, the import should be quick and easy. If you run into issues, contact your CRM vendor for help.

TIP

To get a visual look at the structure of your data, look at your data in Excel, as shown in Figure 7-14. Information is in columns, making it a simple task to see when you have data that doesn't line up properly.

FIGURE 7-14: A simple Excel file layout for easy import into a CRM.

A	B	C	D	E	F
Firstname	Lastname	Email	Company	User1	Groups
Mary	Moore	mary@something.com	ABC Tech	Football,Soccer	Leads, Salesperson A
Barbara	Smith	barb@another.com	ACME Widget	Soccer,Hockey	Leads, Salesperson B
Mike	Jones	mike@widgets.com	Super Widget	Football	Leads, Salesperson A

From any spreadsheet program, you can export your data as a CSV or tab-delimited text file, which should be easy to import into your CRM.

Choosing a master

If you routinely import and export data in and out of your CRM, you can save time if you set up a preference for which data overwrites or "masters" the other data. Doing so prevents old data from overwriting newer, better data. If your team is regularly transferring data, establish a protocol that everyone follows. All CRM platforms have a setting that lets you determine if the imported file takes precedence or the existing CRM data holds precedence.

Triggering automated action by import

Your CRM platform should allow you to activate some form of automation upon importing new records. You can then set up delivery of messages, schedule CRM activities, or do anything else you would like your workflows to activate when a contact is added to your CRM.

One easy way to automate lead nurturing programs is to set up drip campaigns attached to the groups that you add contacts to. Some marketing automation programs use tags, but the end workflow has the same intent. The imported file can drop contacts into those groups, and as a result, trigger emails and workflows to those new contacts. Using new data to start contacts on a buyer journey is an effective way to use your CRM and marketing automation platform's power to generate sales.

IN THIS CHAPTER

» Determining how to get leads

» Pulling leads in through your website

» Tracking campaigns through IDs

» Using sign-up forms on your website

» Filling in contact information

» Automating processes

Chapter 8
Capturing Leads to Build Your CRM Database

Capturing leads and getting them into your CRM is of utmost importance for growing your business. Your contacts are the most valuable part of your business, because your relationship with those contacts drives your revenue and your growth. Whether you are a B2B or B2C company (or both), you want to maximize the chance of gathering qualified leads.

Tracking marketing campaigns and using integrated tools such forms to add new leads into your CRM is critical to growth and efficiency. Whether you ask leads to fill out a form or you automatically gather their data from partners, that data must be easily accessible to your sales and marketing teams. A Complete CRM strategy includes these lead capture processes and makes it easy for you to see which work best.

This chapter shows you how to use signup forms and ticketing forms to gather new leads and add them to your CRM. You also find out how to set up different kinds of automation for your new leads, and successful techniques for organizing them as they come in.

Finding the Best Lead Capture Methods

You can use many strategies and tactics to gather leads. At the very beginning of the process to bring leads to you is advertising, and it has two main components — *awareness* and *perception*. Awareness is letting people know you exist, and perception is the emotional feeling your target market gets when people connect with your brand.

Three types of advertising are useful: pay-per-click (PPC), retargeting, and SEO.

All the variables that go into positioning your ad on search engines make for a large, complex system. If you don't have an in-house expert to manage PPC or SEO (each of these is a different skill set), outsource the work. Most companies charge a management fee for PPC (usually 10-20 percent of your ad spend) or a fixed rate for SEO (usually a retainer based on a minimum number of hours at a specified hourly rate).

Pay-per-click

Pay-per-click advertising is the de facto standard for bringing awareness and leads to your online presence. Google is the dominant player in this market, representing over 90 percent of all search traffic. These ads, listed as sponsored ads when someone searches for a certain keyword on a search engine, provides a link to a specific webpage. This webpage should be a special, targeted webpage (also known as a *landing page*) that correlates to that ad. If you're targeting a market segment, make sure the ad and the landing page are relevant and match their message. Your CRM can automatically assign a campaign ID to people who click certain ads.

The landing page itself should be simple with a clear call to action, as shown in Figure 8-1. Video is a useful medium for communicating testimonials or an overview of what you do.

Figure 8-2 displays paid ads at the top of the page; they're displayed by the amount advertisers paid.

TIP

You can set up pay-per-click ads on other websites such as Facebook, LinkedIn, and Twitter, as shown in Figure 8-3. You can also post ads on content networks. In all cases, you have control over the text and/or imagery in the ad, so be sure the content is consistent with what you're selling and uses the voice and brand you want to represent you.

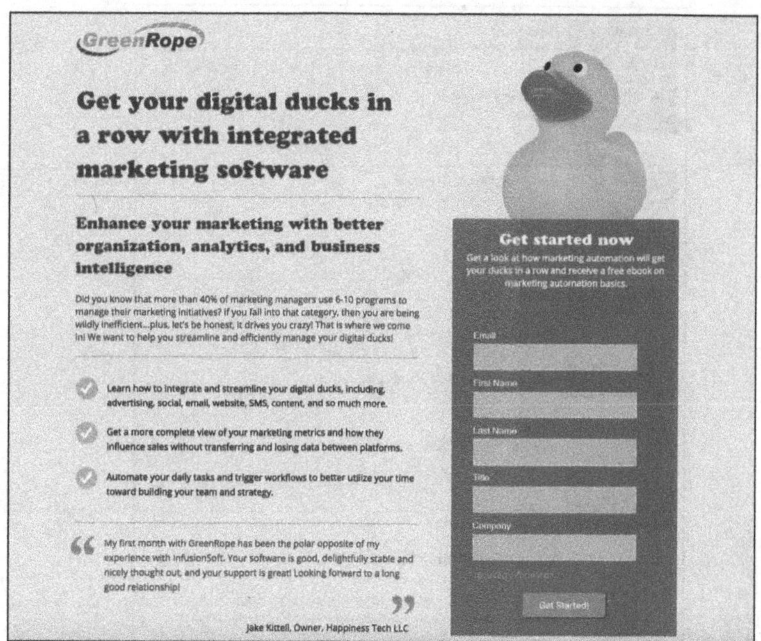

FIGURE 8-1: A landing page with a simple message and a short form.

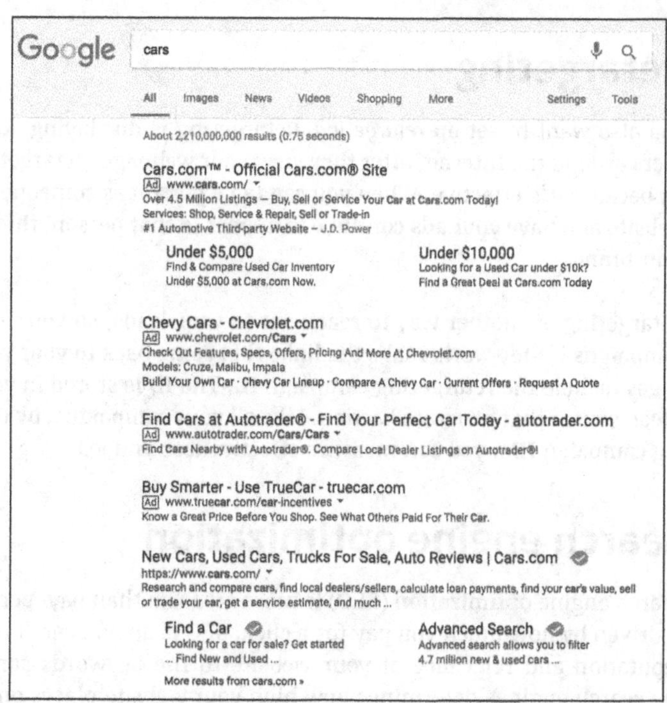

FIGURE 8-2: Paid search ads appear at the top of search pages.

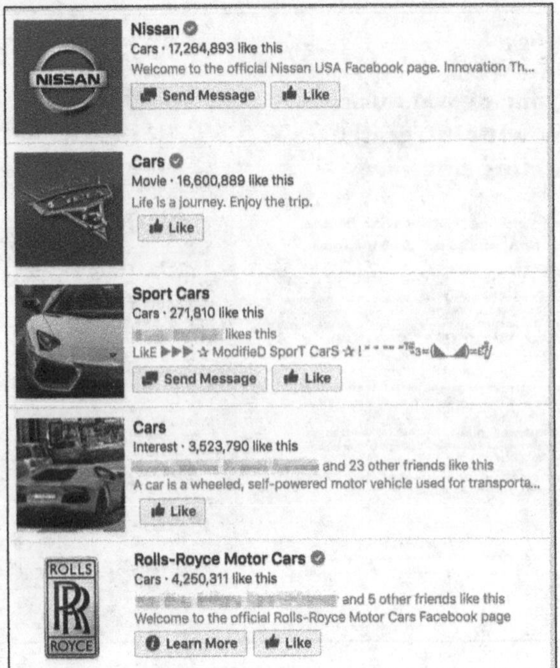

FIGURE 8-3: Searching for "cars" on Facebook.

Retargeting

You also want to set up *retargeting*. Retargeting is displaying ads that follow the users around the Internet after they view your webpage. Retargeting is very popular because it's effective. When you can tag a person as someone who visited your website and have your ads continue to appear to that person, they are reminded of your brand.

Retargeting is another way to reach out to your leads, so you must include these campaigns if they work. Make the links that come back to your website or landing pages include the retargeting campaign ID. The ID is stored in your CRM as being a lead source that generated action. Like all your campaigns, by tracking retargeting campaign IDs, you can measure effectiveness and ROI.

Search engine optimization

Search engine optimization (SEO) is more art form than pay-per-click. While PPC is driven by how much you pay for a click, SEO is about search result quality. The reputation and relevance of your website to the keywords someone types into the search engines determines how high your website places on the search page. The better the reputation, the more likely your website is shown to a visitor searching for something related to the content on your website.

TIP

A popular SEO tactic is to build content (for example, blogs and landing pages) on your website specifically to answer questions that people tend to search for. The more you can answer those questions with useful information, the more likely you are to capture that search traffic.

Creating metrics to measure lead capture performance

When you see reports on how well your lead capture is doing, you want to be sure you're looking at relevant data. First analyze your ads. Look at the different campaigns you're running and measure the click-through rates and costs associated with each campaign, as shown in Figure 8-4.

One important cost to focus on is the early stage conversion. Conversions, which happen when someone becomes a customer, usually have multiple stages, so you measure the amount of money it takes to bring someone into that buyer journey. For example, the cost to get someone to fill out the form on your landing page. If each click costs $1, and it takes 100 clicks to get one lead into your funnel, the average cost for this early stage conversion is $100.

This example represents the average cost to put a lead into your sales funnel. After someone is in your funnel, you can then measure the amount of time and the rate of conversion to each next step of the buyer journey. Progress down the buyer journey may or may not correlate with your cost per click on the ad, as higher quality traffic has more people filling out your form.

Chapter 15 goes more indepth about the different metrics you can measure.

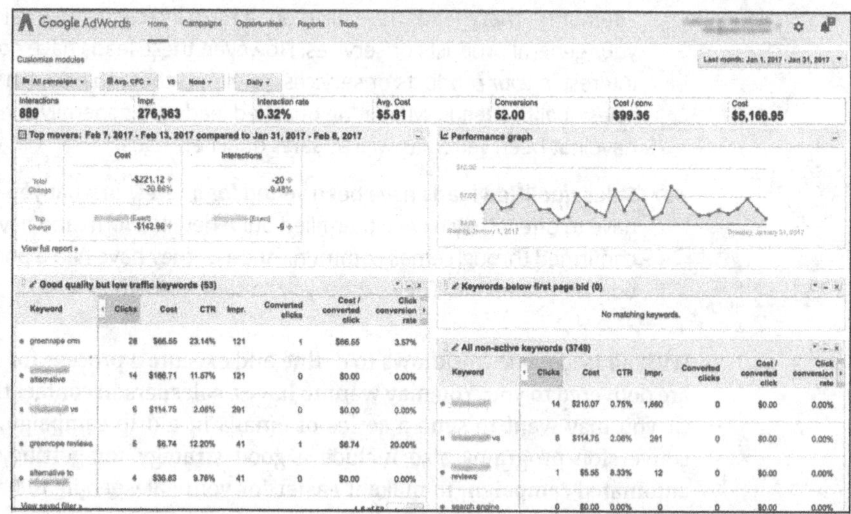

FIGURE 8-4: Google AdWords has robust cost and ROI accounting.

Getting qualitative data from salespeople

Numbers don't lie, but that doesn't mean you should ignore the general feeling from salespeople. They can often give insights that go beyond the numbers, or may provide an explanation for the numbers. Ask your salespeople if leads from certain sources tend to have common characteristics. Are leads from certain market segments generally interested in a certain aspect of what you're selling? Do they tend to be more price conscious? Does their behavior generally track with buyer personas you have developed?

Be careful of bias from salespeople, however. It's human nature to remember the more dramatic encounters they have. Bias is very real, and it's often emotionally driven.

If a particular segment or ad channel brings in a lead or two with strong negative experiences to a salesperson, that salesperson is more likely to think that channel is very bad for business, even if statistically that doesn't make sense. Be sure to back up any conclusions you make about market segments with data.

Buying Leads from Third Parties

Companies specialize in capturing leads and selling those leads. Such websites have forms designed to gather the information of the person visiting the site. Then they sell the leads to other companies. You can purchase two kinds of leads:

- **Marketing qualified leads** are people who fit certain criteria but have not been positively identified as interested in your specific product or service. Oftentimes these leads have filled out a form indicating they're interested in your general products or services. However, these leads have not expressed interest in *your* products or services, so expect them to perform worse than sales qualified leads. Marketing qualified leads are generally cheaper, as they have not been vetted as well as sales qualified leads.
- **Sales qualified leads** have been vetted for interest in what you specifically have to offer. They have either filled out a detailed form and have been confirmed through email communication or they have had a phone conversation with someone. They expect you to contact them.

With all leads, use workflows to define and execute a process for when these leads are delivered to you. You may want to have a salesperson contact the lead by phone. Or you may want to send a series of emails in a drip campaign. Most successful conversion programs also include a good strategy for getting the lead into an automated campaign, to make it easier for your salespeople to handle more leads.

PROTECTING YOURSELF FROM LEAD GEN CHARLATANS

On the surface paying a vendor for leads seems like a good idea. The challenge is that those leads are usually sold to many companies, and if you aren't the first or second company to contact the lead, you often get a cold reception.

If you decide to engage a lead source, be sure to ask how many other companies they sell their leads to, the prequalification of the leads, and if you can focus the leads to come from specific industries or niches that maximize your chance of closing those leads.

As with any vendor, talk to other clients to see whether the quality of the leads the vendors are selling are of sufficient quality. When you talk to their other customers, ask what the most common reasons they found leads were bad. If you hear that leads were non-responsive, or didn't expect the call, chances are the lead generator is just buying lists and not qualifying their leads.

Applying your personas and segments to lead gen rules

In Chapter 4, I discuss creating buyer personas to help segment your market. From there, you determine your market segments, which help guide a lead generation company toward the kinds of clients you want.

Every lead generation company gives you a wide range of leads. Because you have already done your homework on the kinds of leads you want, apply those rules to those leads so you don't waste your time and money on leads that aren't interested in what you're selling. For example, if you're targeting 20- to 25-year-old women in the state of Colorado, the lead generation vendor should be able to provide that.

Lead generation vendors give you a series of options you can use to set rules for the leads they give you. Some of these may be demographic (gender, location, age), some may be interest-based (have they expressed interest in your product or service), and some may be time-based (have they said when they are looking to buy). The more you can narrow your criteria, the more efficient you can convert those leads.

Resolving disputes quickly with lead generators

There are always leads that don't pan out. Take the time to review the lead generator's dispute resolution policy. In case the lead fills out inaccurate information or claims to have never provided information to your lead generation source, you should have a way to inform the vendor and not pay for that lead.

Some lead generators don't have a dispute resolution policy, meaning you have to accept (and pay for) the leads, regardless of whether they fit the rules you defined. Some lead generators require a phone call with someone, which is time consuming for your staff. The best lead generation vendors have an online portal where you can explain why the lead doesn't fit your criteria, and the vendor can then accept or question you.

If a lead is responsive, but chooses not to purchase from you, a lead generation vendor doesn't, as a general rule, issue a refund. However, if the lead doesn't respond or falls into a different demographic than you specified, you may have a case. It's up to you to nurture each lead and use a combination of sales and marketing strategies and tactics to convert that lead into a customer.

Bringing Leads in with Your Website

Your website is one of your best resources for educating and obtaining leads. Your website needs to be fast, easy to navigate, and have clear calls to action. The less a viewer has to think, the more likely she is to contact you and buy your products and services.

Designing a website and filling it with the right content is a combination of science and art. The first step to getting ideas about your site is to look at successful companies in similar industries. Take a look at how their sites are constructed and the content they show to users. This information can often help guide your designers, so they know the general look and functionality for your public-facing website.

Writing your sitemap

When designing a new website, before any mockups even begin, you must develop a sitemap, a structured layout of your website. It helps you understand how people navigate through your site, as well as how you design the structure of your website navigation. It's also important because your website needs to have this sitemap in XML file format for search engines. This file should be automatically generated in case you add new or change webpages in your website.

If your current website does not have a sitemap or a sitemap.xml file, be sure to contact a web developer to build one for you. Many website building platforms (also known as content management systems [CMS]) include automatic posting of your sitemap.xml file as you build your website and its pages.

Making search engine optimization (SEO) work for you

Use keywords and search terms common to your business and industry in your website content. This practice — called search engine optimization — increases your chance of appearing higher in search results for those search terms; the chances of a customer finding your website goes up as well.

Keywords for SEO are an important part of your overall strategy. These keywords determine what people look for when they're looking for you. They also are what drive people to find you, so they can start their buyer journeys toward becoming your customers.

Your CRM should track the keywords used in finding your websites. You can then customize your messaging and workflows when communicating with your leads.

TIP

Write the content for your website to appeal to online readers. Online content tends to be in short paragraphs with graphics, rather than long form articles. Also use short, attention-grabbing headlines with simple text and imagery.

Think about your buyer journeys when writing content for your website. Start with the keywords people are likely to use and build content to address those search terms. Use headlines and text that matches those search terms. Bulleted lists are easy to read and can also be written to include your search keywords.

Consider also how much information you want to have available to the general public versus behind a form that asks people to provide their information. Putting valuable information behind a form gives you a way of collecting email addresses and phone numbers. Just be sure not to ask for too much information — that might turn people away — and that the information you're providing is worth people giving up contact information. People don't like to give up their personal information easily.

REMEMBER

When you have someone's contact information, be sure to get that person into your CRM sales funnel and into an automated workflow. (See Chapter 11.)

This can be a little technical, so if you have the budget for it, I highly recommend finding an SEO company or someone with experience researching keywords to find the searchable words you want to "own."

Using video

Videos allow you to communicate your value proposition effectively. Embed short videos — two minutes is about how long you can keep attention spans — that explain what you do and how you do it, as shown in Figure 8-5.

TIP

Be sure to embed tracking into your videos. Most sites, such as Vimeo or Wistia, track video plays for you.

After you have video tracking in place, you can automatically tag a contact in your CRM when she watches that particular video. You can have this action trigger a workflow, which can give your salespeople an advantage when following up with leads.

Video is an excellent tool from turning a marketing qualified lead into an interested, sales qualified lead, triggering follow-up from someone on your team to have a conversation and determine real interest in your products and services.

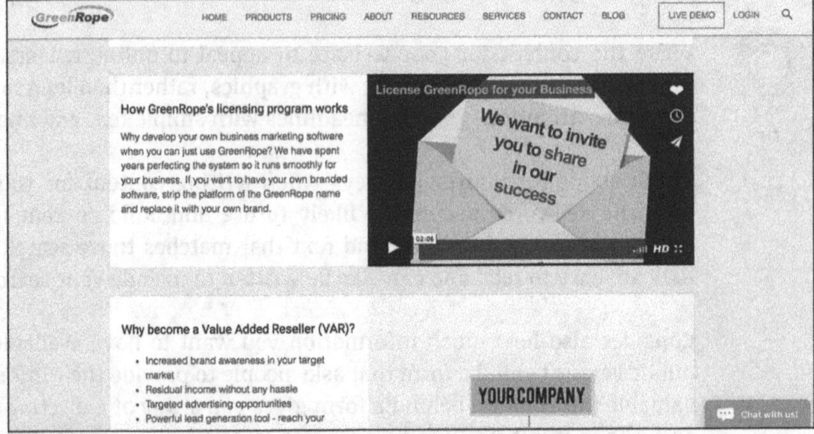

FIGURE 8-5: Video is used as an educational piece on this page about licensing.

Choosing the right framework

Most websites are built on frameworks that allows you to edit content on them without having to talk to a vendor or webmaster.

WordPress is the most popular, but others are out there. Be sure to get an understanding of the capabilities of the various frameworks so you know they support what you want your website to do. Common functionalities include:

- » Embedding forms
- » Managing membership lists
- » Tracking website visitors
- » Embedding live chat
- » Creating standalone landing pages
- » Embedding calendars

Be sure that vendors understand everything you want your website to do ahead of time. Take a look at work they have done in the past and make sure it looks modern. Ask for references, and get a feel for vendors' ability to develop on schedule. Be sure the platform they intend to use supports everything you need.

If you're interested in building your own website without using a web design firm, be sure you research the platform to ensure it can support everything you want to do with it. Ease of use, cost, and flexibility are all important aspects of managing your website you want to iron out first, before you get too far into designing your site and putting content on your webpages.

Using landing pages

Landing pages are single-purpose webpages, designed to capture leads. The headline, the lead capture form, and the form's call to action are the focus on these pages.

Use color to call out various parts of your content but draw the eye naturally to the form. The form should only ask for the minimum amount of information you need to effectively follow up with the lead.

REMEMBER

Every additional piece of information you ask for reduces the number of people who go through the effort of filling out that form.

Using PURLs

Personalized URLs, or PURLs, are a great way to engage with your leads and clients. These pages are dynamically created for individuals. Based on the URL that's provided, the website engine can put special content on the page because it knows who the webpage visitor is.

One example of a PURL is `http://www.yourwebsite.com/JoeSmith`. The person visiting the site is Joe and sees "Welcome Joe Smith" in the page headline (along with any other webpage personalization you would want).

PURLs also work very well with print. If you create QR codes or other landing pages that direct a specific recipient of a printed brochure, you see great improvements in engagement.

Tracking Sources with Campaign IDs

Identifying your leads by campaign ID is critical for understanding the reach and influence of the marketing campaigns you're running. You can also track individuals or companies who refer you business through campaign IDs. Usually these referral sources are called affiliates. Be sure if you're interested in setting up affiliates that you can track and pay for the business they bring you, usually correlated by campaign ID.

Tagging inbound links to automate campaign assignment

Campaign IDs work by either assigning a campaign to individuals when they click a link to your website (for example, `http://www.yourwebsite.com/?cmp=GoogleCampaign21`) or with a CRM workflow. Then segregate your contacts into subgroups of people who are associated with those campaigns.

When you design pay-per-click campaigns, ads to be placed on other websites, or links to your site from social media, be sure to tag as many of those links as possible with unique campaign IDs.

Your CRM uses campaign IDs as a way to segment your contacts. By separating contacts by campaign, you can see how many contacts came from a campaign and how much revenue they generated. When you look at the amount of money you spent on that campaign, you can then easily calculate the ROI of that campaign.

If a campaign is effective (creating positive ROI), that means you should invest more money into it. Invest the most into the best performing campaigns.

Segmenting analytics by campaign

After you have campaign data, study the analytic data to see how well each campaign is performing, and its impact on your funnel.

Remember that for campaign IDs to be automatically assigned, you need to ensure that the website analytics functions provided by your CRM are in place.

You can look at a few analytics to get a deeper understanding of what aspects of your marketing are working better.

- **Average page views of visitors by campaign** tells you which campaigns generate the most traffic on your website after those visitors reach your website. By tracking the average number of page views by campaign, you can see which campaigns drive the most interested leads to you, as shown in Figure 8-6. If you normalize this data with the cost for a click to your website, you can see which campaigns are most cost effective for interested leads.

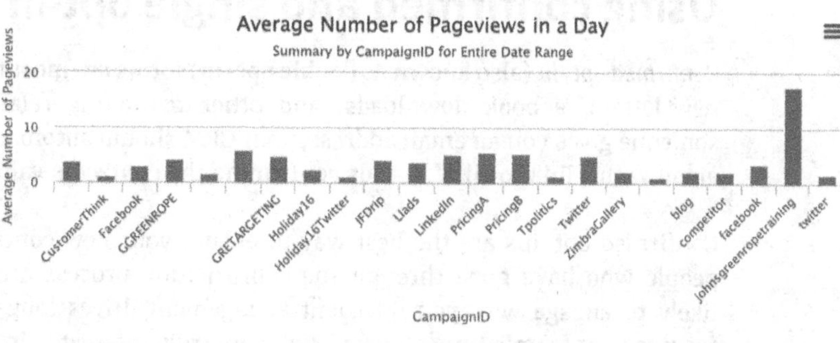

FIGURE 8-6: Average page views generated by different campaigns.

- **Average page views of visitors by campaign by day** is a granular look at the traffic your campaigns drive, as shown in Figure 8-7. Sometimes fluctuations in traffic can be attributed to increased spending or competitive ads, so examining sudden spikes or dips in performance from campaigns might illuminate effective or ineffective campaign strategies.
- **Funnel performance by campaign** is a good way to view the success of the entire customer journey. By examining how effective different campaigns are at converting leads into clients and how long people take to progress through their buyer journeys, you can compare the effectiveness of your campaigns and their strategies. You can see what is working and direct marketing budgets toward better-converting methods of attracting leads.

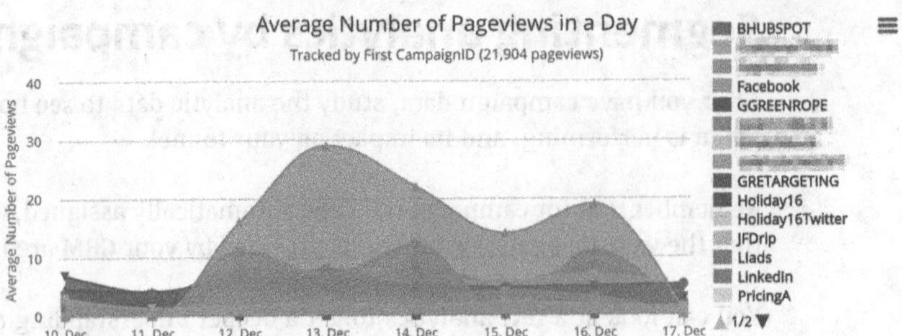

FIGURE 8-7: Average page views per day by campaign.

Deploying Signup Forms

The forms you place on your website are absolutely critical for gathering contacts into your CRM and starting them down the path of becoming clients. Forms generally fall into two categories: confirmed opt-in and single opt-in.

Using confirmed and single opt-in forms

Confirmed opt-in (also known as double opt-in) forms are most frequently used for newsletters, e-book downloads, and other marketing-related content. After someone gives you an email address, your CRM should automatically send him an email with a link to click — thus confirming the contact is valid.

Confirmed opt-ins are the best way to ensure your new contacts are valid, and people who have gone through the confirmation process are 70 percent more likely to engage with you. Efficient engagement drives long-term growth and focuses your team's time on people who are truly interested in working with you.

Because confirmed opt-ins require the person to take action (clicking a link in the confirmation email), some people won't finish the confirmation process. In this case, ticketing forms are a good solution for when you want to ensure someone on your team follows up with every lead (see the "Deploying Ticketing Forms" section coming up).

Single opt-in forms don't require a confirmation email to be sent to the person filling out the form. With single opt-in forms, there is risk that a competitor or person with ill intent could sign up a fake lead or worse, a spamtrap email, that could affect your ability to send email to the inbox. Choose the type of form you put on your website wisely.

TIP

Some email marketing and CRM service providers give you the option to send a second confirmation email, which gives you a marked increase in confirmation rates. While the primary objective of each confirmation email is to get the recipient to confirm, these emails can also include more information about your products and services below that call to action in the message.

After someone confirms intent, you can further engage with him using a lead nurturing process. Part of that lead nurturing can be sending each new lead a sequence of emails, spaced out over days or weeks. Series of emails triggered by forms are often called *auto-responders,* and allow you to send information to your new leads in slower, more digestible chunks. You have many options, including setting CRM activities, sending text messages, and creating opportunities. Be creative and think about how you want to guide new leads from your forms to become customers.

Gathering the minimum amount of data

Forms work best when you make them as easy as possible to fill out. (See Figure 8-8.) You have a balance to make when designing your forms. Your natural instinct is to request as much information as possible, so you can target your follow-ups precisely. But people are less likely to fill out your form when you ask them for too much information.

The more manual typing you require someone to do, the weaker the incentive to fill out the form. Focus on asking for the minimum amount of information on the first form and then work on getting more data later.

REMEMBER

A good CRM includes a form builder that has automatic data appending, so with only an email address, you can get a lot more information without explicitly asking for it.

Get in touch with us!

Thank you for contacting us. Please fill out the information below and we will get back to you shortly.

Regarding: Feedback

How can we help you:

Your Email Address: required

FIGURE 8-8: A simple contact form.

Optional behavior to enhance user experience

If your form responds to the user's actions, you have a better chance of getting the user to provide additional information. Reactive forms are driven by logic and are sometimes referred to as *branching forms*. Improve user engagement with your forms by showing follow-up questions inline. For example, ask what general type of product someone is interested in and then have a more detailed product question appear.

Progressive profiling is another technology that may be helpful in creating better engagement with your forms. The server checks whether a cookie is on the user's computer, indicating the person has been to your site before. If that person is recognized, the server pre-fills the form with information stored in the CRM (such as name and email address). This process can save time in data entry and help the user focus on new information you want to collect.

Deploying Ticketing Forms

Ticketing uses forms to track an "issue" that is created by filling out the form. This "issue" could be interest in your product, or it could be someone having a problem with a product you sell. In either case, you want a person from your company to engage with the person filling out the form and manually close it.

Figure 8-9 shows a form for customer service that can help you with capturing new leads.

Using ticketing forms for capturing leads

Ticketing forms are by their nature single opt-in, meaning no confirmation email is required. When used in the context of sales, they ensure your sales/customer service team always engages with leads. Tickets opened this way must be manually closed, which means you can see at any given time how many tickets are open and who they are assigned to. It's an effective way to enforce lead follow-up, ensuring no leads fall through the cracks. Ticketing forms encourage better lead nurturing and follow-up.

Good ticketing systems also include average response times in their reporting, which helps to ensure fast follow-up when leads and clients reach out to your organization.

GreenRope Use this ticketing form to report a bug or issue to the development team

Regarding: 0-Bug-Urgent

Summary:

Your Email Address: required!

First Name: required!

Last Name:

Request Detail:

required!

Add an Image: Choose File No file chosen

wdsfsi

Enter the letters you see above:

Submit Ticket

FIGURE 8-9: An internal ticketing form.

REMEMBER

In addition to having someone manually close each ticket that is opened, be sure to schedule workflows and/or marketing automation when people fill out your lead capture forms. Ticketing forms create a more consistent user experience and strengthen your brand, while providing a convenient way to provide educational content to the people who fill out your forms.

Using ticketing forms for customer service

Just as you want a human in the loop to confirm a new lead, you also want a human to confirm that when a lead has a problem, it was resolved, and how it was resolved. Ticketing forms gives you this ability and are an effective tool for ensuring the best customer experience possible.

By encouraging your customers to use ticketing forms, you ensure that no issues get ignored. You can measure time to respond to the ticket, as well as ask for feedback after the issue was resolved to measure quality of service. Customers feel valued and their voices are heard, which improves your brand overall satisfaction with your company.

Figure 8-10 shows a summary of a ticket. Your CRM should be able to easily call up tickets to see status and if they were resolved, how they were resolved. Exit ratings for tickets help you get an idea if the customer is happy now.

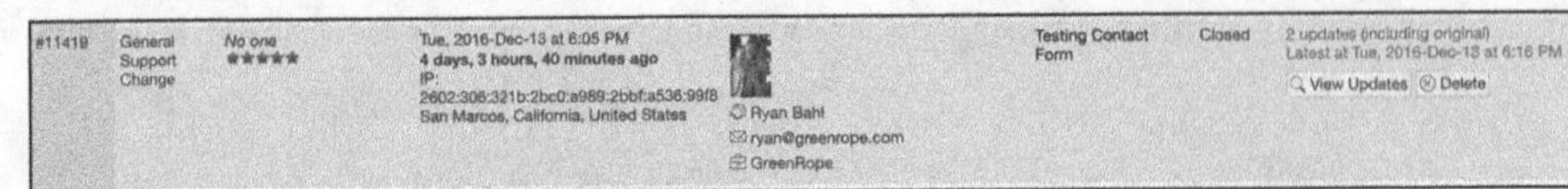

FIGURE 8-10: A summary of a ticket.

Integrating workflows and satisfaction surveys

In both types of applications for ticketing forms, build in automation. For example, a workflow that schedules a CRM activity, sends an email, sends a survey, or any combination, as shown in Figure 8-11.

REMEMBER

Automated follow-up messages to your leads and clients are opportunities to cross-sell, up-sell, and/or educate, but be careful to not overdo the selling part. People who fill out forms, particularly for support, don't want to be inundated with "buy this" messages.

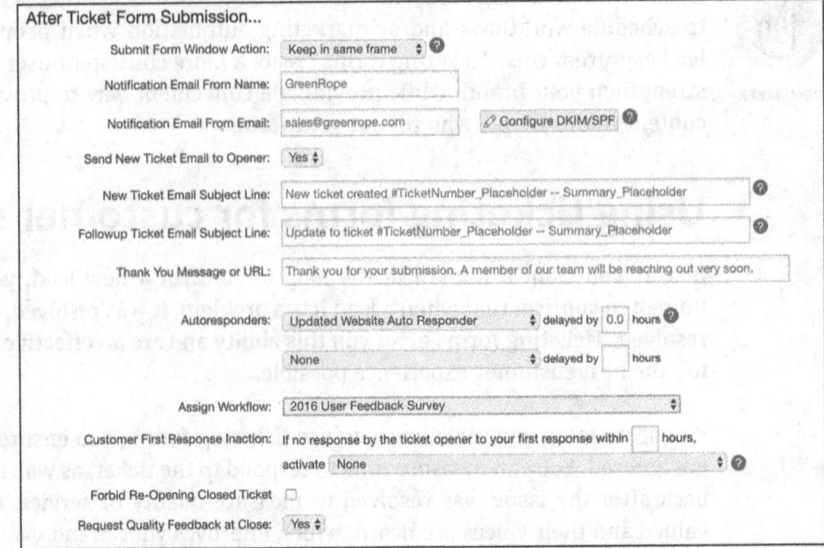

FIGURE 8-11: Ticket form options that customize messaging and activate workflows.

Appending Data

Your forms can only gather the data that you ask for. At a very minimum, your forms collect an email address. You can ask for more fields, but each additional field lowers your response rate. The easier and simpler you make your forms, the more willing people are to fill them out.

Every form also has the ability to capture information about the person filling it out behind the scenes. The browser collects some information, such as the IP address the lead is connecting from, as well as attributes about the computer being used. When this information is collected by an intelligent CRM platform, you can automatically perform a risk assessment of that lead and simultaneously augment your CRM with more information.

Data appending is the process of starting with a limited amount of data about a contact — say the email address — and extrapolating more about the person. This extrapolation is done by connecting to a third-party data source and getting as much information as possible from that provider. A good CRM does this for you automatically.

When you connect automatic data appending to your forms, your CRM can automatically add data that wasn't put into the form. This data is derived from open-source places, such as an email address from a LinkedIn profile, for example. By correlating a wide range of data sources, the third-party data source can append more information to the contact record.

Sometimes the data appended is online, such as someone's Twitter handle or public LinkedIn page. Sometimes the data is correlated to other sources and can pull in offline data, such as number of children, income, and homeowner/renter status.

Another useful function is a reputation assessment tool. These tools, when integrated into your forms, look up the email address and IP address and determine the reputation of the person filling out the form. This process should happen automatically with all your forms, so you can be warned if a bad actor is using your system. Large networks of users drive reputation assessment tools for your benefit. Use this data to influence how you interact with your leads. Your sales team's time is valuable, and you want them to focus their energy on viable leads.

Figure 8-12 shows an email alert received when someone fills out a ticket. This alert informs your customer service team and management that a ticket has been created. Updates can also be sent to the same people, so everyone is aware of how the ticket is handled.

Adding social and demographic data to contacts

The process of taking the data appending and attaching it to a contact should be an easy, if not automatic, one. Your CRM should accomplish this process for you at no cost as an added value. Figure 8-13 shows how the information a CRM has appended to a contact's record.

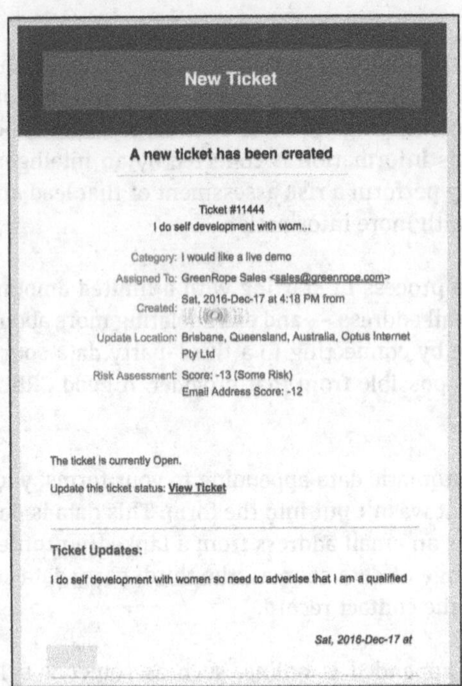

FIGURE 8-12: A ticket email alert with useful information.

Most of the data fields you capture with data appending aren't standard fields attached to the contact record. You likely have to create custom fields to store that data. (See Chapter 7.) Your CRM should also give you the option to automatically create these custom fields when the data for a contact appears. You can then decide where in the View Contact screen that data is visible.

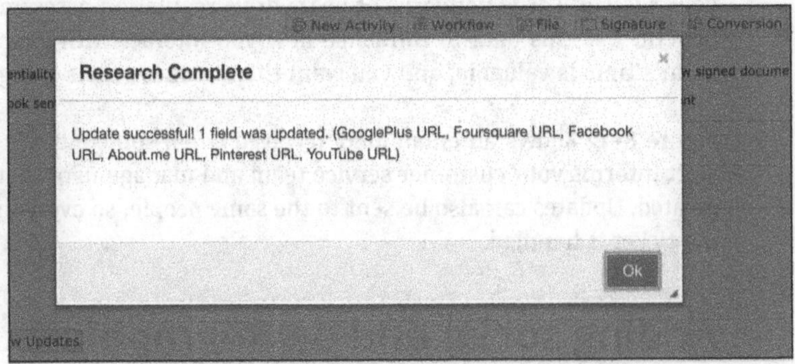

FIGURE 8-13: Researching a contact to append social and demographic data.

Adding data to companies

Sometimes it's difficult to find data and append it to companies. Most people fill out forms as individuals and don't directly represent companies unless they make that clear in the form. In any case, usually company-based data appending requires the company website to confirm which company you're appending, because websites are unique to the company.

Figure 8-14 shows how you can use your CRM to automatically research a company and append the data found to the company's record in your CRM.

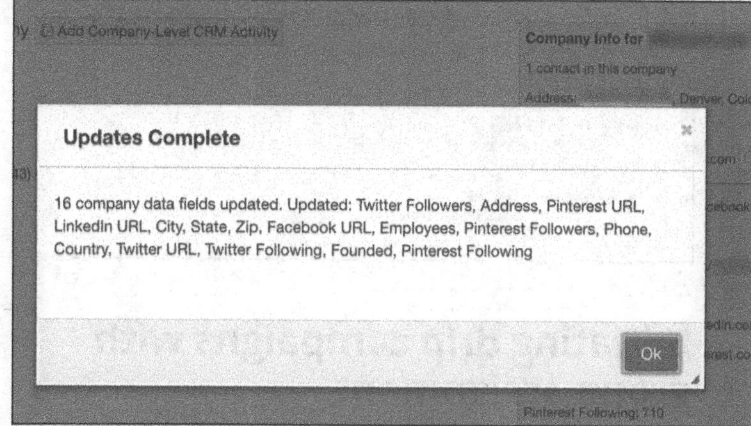

FIGURE 8-14: Researching a company to get more information.

Building Automation into Forms

Every method of lead capture can and should be connected to a form of marketing automation. Marketing automation allows you to engage follow-up with leads and nurture them, and help them on the buyer journey. Lead nurturing is a combination of education and encouraging action, along with measuring what leads and customers do with your messaging.

The goal of marketing automation is to use software to drive people into your sales funnel. Tracking this data gives you insight into what messaging works, while helping your sales teams focus on tasks that they do best — phone calls, personalized emails, and in-person meetings.

Attaching auto-responders to forms

When someone fills out a form, you can trigger emails to be sent to that person, as shown in Figure 8-15. An immediate email may be warranted to confirm the form data was received. Follow-up emails for educational purposes are also helpful.

REMEMBER

Be careful to not inundate leads with too many emails. People want to be followed up with, not harassed.

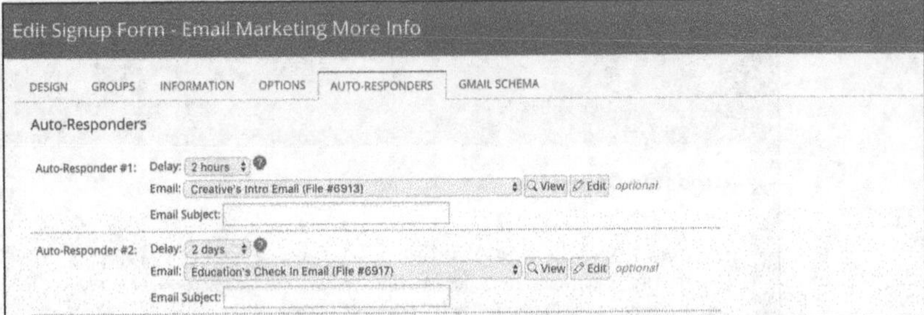

FIGURE 8-15: Setting auto-responders to forms.

Initiating drip campaigns with group assignment

Your forms should give you flexibility to assign a contact to different campaigns or groups. Assigning leads to groups allows you to trigger targeted drip campaigns, or sequences of emails, as shown in Figure 8-16. With your CRM connected to your marketing automation, you have the ability to tailor the content of those messages directly to what the lead is looking for.

Beyond forms, group assignment is a great way to trigger automated workflows and marketing. Allow key members of your team to add someone to a group to engage a campaign to simplify multi-step conversion processes. Build it into your process flows. (See Chapter 7.)

Starting buyer journeys

A customer journey is a model of the path you want your leads to take from when you first track them until they become customers. Marketing automation combined with your CRM guides your leads along their paths. Because everyone's path is likely a little different, build personalization and expected behavior of your market segments into your buyer journeys.

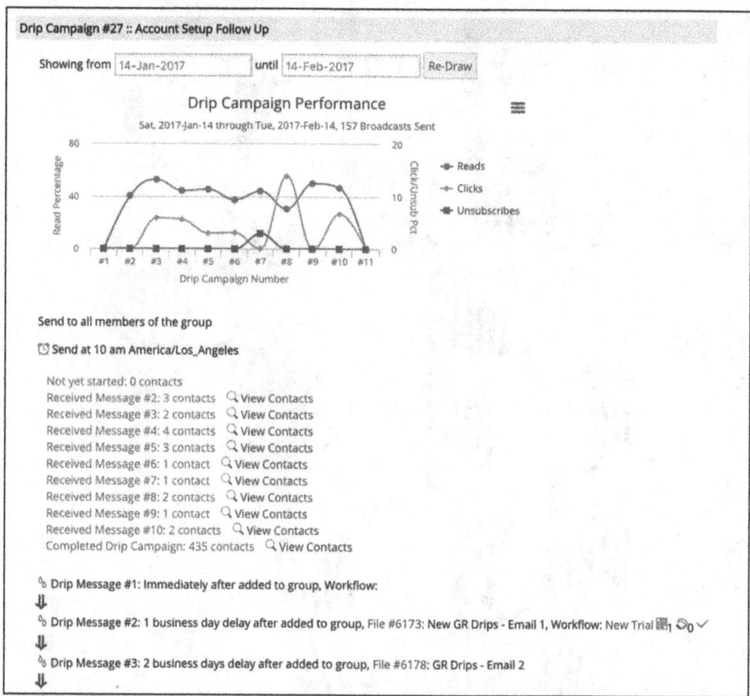

FIGURE 8-16: A straightforward drip campaign activated when a contact is added to a group.

By starting individuals on a journey as a result of capturing their information with a form, you can build in a complex, logic-driven way to convert them from leads to customers. You can also use that as a way to further educate or up-sell existing customers. Journeys are a powerful tool when used to drive people to take action.

Journeys can trigger workflows, which can assign CRM activities, send emails, send text messages, send print pieces, update data in the CRM, change group assignments, or do any number of different actions. Determine what your journeys look like, and then build workflows to match the actions you want your team to take. See Figure 8-17.

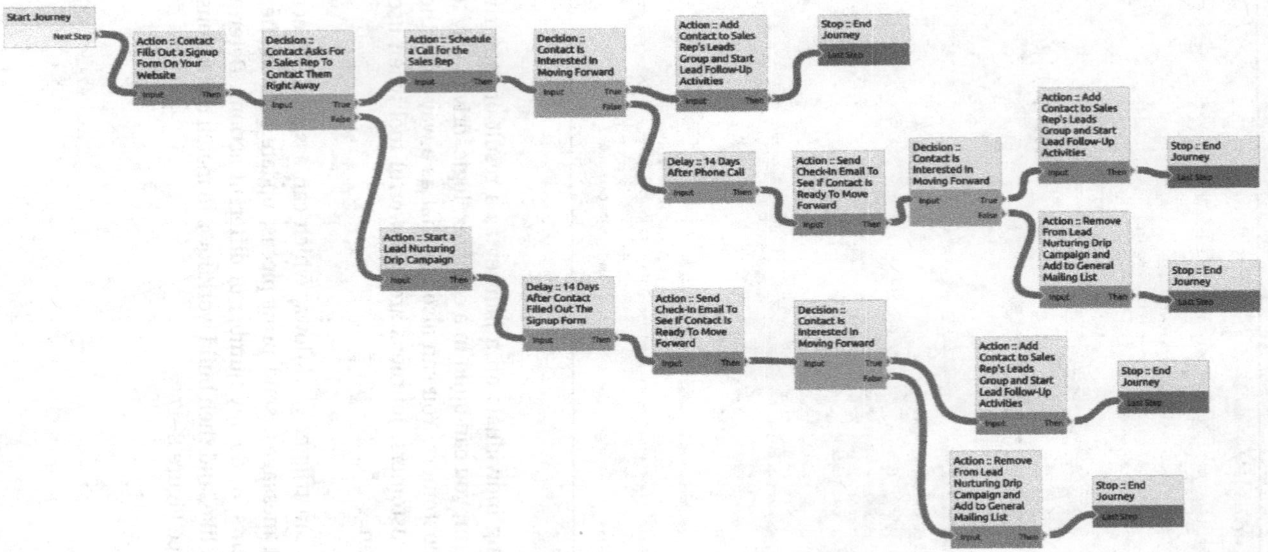

FIGURE 8-17: A journey that starts when someone fills out a form on a website.

IN THIS CHAPTER

» Offering chat hours through your website

» Connecting through smartphones, whether text or live conversations

» Connecting through social media platforms

» Meeting leads in person

» Bringing in leads automatically from other platforms

Chapter 9
Capturing Leads with Other Methods

Many people think of online lead capture as something that can only occur through your website. The world of Complete CRM is bigger than that, and after you embrace a holistic view of your buyer journeys, opportunities are in places you never thought possible.

This chapter details different methods of finding and engaging with leads. Online chat, text message, phone, in-person meetings, and other third-party integrations are all ways your organization can bring in business. Your CRM facilitates and tracks all your lead generation strategies and tactics, and a Complete CRM stores all that data in one convenient place. With the tools I outline in this chapter, you see how a CRM can turn leads into customers, and then customers into advocates.

Interacting with Chat

Online chat is an effective tactic to capture leads and provides an opportunity for both clients and new leads to engage with your brand. Whether for a support issue or a sales inquiry, online chat is easy to use, completely trackable, and can trigger automation to further define or improve the customer experience. Making interacting with your customer service managers easy goes a long way toward giving your leads and clients satisfaction with your company.

REMEMBER

Chat does require a commitment. If you only plan to have chat for a couple hours a day, be transparent about your hours and availability, as shown in Figure 9-1.

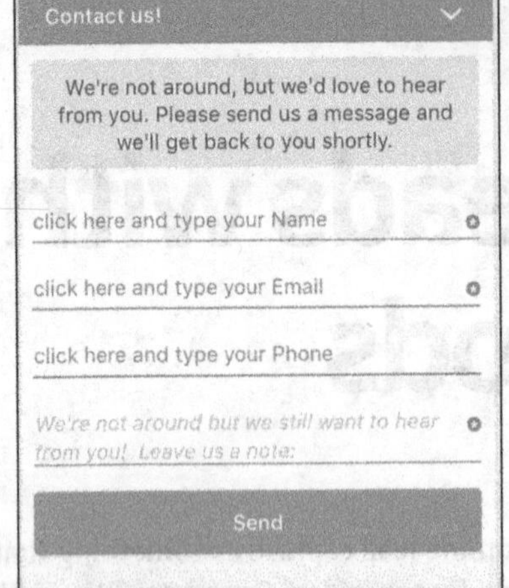

FIGURE 9-1: Good chat software has a form available when no operators are around.

In the modern era of social communication, many people find chatting easier than talking on the phone. You may find chat opens a new channel to capture leads that would have been too timid or too busy to call your salespeople.

Picking a good chat provider

The most important aspects of chat are reliability and integration with your CRM. Look for a chat provider that gives feedback after chats, as well as allows operators to talk to each other in real time. Olark (`www.olark.com`), LivePerson (`www.liveperson.com`), LiveChat (`www.livechatinc.com`), and Five9 (`www.five9.com`) are reputable, business-oriented chat solutions available on the market. Evaluate user experience, cost, and design to determine which is the best for you.

Figure 9-2 shows a form a lead can fill out to start a chat with a live operator. Note the fields are the same kinds of fields you would use in a lead capture form.

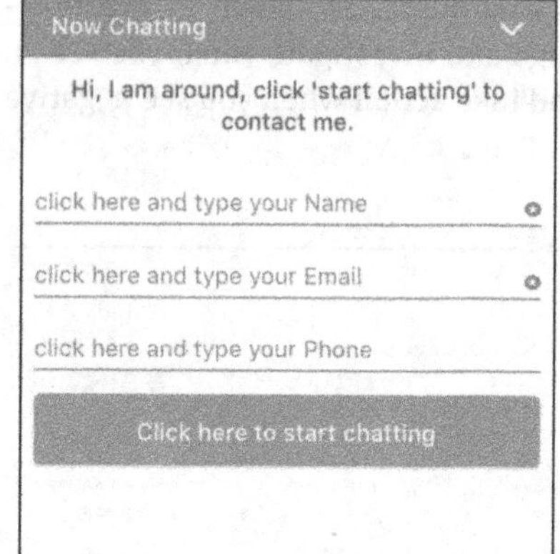

FIGURE 9-2: A chat form with the operator standing by.

Integrating chat transcripts into your CRM

Transcripts should integrate automatically into your CRM, so that conversations are attached to contact records, as shown in Figure 9-3. You can also create workflows for people who complete chat sessions as a way to engage with them after the chat. These workflows might be triggered automatically (in which case limit the frequency because sometimes people open multiple chats in a short period of time), or they may be triggered by your chat operators for frequently asked questions.

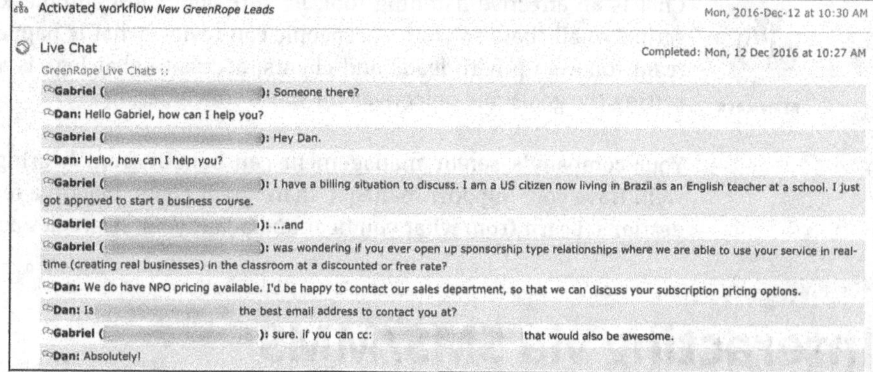

Activated workflow *New GreenRope Leads* — Mon, 2016-Dec-12 at 10:30 AM

Live Chat — Completed: Mon, 12 Dec 2016 at 10:27 AM

GreenRope Live Chats ::

Gabriel ( ): Someone there?

Dan: Hello Gabriel, how can I help you?

Gabriel ( ): Hey Dan.

Dan: Hello, how can I help you?

Gabriel ( ): I have a billing situation to discuss. I am a US citizen now living in Brazil as an English teacher at a school. I just got approved to start a business course.

Gabriel ( ): ...and

Gabriel ( ): was wondering if you ever open up sponsorship type relationships where we are able to use your service in real-time (creating real businesses) in the classroom at a discounted or free rate?

Dan: We do have NPO pricing available. I'd be happy to contact our sales department, so that we can discuss your subscription pricing options.

Dan: Is the best email address to contact you at?

Gabriel ( ): sure. if you can cc: that would also be awesome.

Dan: Absolutely!

FIGURE 9-3: Integration is vitally important for giving information about chats to sales teams.

Measuring operator performance

Chat software allows you to review performance by each chat operator any time you like. Do monthly reviews of your online chat customer service team to see how they rate according to your customers, as shown in Figure 9-4. Set minimum standards for customer ratings and investigate when you see any general trends. Reward positive feedback, and take action when you see negative sentiment in the transcripts.

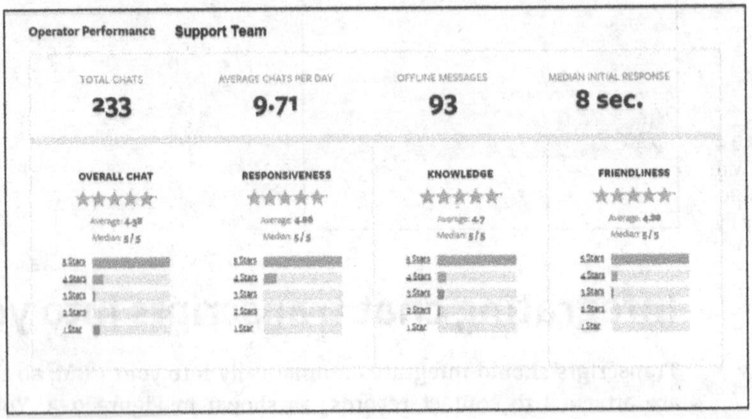

FIGURE 9-4: In good chat software, customers can rate how the service was.

You can learn a lot from reviewing chat transcripts and interviewing your operators. Pay close attention to dissatisfied customers to see what they're complaining about. If one person has a complaint, chances are more people have the same problem but aren't telling you about it.

REMEMBER

Chat is an effective listening tool. Be sure your CRM automatically stores transcripts of all chats so your salespeople can review what is happening. When your team follows up with leads and clients, access to chat logs is a valuable part of setting the goals and objectives for those conversations.

Your company's senior management can benefit from hearing about chats, as well. Have your support manager share great chats, negative feedback, and suggestions. Learn from what you hear and adapt your strategies accordingly.

Interacting via SMS/MMS

When communicating to leads and customers, you may want to consider text messaging. SMS is the easiest and cheapest way, being simply text. MMS is nice because you can send pictures, but it's more expensive because of the increased data sent to each recipient.

Communicating with your leads and clients by messaging is a direct and powerful way to reach out, and as such, records of this communication need to be in the CRM. Likewise, if your contacts send text messages to your company indicating preferences, you want to track that, too.

Broadcasting SMS/MMS messages

When you send messages to a lot of people's phones, you have to be careful to not violate the carriers' terms of use. If a carrier suspects you of spamming, they stop delivering messages. Usually these blocks are temporary and may be based on content, delivery speed, or recipients complaining.

Figure 9-5 shows a simple interface to build and broadcast an MMS message to contacts in your CRM.

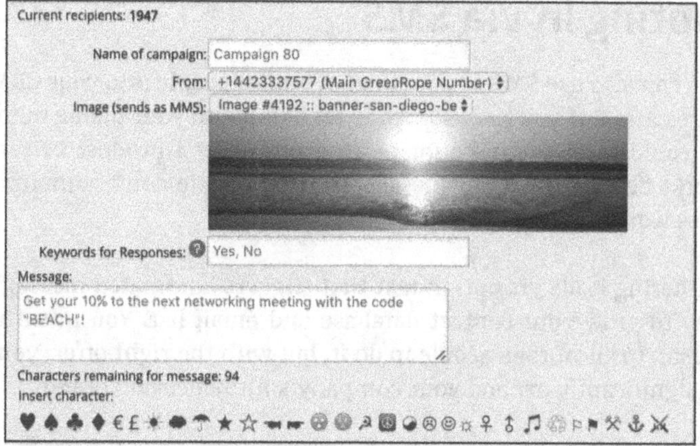

FIGURE 9-5: Sending an MMS message to a group of contacts.

WARNING

If you send text message broadcasts, be sure your recipients have opted in to receive your messages. Do not blindly send messages to lists of people you don't know, or you may face permanent blocks, or worse, legal action from the carriers.

Sending one-to-one mobile messages

Your CRM should allow workflows to trigger text messages to your contacts, opening a new channel of communication for alerts, notices, and ways to drive people to take action. See Figure 9-6.

People tend to treat text messaging with urgent priority; when combined messaging with a workflow, you're almost guaranteed that not only does an important message get sent, it gets read. It's why many companies use text messages for security-related communication. However, because messaging is obtrusive, you want to be very careful with the volume you send. Inundating customers with text messages is a good way to make them angry, so be sure you set up activation limits on those workflows.

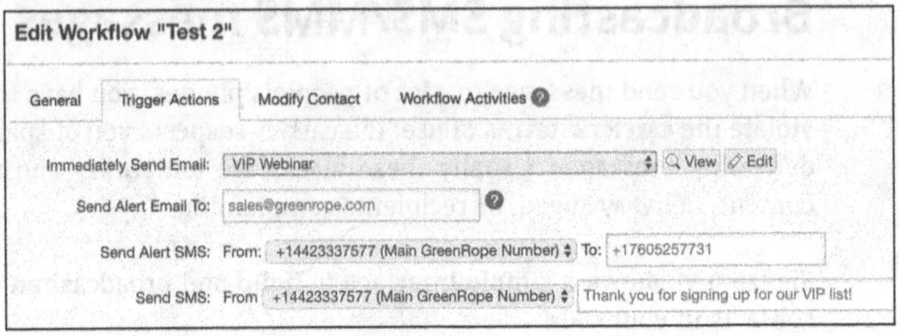

FIGURE 9-6: Using a text message to confirm membership to a VIP list.

Opting in via SMS

You can also use SMS as a method of opting people into your CRM and email communication. If you have someone text "join" to your phone number, for example, he could receive a discount to an event or to a product or service. This opt-in works best with B2C businesses, as most people don't communicate in the business world via text message.

Gathering leads via opt-in text that triggers automated messaging is an efficient way to grow your contact database and email list. You must have a compelling reason to encourage people to do it, but with the right offer, you can use software to significantly expand your company's influence and brand.

Interacting over the Phone

The phone is a powerful method of communication, with only web meetings being more intimate for talking to a lead or client (see the next section for web meetings). You can and should connect phone conversations to your CRM. Automatically recording that the phone conversation took place, transcribing the conversation, and recording it for later playback are all effective ways to link your team's use of the phone to your Complete CRM.

When you store phone interaction in your CRM, it ensures that management oversees the quality assurance and brand consistency. You also save your sales team's time, cutting data entry time and helping them focus on the conversation.

Clicking-to-call contacts through the CRM

Time is extremely valuable to salespeople. Anything you can do to help them work more efficiently is appreciated and improves morale. Click-to-call (shown in Figure 9-7), where the salesperson only has to click a button in the CRM to connect to the contact, is one such way to increase efficiency.

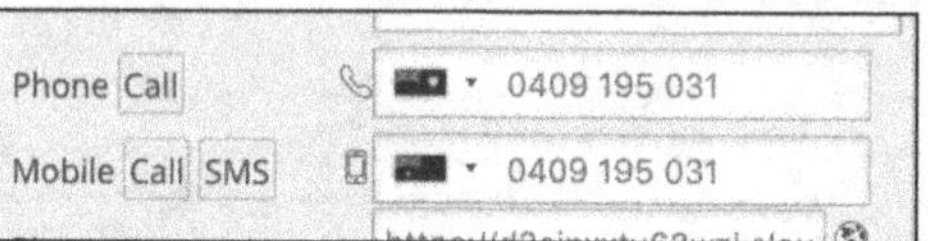

FIGURE 9-7: Easy-to-use click-to-call interface for a contact.

Click-to-call automatically links each salesperson's conversations to your CRM. The CRM activity is attached to the contact, along with the recording and the transcript for easy retrieval in the future.

Increasing efficiency with voicemail drop

Another convenient feature is voicemail drop, which works with click-to-call and allows a salesperson to click a link from within the CRM to leave a prerecorded message after he knows voicemail is going to pick up. After the system hears a predefined duration of silence, it knows to leave the voicemail (a recorded MP3 file) and then hang up. This action greatly improves the efficiency of your sales team's calls.

Managing inbound call routing

You open a world of telephone-based marketing and automation when you control how inbound calls to your business are routed. Technology exists to set up dedicated numbers for your sales and marketing quickly and cheaply.

One application for inbound call routing is for marketing campaigns. You can direct people to call a number to trigger some kind of action. The call itself could have a recording with information or an offer, and you could activate a workflow such as the one in Figure 9-8 for an automated follow-up to the caller.

On the sales and support side, you can route inbound calls to dedicated members of your team. With a connection to your CRM, you can automatically create the CRM activity, record the call, transcribe it, and attach it to the caller's record.

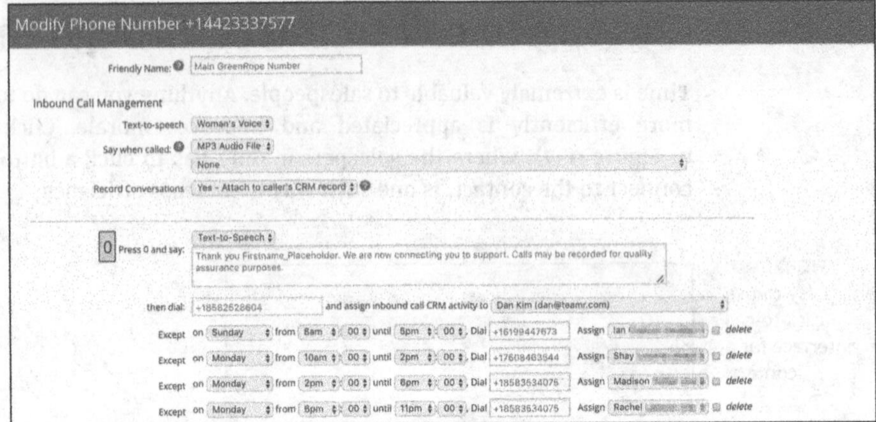

FIGURE 9-8: Managing call routing with a simple phone tree manager.

Recording and transcribing calls

Whether you use click-to-call or inbound call tracking, your software should create the CRM activity and provide recordings in the caller's CRM record automatically, as shown in Figure 9-9. You can then build in lead scoring to add value to leads and clients (see Chapter 6) and predictive analytics and predict when calls impact your ability to close deals (see Chapter 17).

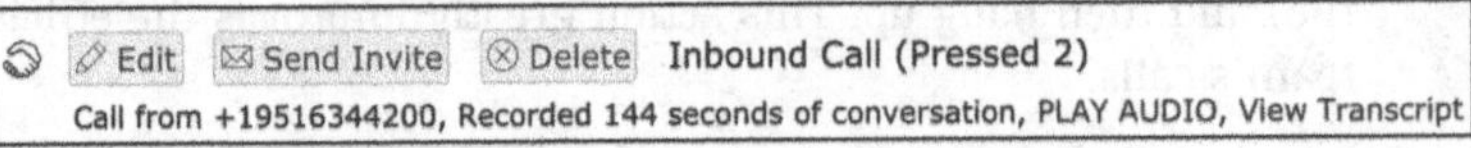

FIGURE 9-9: An entry in the CRM that has a recording and transcription.

Meeting Over Web Conference

As web meeting technology improves, more and more businesses are holding virtual meetings. When you have these meetings, you want to record them in the CRM. Some providers, such as WebEx (`https://www.webex.com`), GotoMeeting (`https://www.gotomeeting.com`), GotoWebinar (`https://www.gotomeeting.com/webinar`), or WebinarJam (`https://www.webinarjam.com`), all have the capability to integrate with a CRM.

Web meetings can be used as informal ways to gather a team together to discuss issues. They can also be an important part of the sales process, particularly if you sell a product with an online component. When a lead is focused on your screen, you often have the best quality of attention from that person.

Webinars are a good way to reach a large number of leads and clients. Useful for education, you should connect webinar attendance to automated marketing follow-up. Send an email to your attendees thanking them for attending, and ask if there's anything you can to do help them. Requesting feedback and ideas for future webinars often results in more interaction with your leads, which can lead to more sales.

In some cases, your team may be comfortable manually entering information into the CRM that describes the topics covered and outcomes of the web meeting. In other cases, you may be able to automate the web meeting attendance information into your CRM. In all cases, be sure the web meeting gets into your CRM and incorporated into your lead scoring and sales management processes.

Interacting over Social Media

Social listening is the art and science of taking what people write about you online and turning it into effective reporting and action. Understanding and responding to mentions of you and your brand is as much a part of your overall marketing strategy as designing your Complete CRM.

When a contact interacts with you on social media, you have an opportunity to engage with a person who is waiting to hear from you. You may want to activate a workflow to ensure follow-up. For example, an alert for your social media manager to respond, or a workflow that assigns a follow-up CRM activity to that contact's salesperson.

Activating workflows from social interaction

Social media impacts both sales and marketing. Your CRM collects this data and gives you tools to take action. Sales can see what their leads care about and judge how they feel about your brand. Marketing can use social data to adjust its strategies and tactics to encourage more engagement.

Your sales and marketing teams should work together to be aware of when leads and customers post messages on your social media pages. If you have ample staff, you can schedule CRM activities to follow up with everyone who makes a comment or shares content you post, as shown in Figure 9-10. If you run lean, recording the social interaction and adding it into your lead scoring and predictive analytics tools may be sufficient.

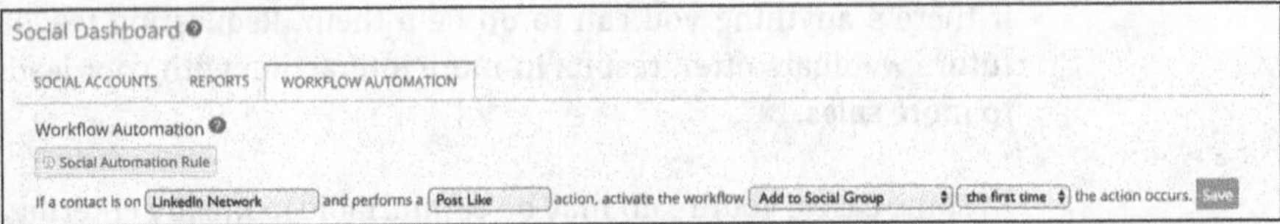

FIGURE 9-10: An automation rule triggering a workflow from a Facebook like.

Getting overall sentiment about your brand

New platforms exist that allow you to see what kind of comments people write about your brand. You can see when people say positive or negative comments about your company, and why. Typically these platforms are targeted toward other consumers, but if you have a large business-to-business brand, you may want to see what the industry as a whole is saying about you.

Google Alerts (`www.google.com/alerts`) is a useful tool for marketers to receive alerts whenever your company, brand, or products are mentioned online. You can react, or just listen, and learn when you're mentioned in content on the Internet.

Meeting Leads in Real Life

The entire world of business doesn't operate online. Many people attend conferences, networking events, and parties, all in the name of making business work.

The business connections your employees make in person should also get logged into the CRM. Entering notes about a conversation is a manual entry process, which is a compelling reason for making sure your sales and events teams have remote access to the CRM.

TIP

If a lot of your business in conducted in the field, a CRM mobile app is critical.

Hosting and attending trade shows: Best practices

If you attend a trade show, you likely collect a good number of business cards and you need to make the most of those leads. One way is to set up a fishbowl to gather business cards, usually for a chance to win something significant.

The fishbowl is a tried-and-true method for gathering business cards, but there are more modern methods:

- Have someone with a tablet ask visitors to your booth for their information. This method should automatically add that person as a contact to your CRM and activate a workflow for the new lead, introducing her to your products and services and getting her started on your buyer journey.
- Scan business cards into your CRM. Some scanner software, such as Evernote, shown in Figure 9-11, uploads the scanned card data directly to your CRM. Other software has an interim step where you create a spreadsheet file to import into your CRM. Others are dedicated mobile apps that work with your phone's camera to take a picture and automatically add the lead to your CRM.

  TIP

  Evernote Premium includes a way to take a picture of a business card with your mobile phone and automatically create a contact in the CRM.

  In either case, having a workflow with automated follow-up message engages with new leads and gets them into your sales funnel and lead nurturing campaigns.
- If your organization hosts larger events, where many people are invited, use an event management platform. Event registration information should link directly to your CRM. Engage with the attendees (and possibly those who did not attend), and target them with email communication or drip campaigns. Use your technology to keep those people engaged with you as you guide them down your buyer journeys.

Whether you send educational material by email or schedule a CRM activity for a follow-up call, use marketing automation combined with your CRM to convert interested leads into customers. (See Chapter 11 for more information about marketing automation.)

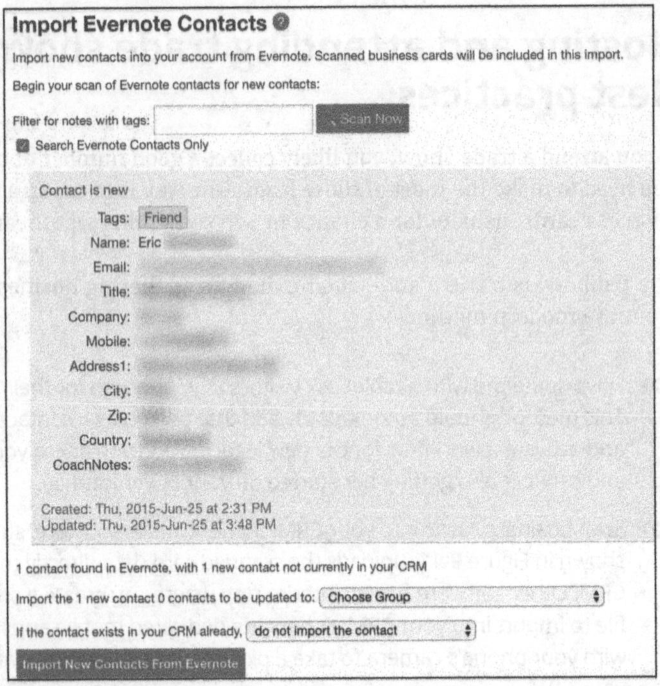

Import Evernote Contacts

Import new contacts into your account from Evernote. Scanned business cards will be included in this import.

Begin your scan of Evernote contacts for new contacts:

Filter for notes with tags: Scan Now

Search Evernote Contacts Only

Contact is new

Tags: Friend
Name: Eric
Email:
Title:
Company:
Mobile:
Address1:
City:
Zip:
Country:
CoachNotes:

Created: Thu, 2015-Jun-25 at 2:31 PM
Updated: Thu, 2015-Jun-25 at 3:48 PM

1 contact found in Evernote, with 1 new contact not currently in your CRM

Import the 1 new contact 0 contacts to be updated to: Choose Group

If the contact exists in your CRM already, do not import the contact

Import New Contacts From Evernote

FIGURE 9-11: Importing scanned business cards from Evernote.

Initiating conversation with a goal

Your team may have some experience with trade shows and networking, but they may not be as focused on your primary goal — to get the people they meet into the CRM. Whenever an employee meets a lead, he should enter the relevant information into your CRM. The goal, especially at events, is to properly place the lead in the right group, activate the appropriate marketing, and maximize the chance of having the lead become a customer.

A business card is a great start, as it contains the key information for contacting each person you talk to. The conversation between your team member and the new lead should be natural, but with a little coaching, everyone in your team can be a part of the sales process.

Every conversation with a lead should be to accumulate information that translates into your CRM. Some of what you learn about the lead is directly attributable to a specific custom data field, such as interests or hobbies or readiness to buy. Get that data into your CRM as soon as possible after meeting the lead.

Integrating Inbound Leads through Zapier

Zapier (`zapier.com`) is a third-party data integration service that helps you connect different pieces of software together; see Figure 9-12. With Zapier, your online applications can talk to each other, keeping data up to date and triggering automation. It works by allowing actions in one piece of software to trigger another action in a second software platform.

The process of building a connector between two pieces of software that are connected through Zapier is a relatively simple one. You choose the trigger in the source software, then activate a "zap" for it, and set up what you want the zap to do. You don't need to do any coding and only have to tell the system what initiates the transfer of data from one system to another.

For example, Zapier connects your CRM to a document creation service like WebMerge. You can then create Word documents through WebMerge. It imports your contact's data and merges it into the document and sends it to your contact.

Another way you can use Zapier is to have a third-party e-commerce engine such as Shopify send transaction data using Zapier to your CRM whenever someone makes a purchase.

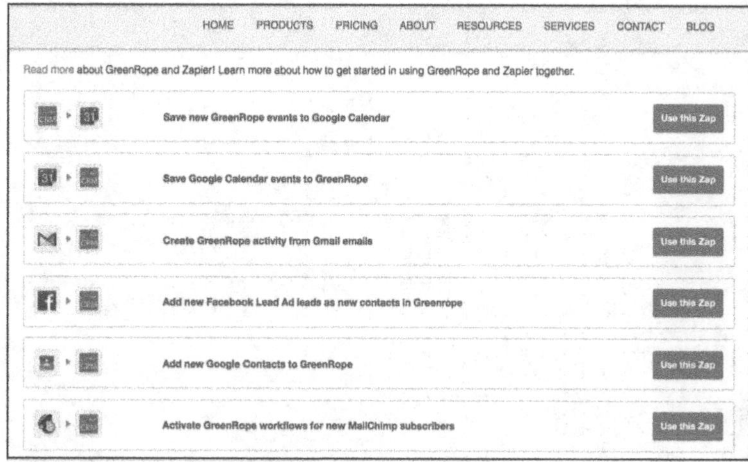

FIGURE 9-12: Zaps connect a CRM to other software.

REMEMBER

The rules you set up when importing data apply when connecting data through third-party applications. You need to ensure these connectors respect the rules you have in place to protect the integrity of your data.

IN THIS CHAPTER

» Setting up your DNS to ensure maximum deliverability

» Knowing the legal requirements for sending email

» Building and maintaining email lists

» Personalizing messages for maximum impact

» Tracking email response and behavior

Chapter 10 Communicating Effectively with Email

Email is by far the most common method of communication, particularly for business-to-business messaging. It's the single most used application for digital communication. Email can be used for personal emails from your salespeople, or it can be part of campaigns from your marketing team.

Email marketing as an industry has been around for many years. People in business are used to sending and receiving emails. Some businesses understand the power of this medium and use that power responsibly. Others don't, having fallen for the false promise of spam and the low cost of sending unsolicited mass emails.

Blasting emails to your contact database is simple and relatively inexpensive, but it must be done responsibly to be effective. Everyone already gets a lot of email, so you must find ways to cut through the noise and be heard. Good timing, relevant content, and working with a reputable email service provider (ESP) open the door for using this medium to communicate, educate, and guide people along your buyer journeys.

This chapter covers everything you need to know about using email. Sending email responsibly, setting up your DNS to maximize delivery to the inbox, and building personalized messages are important to ensure your message is received and read by your recipients. Integrating tracking data in your CRM helps your salespeople understand what their contacts want. Studying statistical data about email performance illuminates how marketers can best reach your market segments, driving leads to become customers.

Avoiding Spam

Spam is technically unsolicited commercial email. I believe the definition is broader. Like art, spam is in the eye of the beholder. If you receive email, you know when it's spam, and it all comes down to the simple recognition of the sender and giving permission to be sent email.

Many companies are lured by the prospect of getting their message to a large audience for cheap. There's a name for that — *spam.* There's also another name for it — *brand suicide.* You don't want to have people remember you and your brand as spammers.

REMEMBER

If enough people report your business as a spammer to their ISPs (especially Google), your emails are blocked temporarily, and maybe permanently. That is a very real cost to not using email responsibly. If your emails end up in the junk folder — or worse, disappear entirely — your business suffers.

Domestic and international laws affect sending emails, as well. In North America, the two big laws you must understand are CAN-SPAM (Controlling the Assault of Non-Solicited Pornography And Marketing) and CASL (Canadian Anti-Spam Law).

If you plan to send commercial email (and you should, as it's an important part of your growth strategy), be sure you're familiar with these laws. If you aren't sure whether certain tenets apply to you, consult a legal professional.

Email marketing has some tried-and-true methods that can grow your business while keeping your contacts engaged. These best practices have been developed over the years and if you follow them, you can grow your reach and influence.

Protecting your brand by being responsible

Remember that your recipients, not you, determine when they're being spammed. They are the ones who click the Spam button in their email clients. If you send your contacts emails that aren't relevant to them, or if you send them too many emails, they can damage your reputation.

WARNING

Do not buy, lease, rent, or sell your contacts. As soon as you engage in this kind of activity, you become a spammer, or are party to spamming, and you will find yourself blacklisted. You may find short-term gain, but in the long run, you'll lose.

The best way to be responsible about email is to follow these guidelines about using email for marketing and communication:

- **Gather leads responsibly.** Collect your leads through confirmed opt-in forms or ticketing forms (see Chapter 8), or when your team meets someone in person. In all cases, communicate that you will be sending emails to them.
- **Keep your list up to date with active contacts.** Be sure the software you use to build, send, and track your emails is tightly integrated with your CRM. This integration makes sure that when someone clicks the Unsubscribe button or calls to be removed from your mailing list that you don't continue to send emails to that person. Sending emails to people who have unsubscribed can have financial and legal implications.

  You also want to cull your contacts for email addresses that bounce emails back to your provider. Your ESP should provide you with this information, and should automatically prevent you from resending to permanently bounced email addresses. These are called *hard bounces* and represent invalid email addresses. Too many bounced emails can affect your reputation, and therefore your deliverability into your contacts' inboxes.
- **Make sure your content is relevant.** The more educational and helpful your message, the better. People want to get something useful when they receive emails from you.
- **Email your list regularly.** If your contacts don't hear from you in a long time, they forget who you are. Your email shows up in their inbox, and because they don't remember giving you permission to email them, they flag your email as spam.
- **Check your message for spammy keywords and phrases.** Your ESP and CRM should include this quality check in the email building tool. Be careful using lots of exclamation points and capital letters, especially in subject lines. Use the word "free" sparingly, as it's commonly used in spam email subject lines.
- **Use responsive design.** Your email should look good on any device (wide-screen monitors, tablets, smartphones). Your email design software should take care of design considerations for you automatically.

» **Use a combination of text and images.** Don't have your email be entirely made up of images. Most people don't load images in their email by default, and when they can't see what your message is about, they may not take the time to load your image.

Following industry best practices

In addition to not sending spam, you should do a few things when sending emails that keep your reputation strong and emails landing in your contacts' inboxes:

» **Honor unsubscribes.** By law, emails sent for commercial marketing must include an unsubscribe link. If someone clicks the link to unsubscribe from your emails, emails you directly saying she wants to unsubscribe, calls your support line, or clicks the Spam button, be sure you never send her email again. You must mark such people as unsubscribers in your email list and keep records of the unsubscribers in your CRM and the ESP prevents you from sending email to them. This step is important, in case you or someone in the future tries to reimport contacts. You want to always keep a log of your unsubscribers. Good ESPs don't charge you to store unsubscribed contacts.

» **Don't resend to hard bounces.** If an ISP (for example, Gmail or Yahoo) finds an invalid email address, it returns a code that says "no one is at this email address." If you continue to send to this email address, it tells the ESP that you aren't paying attention to your email list and are likely a spammer. Good ESPs mark these hard bounces in your email list and don't attempt to send to them again.

» **Pay attention to soft bounces.** After you send an email, look at the emails that didn't get delivered for temporary reasons, such as unacceptable or filtered content. If you see soft bounces, look at the details to find out what is causing them. Soft bounces can often be resolved by communicating with the ISP or following the instructions in the bounce message. ESPs should keep track of your soft bounces and show you the detail for each individual bounced email.

» **Give your contacts the ability to choose what lists they are on.** If at all possible, allow your contacts to opt in or out of different email lists. Give them the freedom to choose when they receive messages and the kinds of messages they receive.

» **Use an established, reputable ESP.** Email delivery technology includes best practices that are invisible to you. They're handled by your email service provider, which should be connected to your CRM. ISPs like Gmail, Hotmail, and Yahoo all have standards for receiving email at specified rates. If you're sending emails to a large group of people, you need to work with an ESP with experience and high standards of acceptable emailing.

USING A DEDICATED DOMAIN

Always use a dedicated domain and send emails from that domain, instead of a webmail address, such as *yourbusiness*@yahoo.com or *yourbusiness*@gmail.com.

One reason for doing so is the perception of you as a real business. Real businesses have their own domains, and if you're sending emails from a free webmail address, there is a high risk of negative perception. People associate free email addresses as tools for personal email use, not for business. Sending email from your own domain, on the other hand, demonstrates you've invested in your own business enough to be legitimate and stable.

There are technical limitations with webmail and free email addresses, as well. You can't use any email service provider to send newsletters. ISPs use DMARC, which checks to see whether you're sending from a server on an approved network. If you're using a third-party domain (such as Google), most ISPs block your email.

Most mail servers also block email with a lot of addresses in the To line. The safest thing you can do is to use an email service provider. A reputable ESP ensures optimal deliverability and more effective email communication with your contact lists.

Knowing the penalties of being a bad actor

There are both legal and practical implication to not following email marketing law and best practices. Always avoid any temptation to buy or send to purchased or rented lists.

Beyond legal ramifications, you're a steward of your brand, and sending spam damages your reputation. If you make the recipients of your emails angry, they may take to the Internet to spread negativity about you. Never lose the trust of your contact list. Not only does it harm your reputation, but it also opens your brand to criticism both on and offline. You also run the risk of being blacklisted, which severely affects your ability to get emails to the inbox.

Adhering to Legal Requirements

You need to be aware of a few things when sending emails. Even if you aren't the person on the marketing team who designs and sends the messages, you have to be in compliance with federal and international laws, such as the U.S. CAN-SPAM Act and the Canadian Anti-Spam Legislation (CASL). You want to take these seriously, as fines from the regulatory agencies in the U.S. and Canada can be steep.

Understanding CAN-SPAM and CASL

A short list of laws you must abide by when sending email to or from North America:

- The subject line of the message must be descriptive of the content of the message.
- A physical address for the sender must be somewhere in the message.
- There must be a way to unsubscribe from further email communication in an obvious link in the email.
- You must honor unsubscribes up to 60 days after sending the message. (The contact must remain active in your email marketing system during that time.)

The Canadian Anti-Spam Law (CASL) is similar to the U.S. CAN-SPAM Act but in 2017 includes provisions for private actions to be taken against your business for up to $10 million if your company doesn't adhere to the law.

Following EU-U.S. Privacy Shield and Swiss-U.S. Privacy Shield

If you do business internationally, two provisions are in place for protecting data you collect about people who live in Europe that impacts your business. Both the EU-U.S. Privacy Shield and Swiss-U.S. Privacy Shield require that you don't share personal data about any contacts in the European Economic Area (EEA).

In agreeing to the provisions of these Privacy Shields, you agree to not sell any data you obtain through email marketing regarding a European. Including capturing reads, clicks, browsers, or any other information about what someone does on your website. This law is important if your business model includes selling any data you accumulate through your interactions with contacts in your CRM.

Employing SPF and DKIM

The best-designed email in the world won't move the needle for you when your email lands in your recipients' spam folders. A number of factors determine whether your email appears in your contacts' inboxes, spam folders, or gets sent to never-never land, never to be heard from again.

The quality of your list determines the success rate of getting your emails in the inbox. If the recipient mail server sees a high percentage of your messages sent to invalid email addresses (bounces), or a large number of people unsubscribe or mark your messages as spam, your emails go straight into the spam folder. Very high rates of bounces and unsubscribes could trigger action by the ISP to not deliver your messages at all.

DNS, or *domain name service*, is a fundamental part of the Internet. DNS tells people where to go when they look up your domain. DNS is also important in routing email.

You must take two actions to ensure email deliverability: adding SPF and DKIM records. Both involve updating your *DNS zone file*, which is managed by your domain registrar (the company you used to purchase your domain). Reputable registrars include a way for you to log in to your domain management interface and update your zone file yourself.

Without SPF or DKIM, your emails may take longer to be delivered, land in the spam folder, or not delivered at all.

SPF (Sender Policy Framework)

SPF, or *Sender Policy Framework*, is a text line in your DNS that lists the valid IP addresses you can send your emails from, similar to this one:

```
@ 10800 IN TXT "v=spf1 include:_.spf.stgi.net
        mx:stgi.netmx:cooleremail.com -all"
```

If you're sending emails with Google Apps or another mail server for one-to-one-communication, make sure you add those IP addresses. If you're doing any email marketing, contact your ESP and get its IP addresses so you can add them to your DNS record. Every ESP publishes its IP addresses for its clients and should be able to help you.

DKIM (Domain Keys Identified Mail)

The other important protocol to add to your DNS is Domain Keys Identified Mail (DKIM).

```
kesq._domainkey 86400 IN TXT "k=rsa/"
p=MIBIjANBgkqhkiG9w0BAQEFAAOCAQ8AMIIBCgKCAExgiBJzQPyItkH
        6uzTN+hQzW0/VER4FAImcGB5RwkQo4
```

It's a cryptologic key that you add to your DNS record to positively identify the emails you send with a signature. The sending mail server knows to sign the message with a key that works with your published key to confirm that you're indeed intending to send messages through that mail server. Your ESP can help you with this important step. There are various strengths of encryption, but be sure to sign with at least a 2,048-bit key for maximum security.

Choosing the Right Email Service Provider

While many ESPs are on the market, and many share strong technology, not all are made the same. The reputation of an ESP has a lot to do with your email delivery. Good tools help you design attractive emails that people want to read. Deep analytics give you the insight to learn from your campaigns.

Evaluating acceptable use policies

Ask your ESP about its policy on contact lists. Each of these policies will impact your delivery, which is absolutely critical to your effectiveness of your marketing.

- Can you send to purchased or rented lists? If an ESP allows sending to purchased or rented lists, it is most likely already blacklisted by many ISPs. Avoid these ESPs at all costs.
- Are you sharing an IP address with other senders? If an ESP sends your messages through a shared IP address, take a look at the reputation of the IP address you will be sending through.
- How does the ESP manage the reputation of its IP addresses? Ask the ESP how it monitors the reputation of its IP addresses, and how often it checks up on its customers' sending habits. Good ESPs constantly monitor and enforce violations of their acceptable use policies swiftly and definitively.

WARNING

Ask if an ESP works with affiliate marketers. Affiliate marketers purchase and trade large lists of email addresses and send spam, which destroys the reputation of the ESP. If the ESP allows this kind of traffic to be sent through its networks, your deliverability suffers with them.

Examining reputation

Your CRM should include full-featured email marketing for designing and delivering your email campaigns. If you choose a separate email marketing platform, be sure to account for the effort required to integrate email marketing data into your CRM.

Part of selecting the best ESP is testing delivery of your emails. Build an email and send it to a small list of friends or employees to see whether it gets delivered and it looks as expected on a computer and mobile device.

TIP

Test every method prior to selecting a vendor, or you risk not getting your messages to your contacts' inboxes.

Testing deliverability of your email vendor is a fairly straightforward process. Test the IP addresses for the email vendor with senderscore.org. The Sender Score you receive is a value between 0 and 100. If the vendor's IP address is below 90, you may have problems with your email delivery.

Figure 10-1 shows what a typical Sender Score report for a good IP address looks like. Note the consistent high score in the chart, representing that the ISP has solid business practices and reputation management.

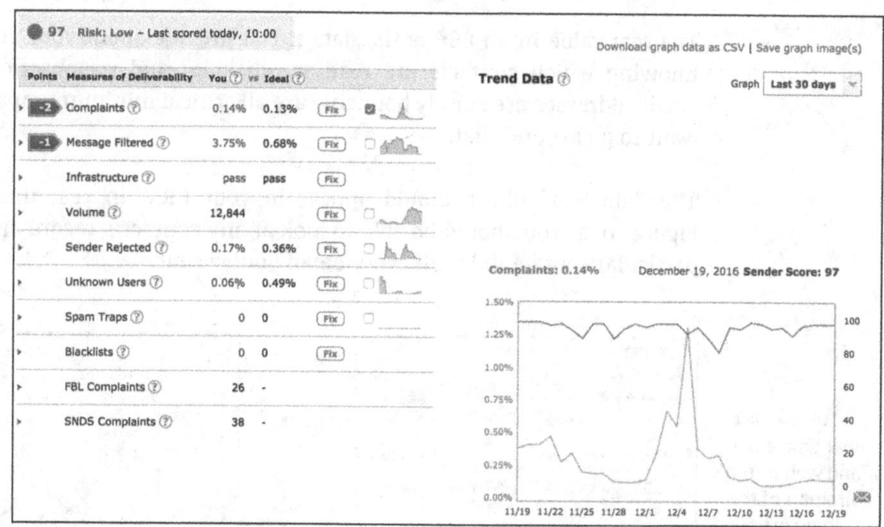

FIGURE 10-1: Sender score report for a domain.

Ask whether your ESP is whitelisted by Return Path (returnpath.com), a third-party service that vets ESPs for appropriate email sending policies and practices. Those who are whitelisted have better deliverability than those not listed.

Red Pill Email (`redpillemail.com/blog`) conducts a comparative study of email service providers every year, which can point you in the right direction. It's an unbiased source with a detailed analysis of the major players on the market.

Measuring throughput and delivery delay time

When you press Send, you want to be sure your emails arrive in a reasonable amount of time. Of course, the definition of "reasonable" is up to you. If your emails are not time sensitive, and you don't mind waiting, delivery delays may not be important to you.

On the other hand, if an email vendor doesn't have the capability to support a large broadcast without clogging up its system, you may get stuck behind unacceptably long delays. Be sure to get actual delivery speed numbers from your vendor, so you have confidence that your time-sensitive emails arrive when you want them to.

Compiling data and learning from campaigns

The real value in an ESP is the data it can provide about your email campaigns. Knowing which contacts are reading, clicking, and unsubscribing, and which email addresses are simply bouncing are all critical minimum capabilities, but you want to go beyond that.

The data you collect should appear in your CRM in real time, as shown in Figure 10-2. You should be able to look at any contact's record and see what that particular contact did with every email you've sent.

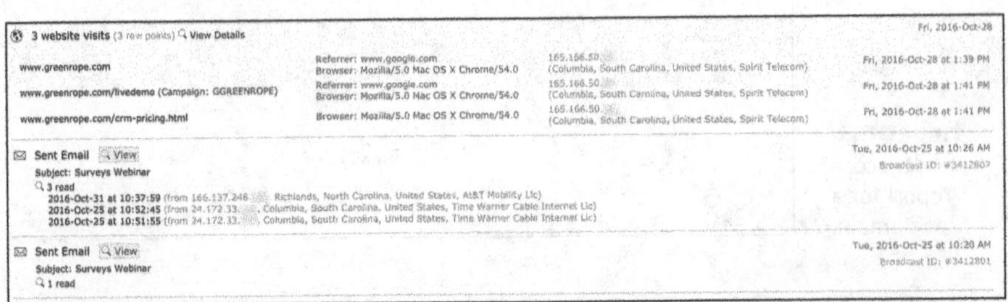

FIGURE 10-2: Real-time email and web traffic are part of the data in your contact's CRM feed.

REMEMBER

Beyond data collection and real-time analytics, you should be able to tie automation to engagement with your email broadcasts. If a lead clicks a link, you may want to activate a workflow, as shown in Figure 10-3. If a lead doesn't read an important email, you may want to schedule an automatic follow-up email.

Tracking your email marketing efforts over time should be effortless. Find out who your most engaged contacts are and attribute lead scores to specific actions they take. Chapter 15 talks more about email analytics.

http://app.greenrope.com/content/buyersguide.pdf 5 points Auto add to GreenRope - Automatically assigns workflow New Trial Edit Delete
http://app.greenrope.com/events/GreenRopesCRM 3 points Add Auto Action Delete
http://app.greenrope.com/events/Jan2012greenon 1 clicks 3 points Add Auto Action
http://app.greenrope.com/events/WebinarGreenRopeWebsites 155 clicks 3 points Add Auto Action

FIGURE 10-3: Activating workflows from link clicks.

Managing Your Lists

All sales and marketing platforms provide tools to help segment your contacts. When you split your contacts into groups, lists, or campaigns, you have the ability to target those segments more precisely and more effectively. This process is important, as each group has different interests, motivations, and receptivity to different kinds of messaging.

Setting up groups for segmentation

Groups are useful for communicating outbound messages as well as analyzing how different segments of your market respond to your messaging. Splitting your email lists into separate lists allows you to

» **Personalize communication.**

- *Set up buyer journeys.* If you sell different products and services to different groups, you can customize the buyer journey for each kind of customer. (See Chapter 5 for more about journeys.)
- *Create personal URLS.* If you have special VIP or membership-driven groups, set up special websites and landing pages for those contacts with special offers or information. (Chapter 8 has more information about websites/landing pages.)

» **Automate workflows.** If you set up automation around these groups, you can precisely trigger emails, text messages, and CRM activities for your market segments. (See Chapter 11.) Use groups for assigning leads to salespeople, so you can personalize the workflows and messaging for each salesperson.

Cleaning your lists

One important part of list management, especially when it comes to email, is to routinely clean your email list of contacts who don't read or open your emails. A good threshold is 6 to 12 months. If you've no interaction in that timeframe, consider moving those contacts into an inactive group or list for a different kind of follow-up.

Your ESP should automatically manage your bounced emails (non-valid email addresses) or when someone unsubscribes from your email list. If a contact clicks the Spam button in her email client, your ESP should also automatically unsubscribe her, to prevent that person from impacting your reputation further.

Filters are a good way to identify groups of contacts who have taken action, or not taken action. You can activate workflows, send follow-up messages, or further segment your CRM based on filters. If you're using an automated buyer journey system, you can set up an automation rule that when an email bounces or someone unsubscribes, a live salesperson makes a phone call to the contact.

Figure 10-4 shows a filtering system that identifies contacts in the CRM who have been sent, but didn't read, an email. You may want to send another email to them with a different call to action as a way to get them to take action and interact with your company.

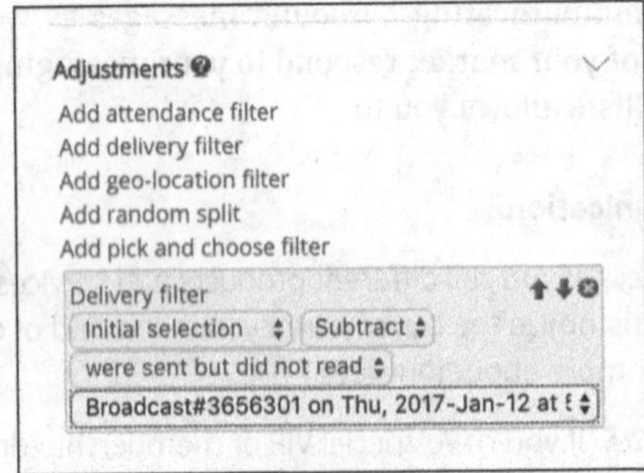

FIGURE 10-4: Use filters to identify contacts who are not responding to your emails.

A/B testing lists

The ability to test your lists gives you insight into your contacts and what drives them to engage with your brand. Knowing what people want helps your marketing team create messages that resonate with your different groups. A/B testing breaks your groups into testable parts so you can see which message works best.

A/B testing works by sending emails to a percentage of any group or email list and seeing how those emails perform. You can do two versions of an email; maybe they each have a different subject line, a different call to action, or a different color scheme. If you pick a small percentage of your list — say 5 percent for each version — you can then broadcast to the remaining 90 percent the version that performed best.

Figure 10-5 shows a simple user interface that would randomly select 9 percent of your contacts for a test. You would send one email to this subset, a second email to another subset. Then, based on results, you would send the best version of your email to the remaining 82 percent.

TIP

If you have a large list, split your groups into more than two. Each test gives you more insight into what content works best and what your contacts prefer to receive in their inboxes.

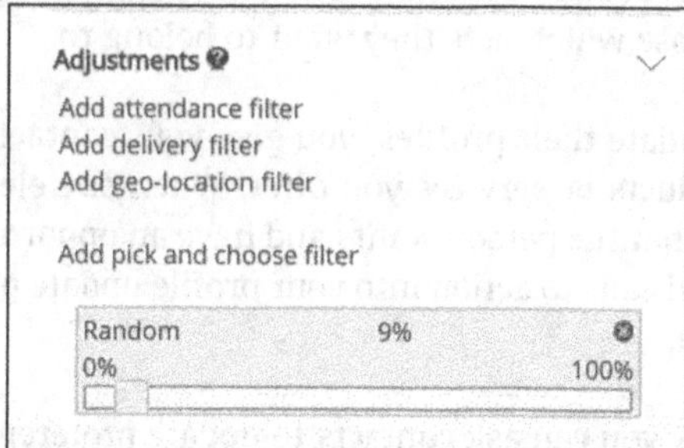

FIGURE 10-5: Random A/B splitting a campaign for testing.

Gathering New Leads

Your ESP gives you tools to help you gather leads and feed them automatically into your CRM. Use these tools to grow your contact lists and potential clients. More leads means more potential sales, which means more actual sales, so take advantage of every means available to boost your ability to generate revenue.

Connecting forms to your email marketing

Web forms are often a key part of any sales process, turning website visitors into leads. Spend a lot of time on them, because they automatically add contacts to your sales funnel and the better they are, the more your business grows.

REMEMBER

It's not enough to just design your forms and hope they're used. Continually monitor how many people visit your webpages, fill out forms, and move along your buyer journeys. The more you optimize and improve your forms, the better they bring you leads.

Forms are useful to getting leads into your CRM and sales funnel. I talk about forms (confirmed opt-in, single opt-in, and tickets) in Chapter 8.

Updating recipient profiles to encourage list subscribing

Most ESPs provide a link you can add to your emails that directs email recipients to a page where they can customize their preferences and update their profiles. Sometimes this page gives your contacts the ability to unsubscribe. A profile update page can also include ways for the recipient to update CRM data, such as preferences or interests. Beyond updating their CRM data, you can also give recipients the ability to choose which lists they want to belong to.

When your contacts update their profiles, you give your contacts the opportunity to see what other products or services you offer. When she elects to sign up for other lists, you learn what the person wants and have an opportunity to cross-sell and up-sell. If you build calls to action into your profile update page, you can drive people to buy from you.

Figure 10-6 shows how you can ask contacts to update preferences with an email profile update/unsubscribe page. You must provide a way to unsubscribe, but having ways to reconfirm intent to be on the list or join other lists is a good way to build more interaction with your contacts.

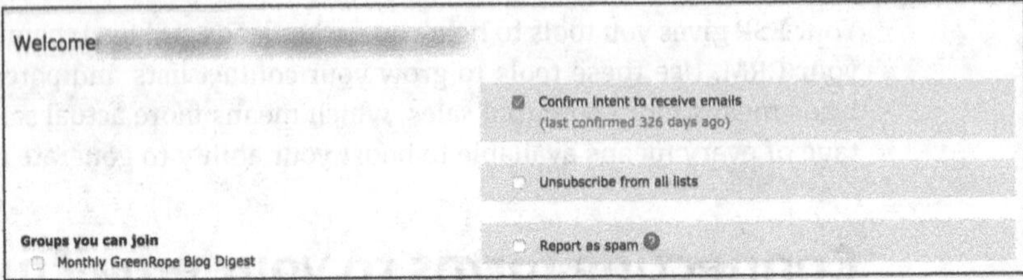

FIGURE 10-6: Profile update page for an email broadcast.

Using forward-to-a-friend

Your ESP can add a link to forward an email to a friend. This link empowers each of your recipients to forward the message to a friend so that the friend can subscribe to your email lists. In the modern era, people are more used to getting emails and don't use these forwarding functions that often. You may still want to include it in your emails, but don't expect your recipients to use that function often.

REMEMBER

Your ESP can't track when someone clicks the Forward button in an email to forward the message. As far as the ESP can tell, the person who received the forwarded message is the same person who received the original message. If you see a sudden jump in reads or clicks from an individual in your CRM, you may be recording reads and clicks from the person who received a forwarded message.

Designing Emails That Work

Not all email marketing strategies are equal, and not all strategies should be applied to the same kind of business or the same type of audience. As with most things in business, "it depends" is usually the answer. Test your marketing strategy and adapt to what your market wants. Over the years, marketing professionals have learned what works. With trillions of emails sent every year, data backs up some fundamentals that can help you get started.

Understanding good design principles

Email design has a few universal rules:

- **Keep it simple stupid.** The old KISS rule holds true with email. People don't want to read a lot when they're on a computer or mobile device. They want information to be relevant and short, not long-winded and hard to understand. Like with most writing, your audience determines the reading level, but usually 6th to 8th grade works best.

  If you're writing email content for technical recipients, you may write at a higher level, but be cognizant that email has a shorter attention span than blogs or whitepapers. Email recipients generally are trying to get through their inboxes and tend to scan, rather than read for deep comprehension.

- **Use a one-column layout.** Traditional print marketing is usually wider, with folds and multiple columns, because the eye has more "real estate" to scan. Unfortunately, email has less real estate. With over 60 percent of emails being read on a mobile device, assume your message recipients scan a single column. A good rule is to design for 600 pixels width at most. If you must have two columns, the left column comes first so put the most relevant information there.

- **Use responsive design.** Email should adjust for the size of the reader's screen. Figure 10-7 and Figure 10-8 show the same email, but sized for different screens. Well over half the emails you send are read on a mobile device. It's critical that you design your emails to respond to a smaller screen while still making your message easy to read.

TIP

  Responsive design can be tricky, so test your design on as many platforms as you can. Check that your ESP makes email within its system responsive, too.

- **Keep articles short with links to more information and video content.** Don't try to cram everything into your email. Get your point across and provide a link for more. Your message is short and you also determine which contacts are interested in learning more about something. This click data is very useful for salespeople and for sending further targeted messages.

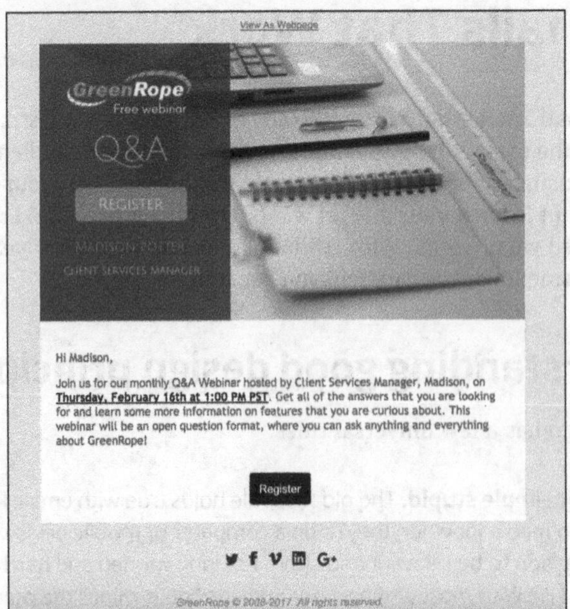

FIGURE 10-7: Webinar invite email on a full size screen.

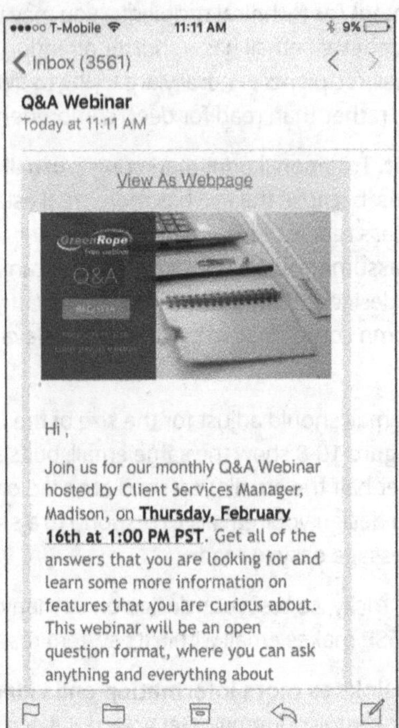

FIGURE 10-8: Same webinar invite, scaled to be read on a mobile device.

- **Make your calls to action clear.** If the point of an email is to drive the contact to take an action, make sure the button or link to accomplish that task is clear.
- **Use images and links to video to make your emails more attractive.** Encourage recipients to click to load images, so you can track when they read their emails. People respond more emotionally to imagery, so use that whenever you can.
- **Educate your recipients.** People don't open emails so they can be sold to. They want to read about something interesting or educational. Help them do something, teach them something, and make them feel glad they are on your list.

Most ESPs have templates you can choose from. Start there and make them your own. You may also want to hire someone to design your email for you. Good email templates should be available to you for a few hundred dollars.

Connecting calls to action to campaigns

When you design an email, your primary objective is to either educate or encourage the recipient to respond to a call to action, or both. If you're driving your contacts to that action, think through the entire process of what you want the person to do.

A positive response should initiate a buyer journey — and if the call to action is to click through to a website, the response should be automated with a CRM workflow — potentially triggering more emails to be sent, an update in the CRM, or more. Be sure the webpage the contact goes to matches what she expects.

Tracking Email Marketing Campaigns

You can measure many aspects to email, each of which should guide your future marketing efforts. These are a few important statistics you can track to learn what is working and why.

Measuring reads/opens

Also known as an open rate, your read rate is the number of people who opened your email compared to the total number of valid recipients. This percentage tells you who loaded images in the email they received. Your open rates reflect why design, content, and a clean contact list are critical. If recipients see a lot of value in loading the images and trusts you, they click to view those images.

Figure 10-9 shows a summary of percentages of results from an email broadcast. Note that you want to compare these figures to other broadcasts you have sent, and similar broadcasts that other businesses send. Your ESP should be able to provide those benchmarks for you.

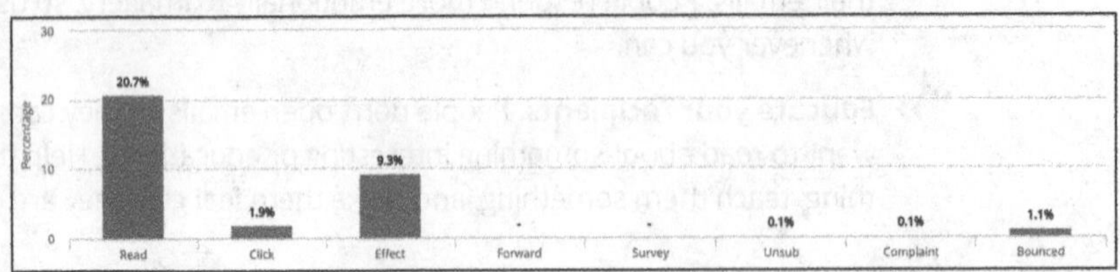

FIGURE 10-9: Summary of percentages of results of an email campaign.

Tracking clicks

Your click rate is the number of people who clicked a link in your email divided by the number of valid recipients. The percentage of clicks lets you know how engaged people are with your content. The more clicks, the more you drive them to your website and toward conversion.

Connected to tracking your click rate is the *effectiveness* rate. This rate is the number of clicks divided by the number of reads. It tells you how compelled your interested readers were to click your links.

Figure 10-10 shows click-related information for an email campaign. In this case, you can see how many times a link in the email was clicked. Your CRM should include allow you to drill into any part of the chart to get detailed information about who took action on your email, and linking that information to that contact's CRM record.

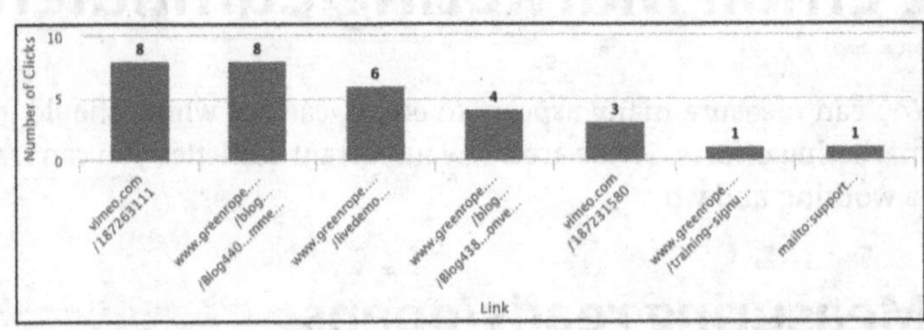

FIGURE 10-10: Comparing summary statistics of an email campaign.

Figure 10-11 shows additional useful data. The top chart shows the activity over time, which is an indicator of how fast people take action. The bottom chart shows the geographic distribution of clicks from the campaign.

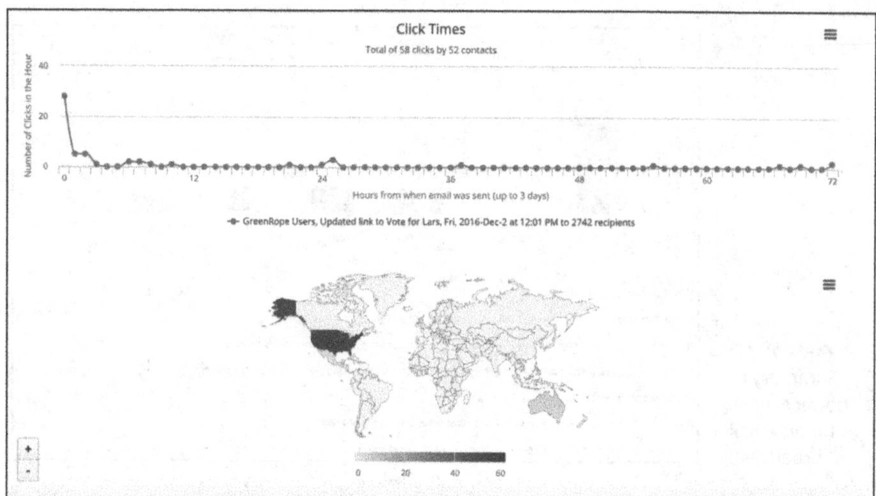

FIGURE 10-11: A report showing when and where email was opened.

Watching unsubscribes

Your unsubscribe rate is all about list quality and your emailing practices. If someone unsubscribes, you can never email her again, unless that person signs up again. Never reset an unsubscribe, unless you're absolutely certain the person made a mistake, and you had a conversation to confirm intent to sign up again. You can incur steep financial and legal penalties for sending email to unsubscribed contacts.

Limiting bounced emails

The quality of your list and the reputation of your mail server is reflected by your bounce rate. Your ESP should give you a summary outlining the reasons why emails bounced, as shown in Figure 10-12. Bounces are classified as hard bounces (the email address doesn't exist any more, or the domain doesn't exist) and soft bounces (rejected due to a full inbox, or inappropriate content). Too many hard bounces to a domain negatively impacts your long-term reputation as an email sender, which is why you need to keep your list up to date.

WARNING

After an email is identified as a hard bounce, never send an email to that address again. Resetting bounces gets you flagged as a spammer by an email provider.

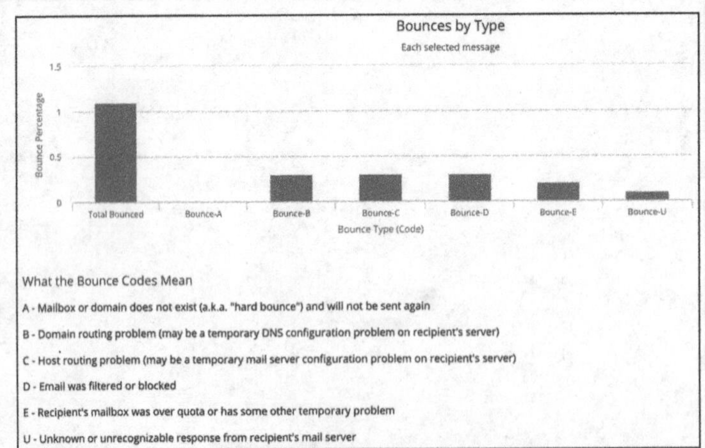

FIGURE 10-12: Summary of bounce types for an email broadcast.

Watching statistical trends

Your marketing team should monitor statistics for both individual broadcasts, and for multiple broadcasts over time. It's useful to look at all your broadcasts as a whole to see general trends in reads and clicks, as shown in Figure 10-13. Get the statistics for a few similar broadcasts (for example, the last several newsletters) and compare them to see whether any performed higher than others.

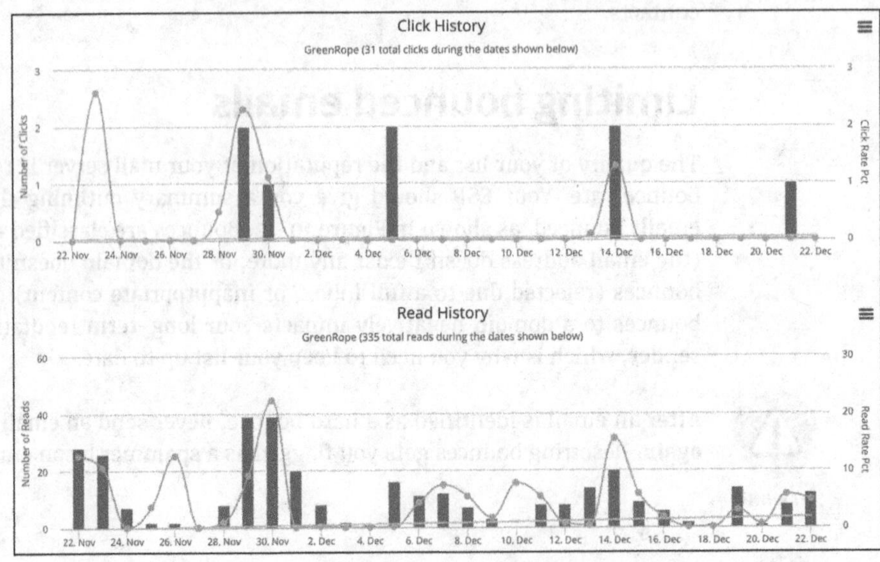

FIGURE 10-13: Summary charts of click and read rates over time with trendlines.

Take a look at vendor-provided benchmarks to see how you're doing in comparison to other companies. List size is the strongest predictor of read and click rate, so your vendor should be able to provide you with relevant stats for your email list size to compare against.

Figure 10-14 shows a chart that can give you insight into how well you're doing overall. If you find you're underperforming, reach out to your ESP or your marketing team to try to figure out why.

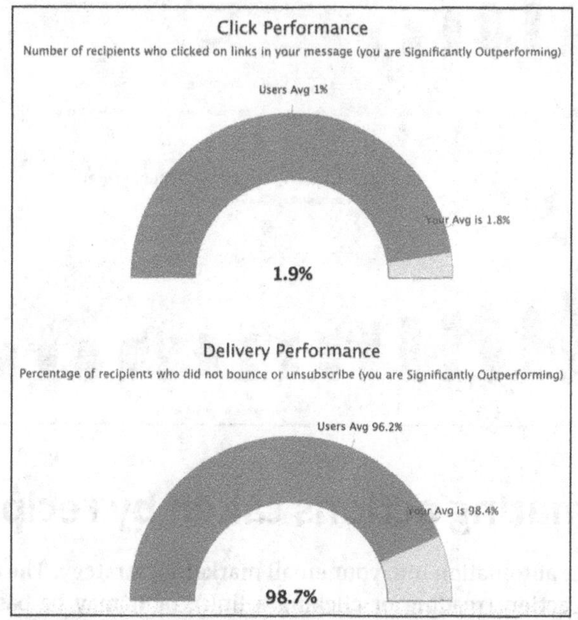

FIGURE 10-14: Benchmarking clicks and delivery against user averages.

Scoring interaction

Scoring is a great way to help you focus on your most engaged contacts. You can target individuals by how many points they accumulated by reading, clicking, or forwarding your message. If you combine scoring across multiple email campaigns, you can target people who have shown repeated interest.

When you identify your hottest leads from scoring, your sales and marketing teams both have opportunities they can take advantage of. For salespeople, a well-timed personal follow-up can reach someone when she's ready to buy. For marketers, knowing someone is interested can trigger a follow-up email with a call to action (for example, a discount code or additional benefits) to spurn a lead to buy.

Figure 10-15 is a hot prospects chart. The top chart shows the contacts who took actions to score those specific scores, while the bottom chart shows contacts who had a minimum score of that number or higher. You can then isolate people based on how interactive they were with the email they received from you.

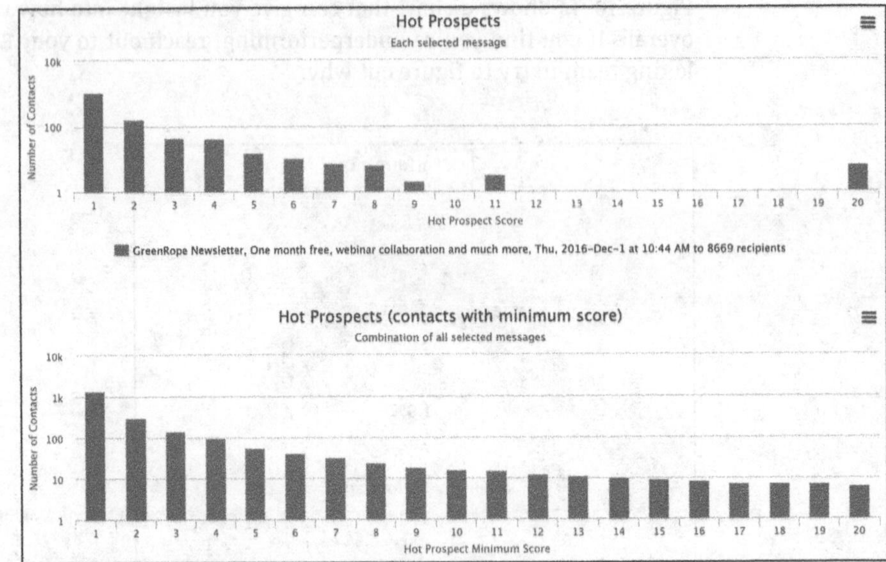

FIGURE 10-15: Individual and minimum score histograms.

Automating actions taken by recipients

Incorporate automation into your email marketing strategy. The trigger may be an individual action (reading or clicking a link), or it may be based on minimum scores, where you may want to target people who are very interested in your message. You may also want to do the opposite, targeting people who didn't read or click your message.

The actions you decide to take should be tightly integrated with your CRM workflows, as shown in Figure 10-16. Workflows allow you to update CRM data, assign contacts to campaigns, schedule follow-up CRM activities for salespeople, and more.

http://app.greenrope.com/cheatsheets/cheatsheet_email.pdf	159 clicks	3 points	Add Auto Action
http://app.greenrope.com/cheatsheets/GreenRope_Account_Setup_Cheat_Sheet.pdf		3 points	Add Auto Action Delete
http://app.greenrope.com/cheatsheets/GreenRope_Email_Marketing_Cheat_Sheet.pdf		3 points	Add Auto Action Delete
http://app.greenrope.com/cheatsheets/GreenRope_Event_Management_Cheatsheet.pdf	3 clicks	3 points	Add Auto Action
http://app.greenrope.com/cheatsheets/GreenRope_Marketing_Automation_Cheat_Sheet.		3 points	Add Auto Action Delete
http://app.greenrope.com/content/buyersguide.pdf		5 points	Auto add to *GreenRope* - Automatically assigns workflow *New Trial* Edit Delete
http://app.greenrope.com/events/GreenRopesCRM		3 points	Add Auto Action Delete

FIGURE 10-16: A link click can activate a workflow.

Setting up automation on emails is part of helping your contacts through the buyer journey. A lead is moving closer toward your goal of conversion, and an existing client is learning more about what you do and moving closer to becoming an advocate for your brand.

Personalizing Your Messages

Message personalization has been around for a long time. In its most basic form, it's saying "Dear *Firstname*" in the opening line of your email. Even this small step goes a long way toward making the recipient feel more valued, as if the message was made for her. As people get more familiar with technology, marketers are expected to take personalization further.

Your marketing staff must be familiar with technology, marketing strategy, and your customers so they can develop a personalization strategy. Gather the data you need to be able to identify recipients and send them the message they want to receive.

Embedding placeholders in your message

The technology that describes the personalization of messages is sometimes referred to as mail merge, a term that goes back to the days of printed mailers. If the mailer was able to include information about the recipient, it had a significant effect on how people responded.

Beyond just replacing the recipient's name, the next step in personalization is to look at other data fields. You can customize an unlimited number of pieces of information with a custom data field. One example is if you want to include personal interests. You could use a placeholder to say, "we see you are interested in *baseball, hockey, and basketball.*" The actual sport a recipient is interested in can be pulled from your CRM. This personalization adds another level to your message that sets it apart from the rest and can help improve your conversion rate.

Using dynamic content

The next level of personalization is rules-based mail merge, also known as *dynamic message content*. You set up mail merge rules to build each message on the fly. Dynamic message content gives your marketing team the tools to personalize messages based on high-level strategies.

For example, if you had a different message for people who lived in California or Nevada or elsewhere, you would create a merge rule with three cases. People in California receive California-related information, people in Nevada receive Nevada-related information, and everyone else receives a generic article that is not geographically targeted.

Triggering Email from Actions

Everyone gets too much email every day. Your emails have to be timely and relevant. Sending an email newsletter once a month to your contacts is a start, but you can do better. Enter the concept of user-triggered communication.

Sending timely and relevant messages can increase engagement by two to four times. Your CRM workflows should include the ability to send emails to people after they take an action. Those emails should be personalized and their content should be relevant.

TIP

As you design your buyer journeys, be sure to think through the kind of messaging you send to your leads and clients. Always put yourself in the mindset of the recipient and "what's in it for me." If you see an opportunity to help a lead become a client or up-sell an existing client through an automated email, think about how to best nurture the lead to do that.

For example, if someone watches a video for more than 60 seconds, she's interested in the content of that video. Trigger a workflow that sends an email to that interested lead with more information and a link to purchase the product with a special discount code.

As another example, if people share your content on LinkedIn, that could indicate they're brand advocates for you, and that may be worthy of a workflow. That workflow could schedule a follow-up CRM activity for a marketing manager to engage further with the contacts on social media.

IN THIS CHAPTER

» **Understanding what marketing automation is and how to use it**

» **Creating campaigns and workflows around automation**

» **Setting up automation around lead scoring**

Chapter 11

Joining the Marketing Automation Revolution

Marketing automation uses software to automate communication and task scheduling. You have the power to set up rules that trigger specific actions based on what your contacts have done. For example, you can have an email automatically sent to a contact who's signed up for your newsletter. Marketing automation saves time and money, while giving your team the tools to focus on what they do best.

Marketing automation and your CRM are tightly linked. They represent different aspects of the same relationship and are components to help you manage, nurture, and engage your leads. Used effectively, they initiate and foster a desire for your leads and contacts to connect to you. The more you harness technology to help communicate, the easier you can sell to your leads.

This chapter explains marketing automation, how to design automated campaigns, and how to integrate your processes into your CRM.

Defining Automation

Marketing automation, when done right, represents the final, ultimate step in using marketing technology to build your business and run your organization as efficiently as possible.

Marketing automation is comprised of two major components — a *trigger* and an *action*. A trigger is a cause, looking for a contact to do something that then causes your marketing automation to create an action. A trigger can have multiple actions, usually executed by a CRM workflow. Workflows can send emails, text messages, or printed material, or they might schedule an appointment for a salesperson in your CRM.

Marketing automation is:

- A way to use software to ensure a consistent experience when people interact with your brand.
- A shift in culture to leveraging technology to save time.
- A revolution in thinking about how you reach out to leads and clients, and how that impacts your entire organization. Everyone is involved and contributing, or it isn't working right.

Marketing automation is not:

- A method to spam people automatically.
- Something you jump into without preparation. Spend time planning and identifying your marketing automation action triggers and actions.
- Something you set and forget. You must constantly monitor how your procedures and communication are working, continually tweaking and improving process.

Knowing when to automate

Just because something *can* be automated doesn't mean it *should* be automated. In designing your automation, first identify all the touchpoints your leads have with your organization. Determine where the human connection is necessary for a profound impact on the buyer journey.

REMEMBER

If the human connection is important at a step in that journey, be very careful with automating communication to save labor costs. Only use automation where there is a small chance of creating a negative experience, and that negative experience is limited in impact.

Be careful automating if you're:

- Selling high-value, expensive items or fundraising large dollar amounts
- Offering services where a high degree of trust is required (such as medical services)
- Marketing anything that is so complex that a back-and-forth question-and-answer session is likely needed

In cases where you don't want to automate communication directly with a lead or customer, use your automation to trigger a CRM activity involving a live person on your staff. It's still a form of marketing automation, as the trigger is automated (for example, filling out a form or visiting a webpage), but the action itself is fulfilled by a person.

On the other hand, if you can easily educate a person by sending useful material on an automated schedule, you save time from having to hire people to say the same things over and over again. Leverage software to communicate relevant, targeted information to ensure consistency of experience and provide a measure of legal accountability.

Avoiding the feeling of being in an automated sequence

People don't like to be treated like they're not important, and your marketing shouldn't oversimplify the buyer journey to the point of generalizing spam. If you send a never-ending stream of emails to every contact you gather, you likely alienate most of them.

Establish a goal with your automated marketing process. Is your strategy helping you reach that goal, or are you sending emails for the sake of sending emails? Each touchpoint must mean something to the lead. Whether it's an automated email or a human touch, be conscious of the messaging and tactic being used. Watch your statistics to see whether your leads are engaging, and be mindful of increasing unsubscribe rates. This way, you ensure you aren't alienating or bombarding your leads with irrelevant content.

REMEMBER

The key to having leads and customers feel like they're valued is to make sure your messaging is personalized and relevant. Personalized messaging makes your leads and customers feel valued and less like a number. Relevant content has meaning to the reader and compels him to engage. Don't distract your reader with information that doesn't help solve a specific problem.

If a contact is interested in a particular product, make the primary objective of your messaging to that person be about that product. If you want to up-sell someone, make it secondary. If you're driving a contact through a customer journey, think about what you can provide him that will want him to take that next step.

Shopping online is a perfect example of how to up-sell without distracting the contact from the primary goal of buying the product he's looking for. Many websites include a "people also bought . . ." section on a product page. This feature is an effective way to up-sell your products and services and to provide relevant content without preventing people from buying what they came to your site for.

Personalizing webpages is a great benefit to the sales process. Use placeholders in your messaging and landing pages whenever possible. Welcome customers back with their names at the top of the page. Remember what each customer likes and display custom information relevant to that person on every page possible.

Your CRM plays an important role in capturing and storing this information for webpage personalization. After you gather information about a lead or a customer, your website should display information based on what you know about the contact.

When a prospect see he's on a page designed for him, you tell him that you're listening. The message contacts receive is that you're committed to providing them with the service they're looking for.

Designing Your Campaigns

A campaign is a programmed effort to create awareness about your products and/or services to a defined group of people with the intention of driving them toward a conversion. A good campaign is planned out, with a journey model and people to support leads as they progress through their journeys.

Campaigns can be designed to be almost anything you can imagine, but I focus on a few standard, effective methods of coming up with your automations. All campaigns should have goals; bring sales, marketing, and operations teams together to discuss and agree on their responsibilities in bringing leads through their journeys to meet those goals.

Using the delay-decision-action model

Building a model of your campaign is important, both from a planning and an execution standpoint. A comprehensive campaign model demonstrates to management that your goals are in alignment with your overall business strategy. A good model also involves everyone who supports the contacts receiving the campaign communication, so your employees know what is happening and why.

Complete CRM gives you the ability to connect every part of your business with the campaign process. Campaigns start with marketing to your target market, but they also involve follow-up marketing communication, interactions with salespeople, and operational elements such as customer service or attending events.

Build as many components into your campaigns as possible. Personalize the experience around demographics, preferences, and actions. All of these are captured in your CRM, so use them to your best ability.

When you build a delay-decision-action campaign, the entire buyer journey is set up like a flowchart. Journeys contain these three elements:

- **Delay:** A delay gives the lead or customer time to make a decision or take an action. A delay is useful when you need to give the contact time to think, or have something happen asynchronously. An example of a delay is waiting for a recipient to read an email.
- **Decision:** The contact needs to make a decision at this point. It can be something active, such as visiting a webpage, watching a video, or clicking a link. It can also be something passive, such as using demographic data associated with the contact.
- **Action:** An action you take, such as sending an email, sending a text message, altering data in the CRM, scheduling a CRM activity, or sending a printed marketing piece.

This model shows the entire buyer journey and anticipates all the things a contact can do along the way, as shown in Figure 11-1. Use this model to anticipate fast-movers (your most interested buyers) and your reluctant buyers. If you can use automation to address the needs of people on your journey, do it.

Your CRM plays an important role in applying this model to real life. You may have places in the journey where a salesperson calls on a lead. Make sure that salesperson has the information and tools needed to effectively follow up. A good CRM implementation provides the demographic and behavioral information that a salesperson needs to make the most of the time spent communicating with the lead.

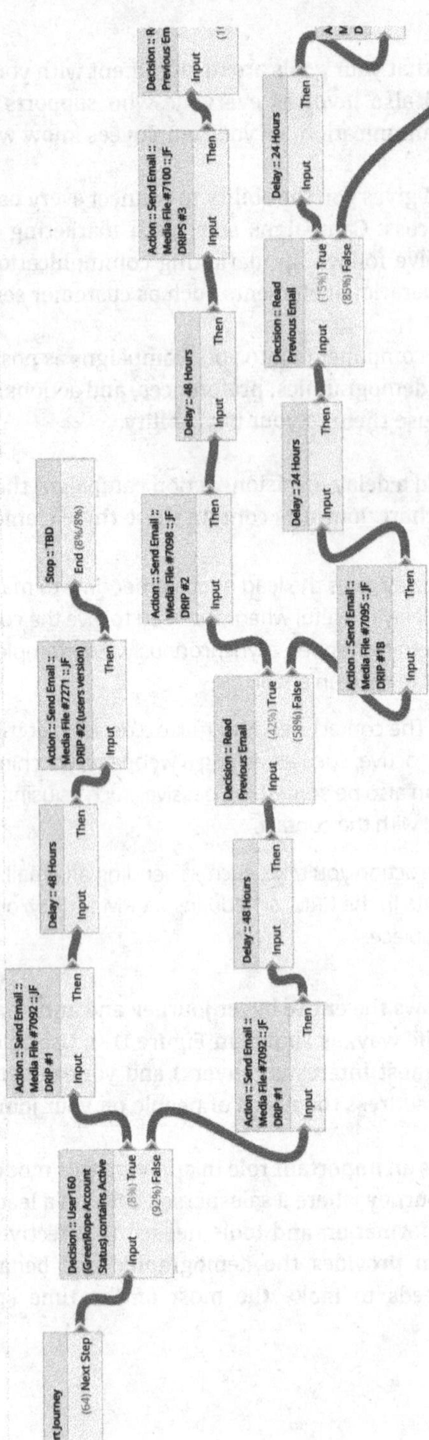

FIGURE 11-1: Part of a journey that includes all three elements of a model.

Educating and marketing with drip campaigns

Drip campaigns are automated sequences of emails or workflows. A specific action or date can trigger a campaign, such as when someone fills out a form, or someone pays for a membership. Because drip campaigns are generally linear in behavior, they tend to not have as much logic built into them, like a journey does.

TIP

A great use for drip campaigns is client onboarding. Ensure a new client receives a sequence of emails that shows her how to use your product. A drip campaign can send that information in smaller, easier-to-absorb emails.

Tracking of drip campaigns over time can also illuminate how people engage with your messages. If you notice that certain stages in your drip campaign perform exceptionally well or badly, dive deeper to find out why.

Figure 11-2 shows a typical drip campaign overview with summary performance data, as well as basic structural data about the emails and workflows associated with the drip campaign.

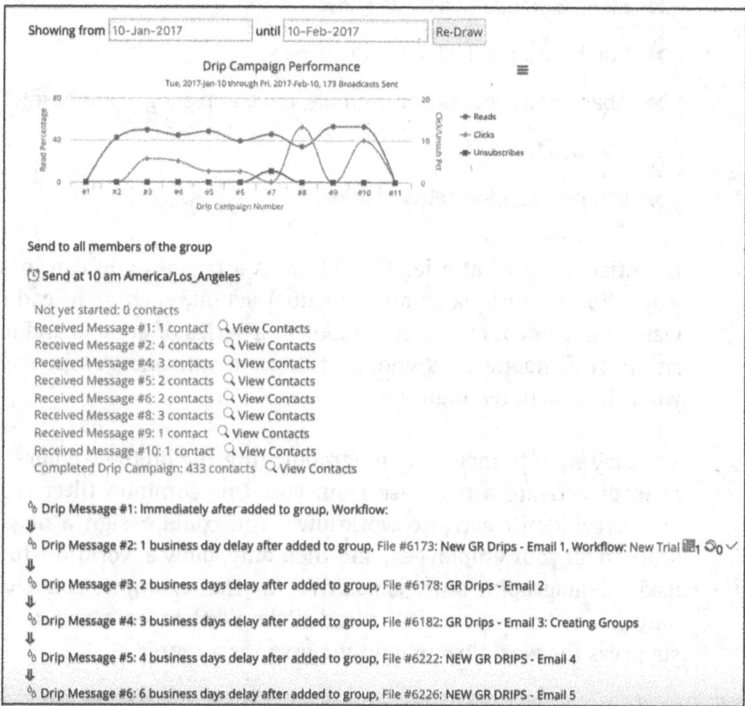

FIGURE 11-2: An overview of a drip campaign.

Setting Up Triggers

Triggers are an important part of modeling the buyer journey. They're the impetus for causing you to take action. A trigger is when a lead does something that causes you to take an action in response.

Triggers are possible whenever you can measure a contact's action. Your CRM must capture these actions to be able to activate a workflow, so you must gather as much data as you can. Email, website traffic, forms, and anything your CRM touches can be part of the triggering process. Some examples of triggers that clients can take are:

- Read or click a link in an email
- Visit a webpage
- Watch a video
- Share or like a social media post
- Chat with a customer service rep
- Meet someone at a trade show
- Purchase a product from an online store
- Abandon a process (for example, not completing a purchase)
- Fill out a form
- Initiate a support request ticket

In anticipating what a lead could do as a trigger, you can look at it in a couple ways. You could look at an individual action, such as a lead clicking a link, or watching a video; or you could look at a series of actions and use a scoring algorithm. If someone does enough things to warrant a response from you, set up what those actions might be.

You may want to include demographic filtering on the triggers; only certain types of leads activate a response from you. One common filter is making sure your employees don't activate workflows. You could assign a negative demographic score to all your employees, and then only allow a workflow to be activated if the lead's demographic score is positive. Another example: You have a product that is only sold to homeowners; if a lead clicks a link to learn about the product, you can suppress the workflow when the person is a renter.

Surveying your processes for triggers

When you use a tool like JourneyFlow to document your processes, you can identify opportunities where a trigger can help a buyer along a journey. This opportunity may include automated communication, or it could flag a contact in your CRM for follow-up by a salesperson. Your CRM tracks when these triggers are activated and what happens afterward.

Limiting over-automation

When you set up your triggers, you want to be careful that there is not too much automation happening at once. You can establish workflow limits in a couple ways:

- Design your triggers in critical steps where people are likely to only go once (for example, relying on scoring instead of an individual action that a lead might take several times in a row).
- Limit the activation rate of your workflows, so that they can only be triggered once a day, or once a week.

Use one way or a combination of them, but it's important to think through your interactions and ensure you maintain a healthy balance and frequency of touchpoints with your leads and clients.

Encouraging Leads to Activate Triggers

When you have built your triggers, you're creating ways to engage your contacts efficiently. For triggers to work, they have to be timely and relevant. In building your buyer journey, evaluate each step for places where triggers make sense.

Designing to support your process

Look at each trigger individually and ask yourself what kind of lead you want to activate that trigger. Put yourself in the shoes of your buyer personas. At each trigger, ask yourself if now is a good time to reach out to that lead.

Take, for example, a lead scoring trigger. This trigger activates a workflow when a lead generates a minimum threshold of lead scoring points in a day. Would you send an email to the contact right away? Probably not. Some of your leads might find that a little creepy. However, if you schedule a follow-up in your CRM for a salesperson in the next 24 hours, you would be striking while the interest is high, while avoiding the impression of knowing too much about that lead's activities.

TIP

If you're targeting new leads, think about campaigns that start your leads on your buyer journey. A campaign might bring someone to a landing page, but be cognizant of where the leads are coming from. Some leads may require different kinds of attention. Higher-value sales generally require more handholding, so trigger CRM activities for those kinds of interactions. Consider having different workflows activated if your campaigns target different market segments.

Figure 11-3 shows a simple flowchart of a lead converting, or not converting. A contingency is built in when someone doesn't complete the process.

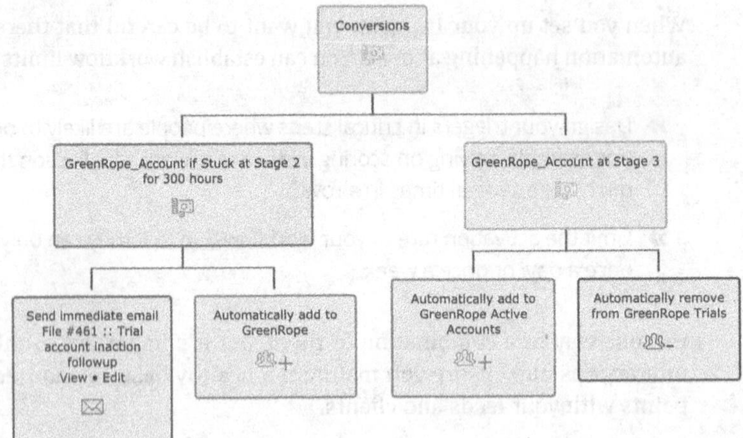

FIGURE 11-3: A click can activate a workflow.

Preparing for process abandonment

Whenever you're tracking a lead through a buyer journey to conversion, a certain percentage of people don't convert or are stuck at a particular stage. Set up process abandonment automation to recapture as many people who appear to drop out of the process.

Whenever someone doesn't progress along your buyer journey, think about how you can keep the process moving. Remind and/or incentivize your leads of what you want them to do.

Usually the perception of someone leaving a conversion process is measured in time. If you expect someone to go from one stage of your buyer journey to the next within a week, but he doesn't, set up a workflow to "catch" that person. Your automated reminder may be an email with an explanation of benefits, a financial incentive, a CRM activity for one of your salespeople to follow up with your lead, or a combination of these.

Automating Workflows Around Lead Scoring

Chapter 6 goes into detail about lead scoring. Scoring assign points to contacts in your CRM based on actions those leads take. Your CRM should store both demographic and activity lead scores for each contact, so your marketing and sales teams can use that information.

Updating your CRM with lead scoring data

Create a custom data field to store demographic and activity lead scores. Those fields update when you update the CRM with new data or your contacts take actions, such as reading an email or watching a video.

Be sure you're familiar with your CRM's ability to sync those user fields with their lead scores. Different CRMs update at different frequencies. Keep that in mind when selecting a CRM vendor.

Figure 11-4 shows an example of how you can automate the connection of lead scoring to your custom data fields in your CRM.

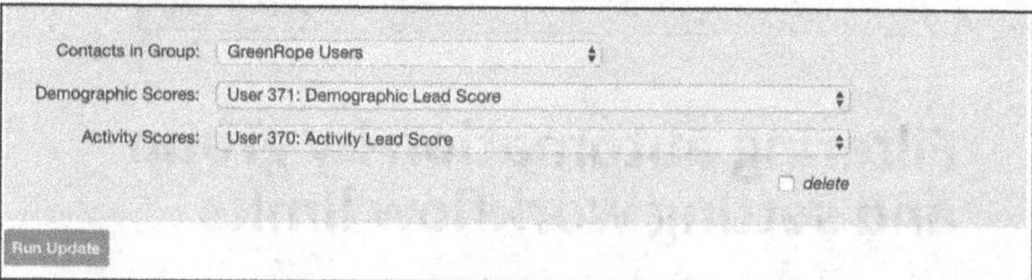

FIGURE 11-4: Automated assignment of lead scores to user fields.

Triggering hot and cold lead scoring automation

You want to set up automation based on the points your leads and clients accumulate. There are two ways to trigger automation based on lead scoring.

Setting up hot automation

Hot lead scoring happens when a contact generates a minimum number of points in a fixed time period. If a lead is very active in a day, you want to know about it right away so that your sales team can follow up, or your marketing team can send something to spur an action. For example, "if one of Austin's leads generates more than 20 points in a day, activate workflow X." (See Figure 11-5.)

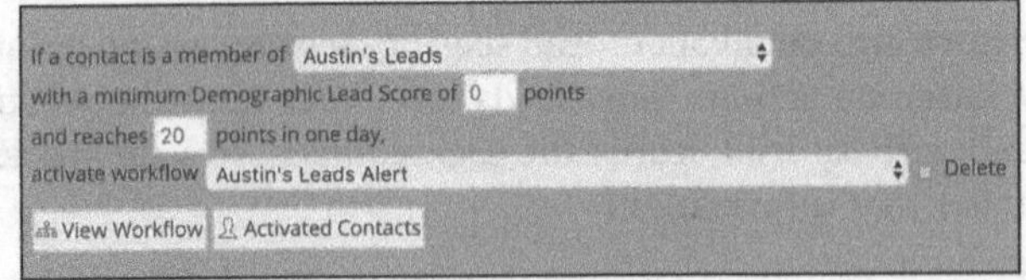

FIGURE 11-5: A hot automation rule for a group of sales leads.

Setting up cold automation

Cold lead scoring is useful when you have a smaller client base that you stay in regular contact with. If you want to ensure your company communicates with your clients every quarter, for example, you could set it up so that if there aren't at least two points of activity generated every 90 days, the "salesperson follow-up" workflow is activated, such as shown in Figure 11-6.

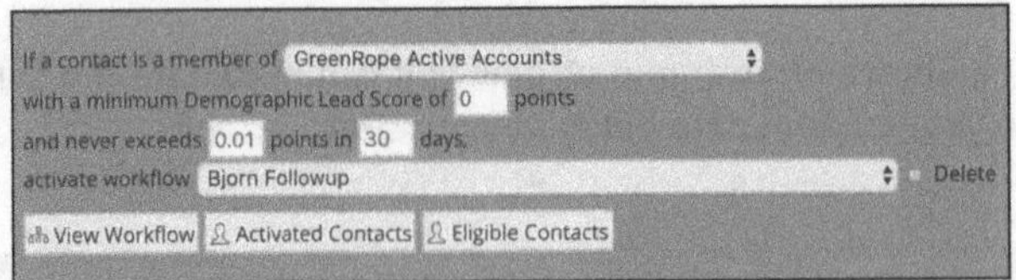

FIGURE 11-6: A cold automation rule for existing clients who aren't active.

Filtering automation by group and setting workflow limits

You may want to set up different workflows depending on which group someone is in. You may also want to prevent workflows from triggering too often, to keep your contacts and your own team from getting overwhelmed. It's important to make sure you have a complete picture of all the automation you define for your entire organization.

Designing Workflows

A *workflow* is an action or a series of actions. Workflows are the execution step that connects sales to marketing and vice versa. The more complete your CRM, the more powerful your workflows. When your CRM incorporates all your sales, marketing, and operational activities, your workflows can automate all of them. Figure 11-7 shows the kinds of actions a workflow can take for you.

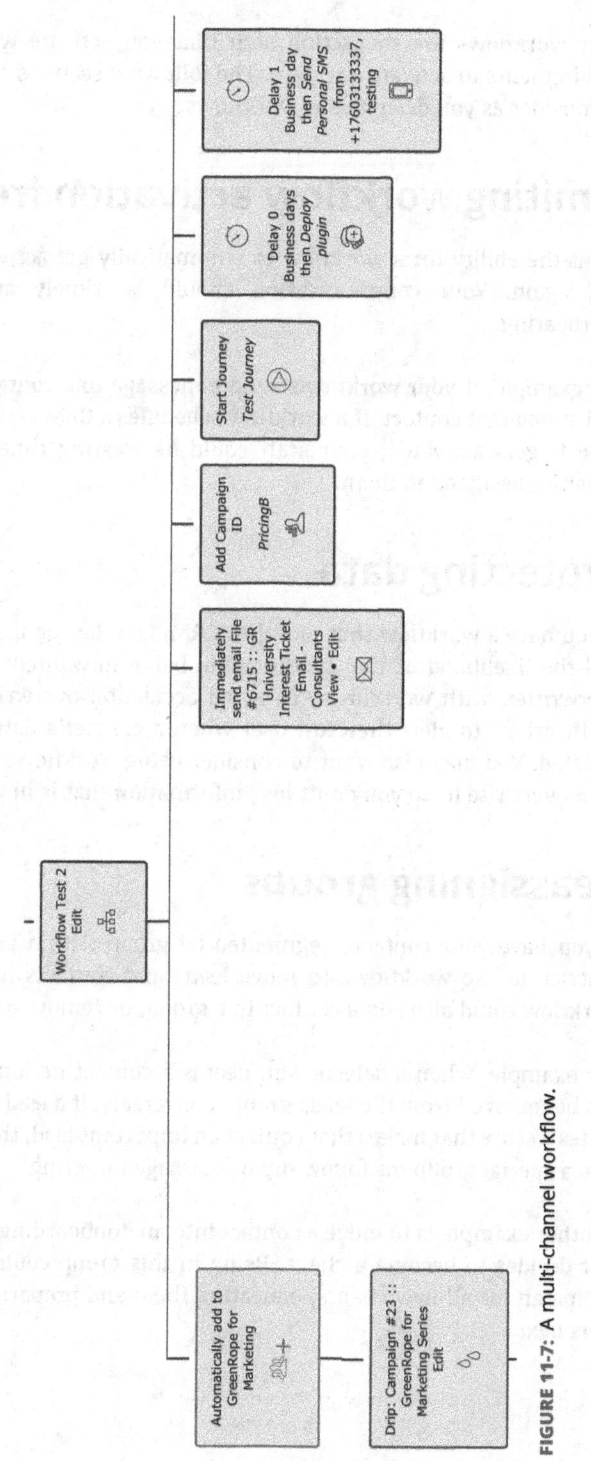

FIGURE 11-7: A multi-channel workflow.

Your workflows are the action step that you activate when a lead meets the requirements to activate a trigger. The following sections cover important factors to consider as you design your workflows.

Limiting workflow activation frequency

Limit the ability for a workflow to automatically get activated too quickly again and again. Your communication should be timely and relevant, but not overbearing.

For example, if your workflows send a message to a contact, repeated activation will annoy that contact. If a workflow schedules a CRM activity for a contact every time it gets activated, your staff could be wasting time deleting unnecessary activities assigned to them.

Protecting data

If you have a workflow that modifies CRM data, be cognizant of what triggers it, and the likelihood of that modification being unwanted. Ensure that data isn't overwritten with workflows. To avoid accidental overwriting, set up real-time notifications to alert the CRM user when a contact's data has been changed or updated. You may also want to consider using workflows to append data, rather than overwrite it, so you don't lose information that is in your CRM.

Reassigning groups

If you have your contacts segmented by group within your CRM, it's common practice to use workflows to move leads and contacts into different groups. A workflow could also add a contact to a group, or remove a contact from a group.

TIP

For example, when a salesperson deems a contact no longer viable, the contact can be removed from the leads group. Conversely, if a lead takes an action or generates a score that makes that contact an important lead, the contact can be moved into a special group for follow-up or message targeting.

Another example is to move a contact into an "onboarding" group when the contact decides to become a client. Being in this group could in turn trigger a drip campaign for all new clients, educating them and preparing them for what happens next.

Creating CRM activities

Use workflows to create a CRM activity for someone on your team to follow up or meet with that client. Workflows triggering CRM activities are a great way to convert clients who are engaging positively with your buyer journey. CRM activities themselves can appear on a calendar and are easy to track for salespeople and management.

Creating opportunities

Opportunities are created for high value, high touch sales. If a lead indicates interest in something that you're selling that is of high value, you can create an opportunity to track that sales process. Opportunities also create a deeper level of accountability to the salesperson or team responsible for closing the deal.

Sending emails, text messages, or variable print

Workflows are a perfect way to trigger messages to your leads and contacts. Depending on the message content and urgency, you may want to send that message by a different medium. Here are the advantages and disadvantages:

- **Email:** *Advantages:* ubiquitous for B2B communication, free, with a good CRM is likely to be delivered to the inbox, can track reads and clicks, a lot of content can be included in an email with opportunity to explain complex ideas and up-sell the recipient. *Disadvantages:* may be filtered, likely to be viewed as less urgent and read when the recipient gets around to it.
- **Text message:** *Advantages:* immediate delivery, inexpensive (though not free), very likely to be read, include images, may include links for more information. *Disadvantages:* recipients sensitive to spam, less content included in message, may get filtered by carrier, cannot track read or delivery.
- **Print:** *Advantages:* not as common a medium, can include more content with different display options, some tracking possible with QR codes or personalized URLs. *Disadvantages:* expensive, difficult to guarantee delivery to the intended recipient, delivery delay may take days.

Alerting the right people

When a workflow is activated, someone on your team may need to know about it. A salesperson can be alerted when a lead triggers a workflow, or a sales manager can be alerted when a CRM activity for a lead is assigned to a salesperson.

TIP

In any situation where someone must execute a critical step, alert that person on your team. This alert is even more relevant if that step is time sensitive. If you rely on your employees to check the CRM for their to-do lists, they may not check often enough to guarantee that timely steps are executed on time. Alerts are a good way to send these alerts and can be sent by email or text, as shown in Figure 11-8.

Send Alert Email To: sales@greenrope.com

Send Alert SMS: From: +14423337577 (Main GreenRope Number) To: +17605551212

FIGURE 11-8: A workflow with email and text alerts.

IN THIS CHAPTER

» **Creating a repository of information for easy access by your team**

» **Protecting your internal knowledge base**

» **Making your knowledge base available to your leads and clients**

Chapter 12
Managing Your Knowledge Base in Your CRM

Intellectual capital often describes the special sauce that your company and employees bring to the market. Your team's knowledge, expertise, and professionalism in your market is why someone pays you or your company instead of a competitor.

Your CRM can be used to store this knowledge in an easily accessible format, connecting your internal processes and documentation. The way you manage your sales, marketing, and operations with your CRM is unique to you. The better you document the way you do business, the easier new people learn your processes and the faster your team can look up helpful reference documentation.

A knowledge base is a searchable database of useful processes, facts, and documentation for your team to use. This chapter covers how to set up a knowledge base for you and your company. When directly integrated into your CRM, a knowledge base provides access to information when needed, without overwhelming your team with massive, hard-to-find documents. You can also control access to your company's documents, by using the same permission systems you use for your sales, marketing, and operations teams.

Knowing What to Put in Your Knowledge Base

Your knowledge base is an extension of the collective knowledge of your team. It's important to document anything you can, to avoid the possibility of employees taking their knowledge when they leave your company.

Store publicly distributed information in your knowledge base. Public corporate documents such as your mission and vision statements, company history, organizational chart, and frequently asked questions are all useful, as shown in Figure 12-1. You can also store internal "how-to" documents, so no individual is the only one who knows how to do something.

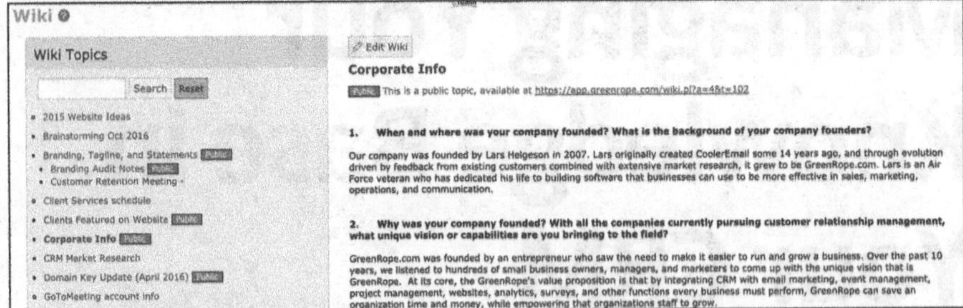

FIGURE 12-1: Topics are helpful to store in a CRM.

REMEMBER

In many ways, a knowledge base parallels your CRM, where you store useful information into a software system for easy recall. Rather than storing sales data about contacts, or marketing data about campaigns, your knowledge base is similar to a company-wide resource for documentation and process.

Knowledge bases are becoming increasingly popular, with the largest example being Google's search engine. When effectively implemented, knowledge bases cut down on paper, reduce time to research answers to questions, and avoid making mistakes that have already been solved in the past.

After you commit to a knowledge base, you need to maintain regularly. Figure 12-2 is an example of how you can store information in an easily accessible directory and make some articles available to the public. It's a convenient way to share your knowledge base with leads or clients.

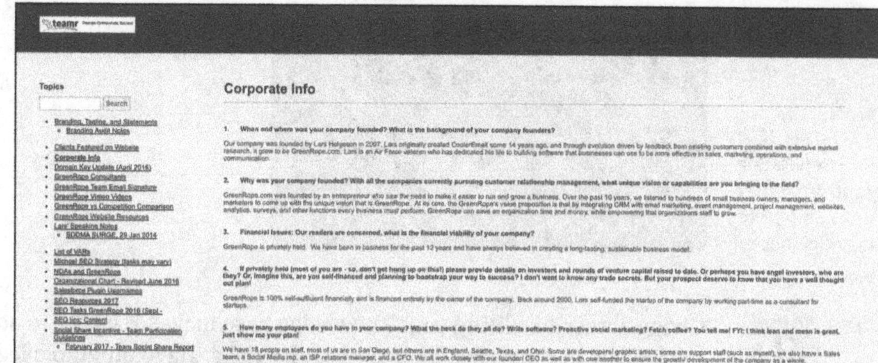

FIGURE 12-2: Store any resource documents in your CRM for internal or public use.

Building Access Levels for Information

Just because you can store information in a private knowledge base doesn't mean everyone in your company should to see it all. Some information you store isn't relevant to everyone. Some is simply private information.

Separating knowledge by group

Your CRM's group architecture is key for protecting information from various leads, clients, and internal team members. You can restrict access to knowledge by the members of the groups you define in your CRM. You should have separate groups for internal team members and your leads, clients, and vendors. (See Chapter 7 to set up groups.) Use these groups to store relevant information to the contacts in those groups, as shown in Figure 12-3.

For example, you can store helpful onboarding documentation in a group dedicated to bringing in new clients. You can make some documents publicly available, some documents available only to the members of that group (your new clients), and some available only to the support team managing those new clients. Using groups to segment access prevents information from being distributed inappropriately.

Allowing contributors to modify content

Depending on how rigorously you want to control your knowledge base content, you may want to allow a collaborative approach to your knowledge base. Give people you trust the ability to add articles or update existing content.

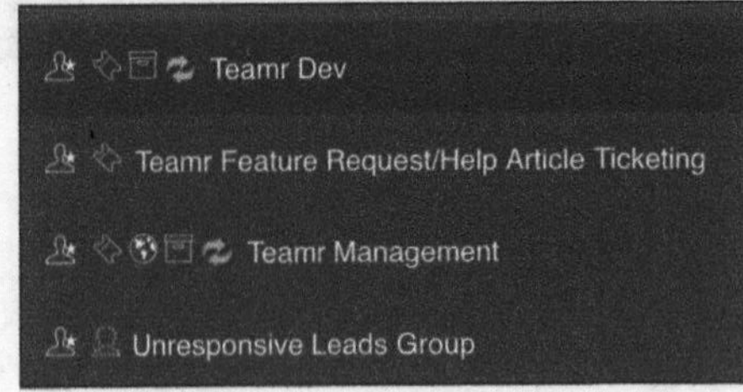

FIGURE 12-3: Separating groups that may have different knowledge bases.

WARNING

Giving access to editing your knowledge base makes it easier to add more content to it, but you must also be aware of the risks. Have an employee you absolutely trust to review updates to ensure information stored is relevant and useful.

Making articles public versus private

When you build your knowledge base, you may want to share some of it with the public through a URL. Documentation on how to use your product or service is a common application for a public knowledge base.

Other articles are for internal use only. These would be operational guidelines for accomplishing common tasks, organizational charts with employee information, and other things you and your team reference on a regular basis.

CRM software comes with an editor in which you can compose your documents, as shown in Figure 12-4. Editors allow you to control who can contribute or edit, designate whether the article is public or private, and where in the hierarchical structure the article should go.

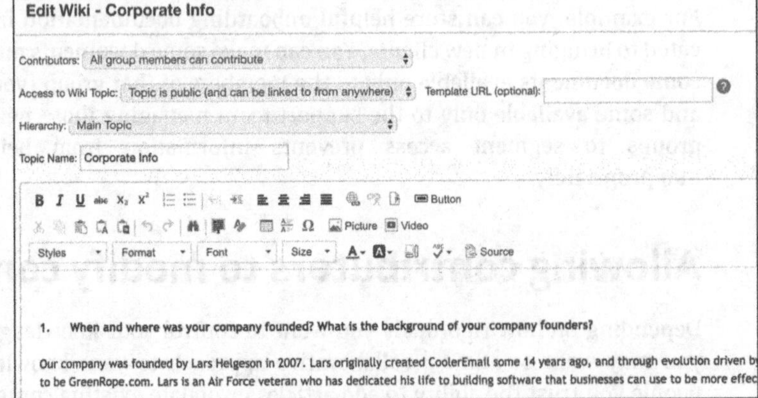

FIGURE 12-4: Knowledge base article editors should be flexible.

REMEMBER

If you're writing for external consumption (people outside your company), spend more time to ensure proper grammar. You also want to write with a friendly tone, which takes more time than straightforward language. Keep your messaging in mind, as any public documents reflect your brand.

Structuring Knowledge for Internal Consumption

When you know your team is going to access your knowledge base on a regular basis, take the time to intelligently design the structure of how it's built. A good design for a knowledge base minimizes the effort required to look up information.

- **Include an index.** Just as a table of contents is key to navigate a reference book, so must your knowledge base have a useful index. Beyond structuring your knowledge base by group, individual groups have categories of information they need to find. You may want to set up multiple levels of indexing, as well.

  Indexing a knowledge base means separating your documentation into categories, and subcategories beneath those categories. Be descriptive, and make sure each article in your knowledge base is relevant to the category it is in. If the document pertains to multiple categories, include all relevant keywords so the document can be easily searched.
- **Use straightforward language.** When writing for reference, it isn't necessary to use flowery language or long, complex sentences. A knowledge base is built around fast, easy access to information. Short sentences, obvious headings, and bullet lists are the easiest way to provide that information for internal use.
- **Include links to other helpful resources.** When building your knowledge base, reference other webpages or documents. Doing so is useful when external sources are updated by other people, or when you want to keep your knowledge base article shorter.

  TIP

  Cross-link your articles, so that when one article references another, all the viewer has to do is click a keyword to view that article.

Sharing Knowledge with Leads and Clients

Your knowledge base for external consumption is just as important as your marketing messages. Bad spelling and grammar, nonintuitive structure, or misinformation reflects on your brand just as outbound messaging does.

TIP

Oftentimes, companies share product details, features, and capabilities with the general public. This information helps answer questions that your leads and clients have without burdening your customer service team. If someone does ask a question of your customer service professionals, they can suggest that the information is available online through the knowledge base. Giving access to information empowers the public to conduct research on their own, allowing you to work more efficiently.

Two actions can save your employees time:

- **Integrate your knowledge base with customer service.** Your chat and support ticketing systems should be able to reference your knowledge base, as shown in Figure 12-5. Even if not directly integrated into the software, if your support team can easily find, copy, and paste information from your knowledge base into responses to customers, your organization saves time and ensures consistency.
- **Link to your knowledge base from your website/emails.** Prospects and clients should be able to gain easy access to your publicly available content with a URL directly linking to your public-facing knowledge base. Direct access to information provides a convenient, useful way to educate people. By embedding these links in your emails and web content, your contacts can find that information on their own, limiting the burden on your support team. In turn, you can handle support with fewer resources, saving you considerable cost.

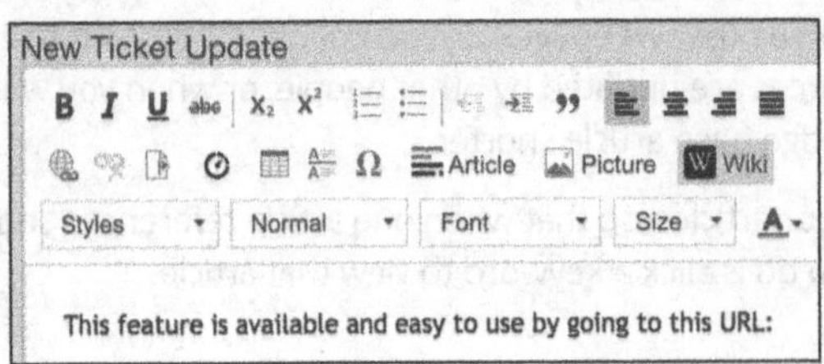

FIGURE 12-5: Connecting your knowledge base wiki to your ticketing system is key.

IN THIS CHAPTER

» **Setting up a project management system for your team**

» **Holding your team accountable to complete tasks and projects on time and budget**

» **Integrating project progress with your CRM for easy management**

Chapter 13
Managing Projects with Your CRM

Project management is a science unto itself. Done right, your team is unified in purpose and efficient in execution. Management has insight into progress and can run reports and bill clients for work done. The right project management system is a powerful tool and every organization benefits when implemented correctly.

Some projects revolve around internal work. Software development, building things, even implementing your CRM can all be considered internal projects. Other projects are external facing; members of your team work together to accomplish a project for a client.

This chapter covers the principles of project management, starting with how and where you set it up for your organization. Connecting your projects to your CRM enables better tracking and accountability on both sides of the project, helping with communication and improving the customer experience.

Setting Up a Project

As with CRM, project management can have a far-reaching influence in your organization, so you want to think about how you set it up before you start using it.

Managing projects: A case for software

When many people work together on a project, the complexities of managing who should do what and when can be daunting. Even when one person works solo on a project, software aids in putting all the moving parts into easy-to-manage compartments.

Each project has a start and end date, representing when planning begins and when the wrapping up is complete. Between those dates, tasks should be done and milestones represent significant accomplishments.

Figure 13-1 shows a summary of ongoing projects. It gives a high level overview of the long-term work a team is collaborating on to complete.

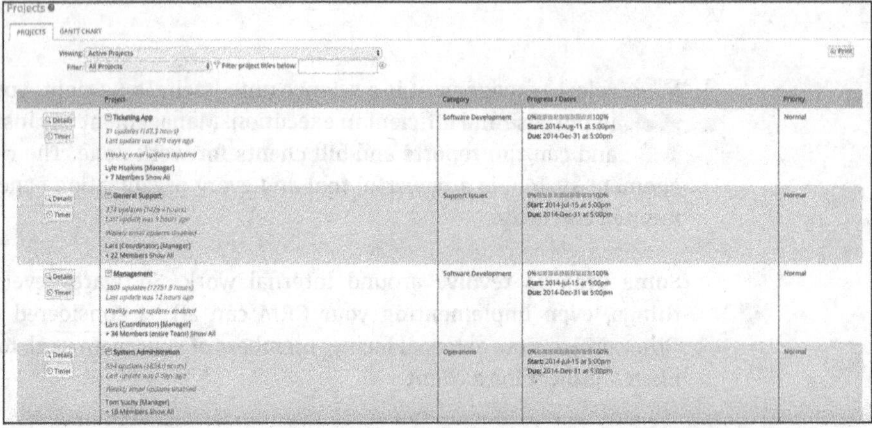

FIGURE 13-1: A few ongoing projects.

A commonly used chart in project management software is the Gantt chart, as shown in Figure 13-2. It's a visual representation of the project, with tasks and milestones shown as component parts to that project. *Dependent tasks* — a task that can't start until a previous task is completed — are depicted with arrows connecting them. It's a good management tool for tracking progress within your project.

FIGURE 13-2: The same projects on a Gantt chart.

Defining requirements

Building your project is not something usually done by a single project manager. Most projects involve several people working together as a team. If you're working on a project for a customer, that customer must also be involved in the initial scoping of the project.

The first phase of any project is to define the requirements (the *what)* of the project — what must be accomplished, and by whom?

REMEMBER

The better you can define your requirements, the less ambiguity happens as the project progresses. Ambiguity causes people to make assumptions. It also causes people to take shortcuts to save money, often to the consternation of the customer, with ensuing arguments.

Setting realistic target dates

Every project has start and end dates. The project also has individual tasks, each with their own deadlines. The more you can define realistic dates, the less worry about overrun you have. If your dates are not realistic, and you overrun, it may impact the rest of the project.

With accurate dates for projects and tasks, you can allocate resources to accomplish those tasks. When individuals know when they're needed ahead of time, you don't have to worry about a different project taking priority or competing for the same resources.

When a project relies on a task to be complete before the project can progress, that task lies on the project's *critical path.* The critical path of a project is very important to accurately budget a project, as mistakes directly impact the date the project is completed.

Defining tasks within projects

Tasks within projects are specific activities that must be accomplished to complete the project. While many people may work on a task, each task should have a person in charge. That person is accountable to the project manager if that task is not completed on time and within budget. Project management software lists the tasks and person in charge of that task, along with other important details, as shown in Figure 13-3.

There are 41 closed tasks in this project View Closed Tasks

☐	Edit	Task ID#884:	1-Feature Enhancement :: Create unit test suite for media image library using qunit and phantomjs. Estimate 3-4 hours.	Eric Christianson	
☐	Edit	Task ID#959:	1-Feature Enhancement :: Performance enhancements in Media Library. Reduce image loads.	Eric Christianson	Hours spent on task so far: 26.5 ($1,060.00 USD billable) of 30.0 budgeted hours, 88% of budget
☐	Edit	Task ID#960:	1-Feature Enhancement :: Re-work files, articles and videos Combine to one list to manage all content with filters.	Eric Christianson	Hours spent on task so far: 152.8 ($6,112.00 USD billable)

FIGURE 13-3: Tasks in a project.

Each task has a start date and an end date. These dates may be fixed dates, or they may be dependent dates as a part of another aspect of the project. For example, a task start date may occur the day after a previous task is completed. Dependent tasks are more flexible, but may cause problems with resource allocation if a fluid task starts on a date different from what is expected, and resources have been given to another task.

TIP

Integrating your CRM with your project management system means you can see project tasks right in the CRM record. By putting your own employees in the CRM, you can track their tasks along with other CRM activities they're assigned to complete. Managing people is much easier, as this data is consolidated into a single place.

Categorizing projects and tasks

Categorizing the work done in a project helps with setting billing rates and reporting. If you do contract work for customers, you likely bill a category of work at a specific rate. Categorizing tasks and having your labor bill against those tasks in that category makes it easy to invoice clients, as shown in Figure 13-4.

For example, you can set up categories of tasks for your team based around the kind of work they do. If you manage an advertising agency, you have people on your team who do graphics, HTML, and strategy. Each category of work is done by different kinds of people, all collaborating on a bigger project to serve a client. Reporting on the number of hours spent on each category of work is important for the client to see, as well as for your own internal project management.

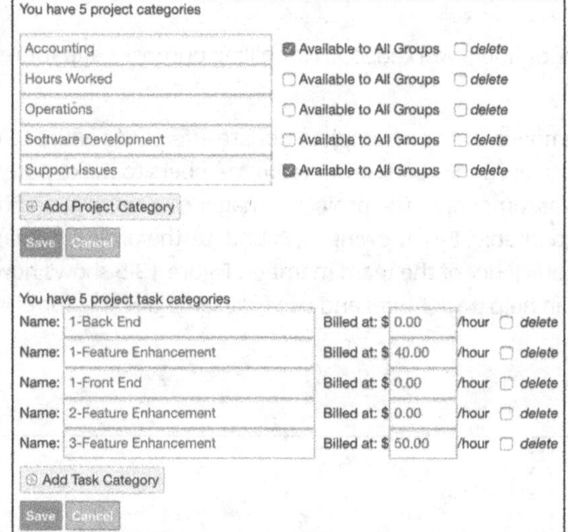

FIGURE 13-4: A simple categories manager.

TIP

Categorizing also allows you to create reports by category. You should be able to see what your labor utilization rates are by category. I cover how to calculate this rate in the next section. It's important to measure how much of your team members' time is spent on projects, so you know if you're spending money on labor appropriately.

Leading Your Project Team

Choosing who leads a project requires a thorough understanding of the person and her capabilities. The project manager must be a good communicator and a good listener, able to translate what is happening in the project to management, and accurately assess how the project is going.

A good project manager

- **Defines the project requirements:** A project manager doesn't have to know how to do every task, but must understand tasks well enough to know when the person responsible for that task isn't performing.
- **Keeps members accountable for the project:** The manager makes sure each person working on a project enters daily updates so that the other members of the team know what's happening. Updates should also include

the number of hours worked, both for billing purposes and for resource utilization.

A team member's late or incomplete update affects the entire team and slows down the project and causes other team members to make potentially dangerous assumptions. The project manager must step in and hold that person accountable. By reviewing each update, the project manager can also assess the efficiency of the team member. Figure 13-5 shows how a project manager can help track hours and use that same tracking for billing a customer.

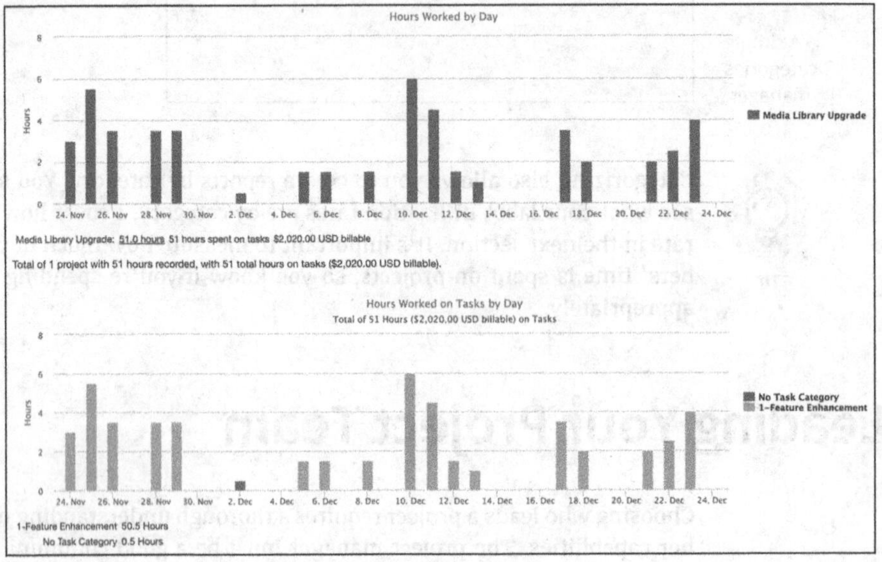

FIGURE 13-5: Hours tracking and reporting.

TIP

One way to have team members track time on a project is with a timer. It keeps track of their work down to the second, even if you only bill in specific increments. Figure 13-6 shows a timer that your team can use to keep track of the work they do on a project during the day. It automatically enters hours, while providing an easy interface for entering work done.

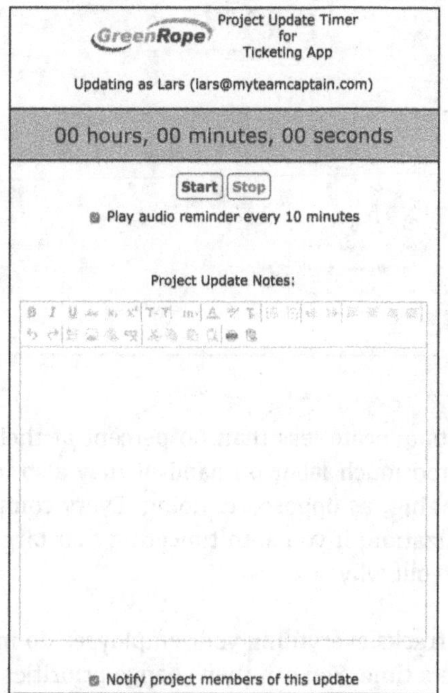

FIGURE 13-6: Simple project update timer that auto-updates a project.

Measuring Important Metrics for Your Team

As a project progresses, your project manager reports on how the project is doing. It's important to watch the right metrics, so your management understands the health of the project without getting bogged down in details.

Tracking resource utilization

Resource utilization is a measure of how well your labor force is being used. The calculation for this rate is simple: billable hours divided by the total amount of hours you pay your employees. The higher that ratio, the more fully utilized your labor is, and less time employees aren't getting reimbursed by clients.

Figure 13-7 demonstrates how you can easily see how full someone's schedule is, and how much time he's spending in management versus working on billable projects. As a manager, you want to see how much overhead is spent in management and if your people are overloaded or underutilized.

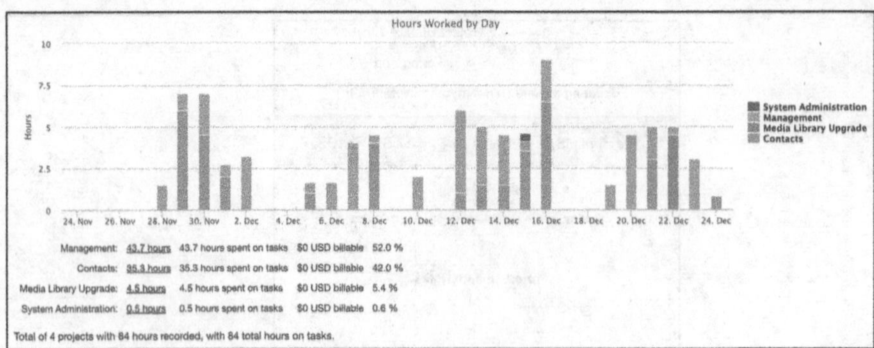

FIGURE 13-7: Tracking resource utilization for a developer.

TIP

If people on your projects allocate less than 60 percent of their time to billable projects, you may have too much labor on hand. It may also indicate too much overhead spent on managing, as opposed to doing. Every company has a target number for resource utilization; if you aren't meeting that target, review project updates and notes to find out why.

If your project manager tracks everything your employees do internally, you can see what is taking people's time. You can then change priorities and processes.

Viewing overdue tasks

Every project management system shows overdue tasks. If these overdue tasks are on the critical path, they directly affect everyone else associated with the project. There may be an ineffective project manager, poor budgeting or forecasting, or changing requirements. The project manager should be able to articulate the reasons for tasks being overdue and take steps to alleviate the problem immediately.

Budgeting projects and tasks

Budgeting can be a bit of an art form, particularly when it comes to technology. Oftentimes, people are overly optimistic on how long a task or project should take, and the budget may not allocate enough time for testing and getting a product ready for the client/consumer. To be on the safe side, if you're starting a new project and you're not sure how much time it will take, double or triple any estimate.

REMEMBER

The better you can break down requirements, the easier you can estimate the amount of work required. Each piece adds up, as you design tasks and connect them together.

IN THIS CHAPTER

» Hosting events with registration and payment

» Connecting event attendance to the CRM and marketing automation functions

Chapter 14

Managing Events with Your CRM

Hosting and attending events are a part of your business that connects the real world to your CRM. They are a powerful way to build relationships and track interest in your brand. Event participation is also a great trigger for marketing automation. (See Chapter 11.) Setting up an event system that connects directly to your CRM is important in fostering deeper relationships with your leads, clients, employees, and vendors. Event sponsors, staff, and attendees all contribute to these relationships; store this information in your CRM to effectively use events for marketing and sales.

You most likely are familiar with event software, such as Evite (`www.evite.com`). Setting up more complex events and storing that data in a CRM for later use may be something new. Tracking your event data has long-term benefits for all kinds of organizations, not just event-focused companies. Attendance and registration can tell a lot about a person and their interest in your company, products, and services.

TIP

Use the same software for internal team meetings and conferences. The idea is the same — keeping long-term track of attendance and participation in the CRM helps as a management tool for your own team.

In this chapter, you connect your event marketing, registration, and attendance to your CRM. Integrated event management and CRM helps you gain maximum exposure for your event, while gathering important data for use in growing your business. Events, as in other parts of your CRM, are a tool for insight and expanding your footprint in the world.

Bringing People to Your Brand

An event is a great way to expose your brand to a lot of people. While events may not have the reach of online advertising, the quality of the engagement is much higher. People spend a lot of time at events, and if you're hosting, sponsoring, or even just attending, your emotional connection is likely to be much greater.

Driving awareness with events

As a business that either hosts or sends your staff to events, you have an opportunity to expose your brand to your market in an emotional, visceral way. This awareness can be used to bring you more leads, and ultimately drive revenue. Common methods you can use to promote awareness are:

- **Sponsoring:** Many large events, such as conferences, provide opportunities to sponsor an event in exchange for promotion. Be careful with this approach. Do your research. Make sure you sponsor events that your target market attends. Many sponsoring brands are forgotten as soon as attendees leave the event. If you spend money sponsoring, ensure you can measure the return on investment (ROI) by obtaining data about the attendees or having your brand exposed to them before and after the event. As with most investments, the more you spend on an event, the greater likelihood attendees remember you and become leads.

  TIP

  Make realistic calculations based on the number of attendees, the percentage who are potential clients, and the likelihood you get them started on your buyer journey.

- **Setting up a booth:** Large meetings and conferences often have booths as part of the event. Be sure you're prepared to meet as many people as possible and have a strategy for following up. Your booth should look professional to attract attendees. Employees working the booth should be assertive, but not too pushy. Your primary objective is not to sell there but to capture the attendees' information so your sales team can do a proper follow-up. Either have a fishbowl to collect business cards or a scanner to scan business cards directly to your CRM. (Chapter 9 has more information about getting the contact information you collect into your CRM.)

- **Attending:** When you attend an event, your goal should never be to hand out as many business cards as possible. Meeting people in person is about listening, and then thinking about how you can help that person. Your team can get much further by establishing a few strong relationships, and not having a competition about who can meet the most people.
- **Hosting:** If you host an event, you control the environment. Large or small, putting effort forth to bring people together opens the doors to many people and companies to know what you do and how you can help them.

Educating leads and clients through conferences

Many businesses hold meet-ups or conferences to bring together clients and share valuable information. When you have the opportunity to educate your peers and potential clients, examine the ROI of that carefully. Speaking to a group of people establishes you and your brand as thought leaders and experts. That naturally draws people to you, as you're the source of answers to their questions.

If you aren't hosting the conference, and are attending the conference, think about the educational benefit of having a booth. Your primary objective should be to educate people at the conference. Education may be about your business, but think about how you can give people knowledge they can walk away with that helps them do their jobs better. It might be a free informational brochure, or a giveaway that helps them in their job.

In all cases, only in special occasions should you attempt to directly sell someone at a conference. You can give an attendee a discount or promotional code or a free promotional item, but unless you're selling a product at the conference, the relationship is far more valuable than whatever you're selling.

Hosting Events

Events should create a lot of value for both your attendees and your business. To track your efforts and results, you need to implement the right software. Your CRM should capture everything about the event and its attendees, so your sales and marketing teams can make the most out of the time and money you invest.

Figure 14-1 shows an event registration page, designed to capture information and add it to your CRM. After the registration information is recorded in your CRM, you can set up any automated follow-up and track any further interaction with your brand, such as emails or website visits.

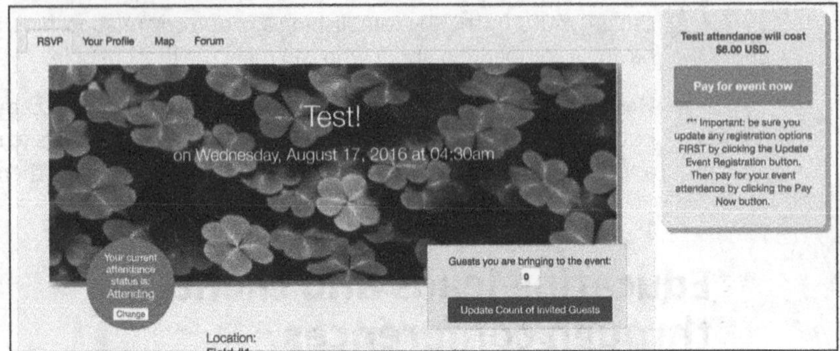

FIGURE 14-1: A simple event registration page.

As with all requests for someone's time, event attendees must feel like they're getting a return on their investment. Value can be found in new relationships, education, or brand exposure, and you must clearly communicate this value in any marketing you do for your event.

Establishing benefits of membership

With your CRM integrated into your event management software, you can use data from your CRM to help manage the event. Set up special automatic discounts for members of certain groups, or limit awareness and invites for events to the membership of a specific group.

If you're a membership organization, or trying to build a long-lasting relationship with your contacts, communicating value by hosting or attending repeated events is a good strategy. Some organizations encourage membership by giving discounts on events, and some provide access to special members-only events.

A goal of many membership organizations is to create strong bonds between members. You may also want to provide a level of vetting, implying that members of your organization adhere to certain higher standards of conduct or proficiency. In all cases, a person is likely to become a member if the membership has a clear value.

Matching attendees by interests

The software you use to manage the event should be tightly connected to your CRM. All the attendees should be recorded in your CRM, along with any preferences you learn about them through their registration.

One way to drive event attendance is to give attendees insight into who else is attending. You can do that by publishing the entire attendance list. But if you want to protect attendees' privacy, you can simply provide a list of the bigger brands that are attending to give attendees a general sense of who is coming and why.

TIP

Another solution is to offer *attendance matching*, telling an attendee who RSVPs that another attendee has similar interests, as shown in Figure 14-2. Familiarity and a sense of belonging with people with like-minded interests goes a long way toward bringing people together. Your event management tool should use your CRM data to make connections between your event attendees.

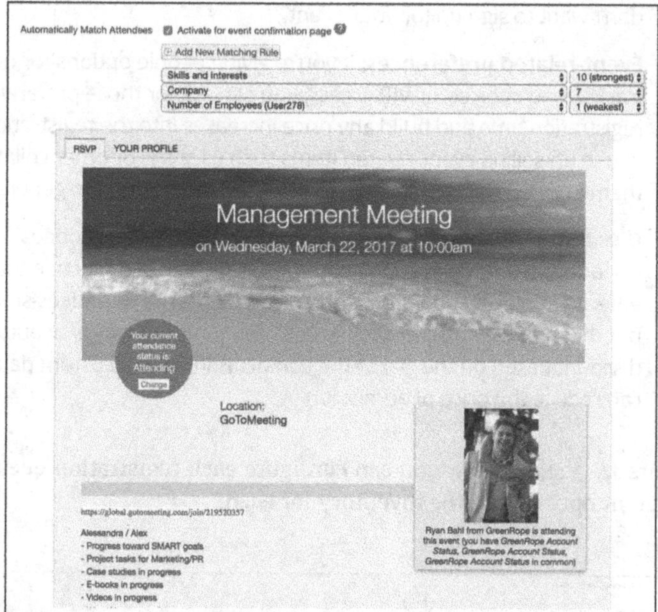

FIGURE 14-2: Building attendance matching rules for event attendees.

Setting Up Registration Options

Every time someone confirms attendance, you have an opportunity to personalize the attendee's event experience. The registration options you ask for should correlate to services you provide to the attendees, but you also have an opportunity to gather more information for your CRM.

For example, an event registration page may ask an attendee what topics that attendee is interested in learning about. It helps drive experience at the event, but it may also come in handy for your sales team in better understanding a lead's interests.

Determining what to ask for

You should have the ability to completely customize your event registration. Gather information that helps better serve your attendees and customers. A list of common options to consider when setting up your event are

- **Contact details:** This data translates directly to your contact data in the CRM. Email address and name are common fields to request, but you may want to dig a little deeper. Asking for general preferences may help you segment your market. The more you ask, the better you can segment your marketing, but you don't want to make registration so challenging that people don't want to sign up for your event.
- **Event-related preferences:** If you're giving people options for different tracks, food choices, or VIP access, you can ask for those preferences at registration time and build any price increases into the registration process. If you're up-selling event-related items such as shirts or other collateral, include them in the online registration to give you another way to generate revenue.
- **Discounts:** You may want to give reduced pricing to attendees. You can offer discounts in a few ways. One common way is a discount code that can be entered at registration time. You do run the risk of attendees sharing codes, but that may be an acceptable risk to you. Another way is to automate the discount based on the group the contact is in; or in a custom data field, you can reduce the price of admission.

Figure 14-3 shows how you can configure each registration question, setting the different options and the inventory for each.

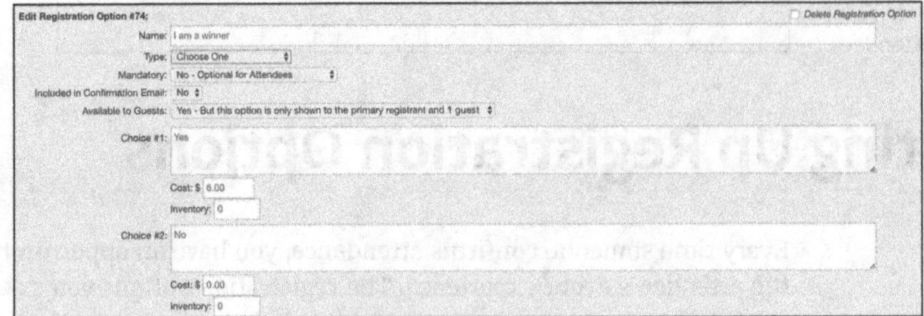

FIGURE 14-3: Managing a registration option for an event.

Using logic to show only relevant options

To streamline the registration process, show only certain registration options if they're relevant. For example, if an attendee says she wants to purchase a t-shirt, you only show the shirt size preference after she confirms interest in the shirt. Only showing relevant information relevant to the registrant is important for making the best user experience.

Automating Responses and Follow-Ups

When someone registers for an event, you want to do automated sales and marketing as a way to encourage interaction with your brand.

Every event management software platform includes attendance tracking. You may want to activate some automation for attendees. Automation is a great way to ensure every attendee receives follow-up information about the event. For example, you could send a recap or pictures from the event, or you could email discount codes to future events.

You can also activate a workflow for each attendee. The workflow could schedule a follow-up CRM activity, send a text message, tag the contact, or send a printed thank-you note after the event.

Figure 14-4 shows a simple way to set up automation triggered for attendees after the event takes place.

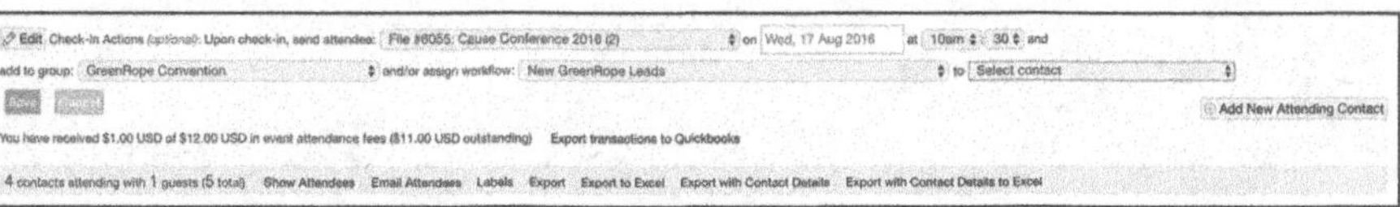

FIGURE 14-4: Automated actions that happen when attendees are checked in to the event.

A common mistake that many organizations make is to think that after an event is over, they can relax and forget about it. If you do so, you miss out on an opportunity to reach out to all your leads. By scheduling follow-ups, you open the door to continued interaction, which builds your brand strength and keeps your business top of mind.

Connecting with Calendars

Modern technology allows people to access and manage calendars directly from smartphones or tablets. Many people rely on Outlook and Google to synchronize their personal and business lives so they can manage all the things they have to do. You can use your CRM in the same way.

- **Keep calendars in sync.** Webcal is an Internet standard that keeps different calendars in sync with each other. Every online calendar program periodically reaches out to the calendars and updates their events so everything is up to date. Your CRM should allow you to share your calendar of events with everyone on your team and the contacts who are interested.
- **Schedule appointments.** If you manage one-on-one appointments, a booking calendar that connects to your CRM is a useful tool. A booking calendar provides a public calendar that a lead can use to book an appointment. The booking process adds the event to your calendar and informs the requestor automatically. This action can also trigger workflows and any other automation you would like.

4

Analytics and Improvement

IN THIS PART . . .

Build Key Performance Indicators (KPIs) and track high-level performance with your Complete CRM.

Deploy forms for supporting your customers and gathering feedback.

Set up analytics for real-time understanding of how your business is doing.

IN THIS CHAPTER

» **Defining sales funnels for tracking the sales process**

» **Developing testing techniques that teach your business how to grow**

» **Designing marketing metrics to guide your sales and marketing investments**

Chapter 15
Measuring Business Performance with CRM

Marketing, particularly digital marketing, is a closed-loop process. Success depends on your ability to listen. Focus on the feedback you receive from every marketing investment you make. As technology advances, you can gain more access to learning from what your leads and clients do in response to your marketing efforts. Everyone responds, engages, and converts in their way; the better you understand how and why, the more your business grows.

The knowledge you gain from sales and marketing is continuous and constant. Being data-driven in your sales and marketing keeps you ahead of your competition. Building your business around a Complete CRM platform sets you up for long-term success.

In this chapter, I talk about various methods you can use to track the performance of your marketing campaigns and sales processes. I cover testing techniques and ways to track website traffic, email marketing, and social media. You can use this information to predict what your leads and clients will do, a powerful edge that can influence the way you design your sales and marketing processes.

Constructing Funnels

Funnels are useful to measure the progress of leads as they move along your buyer journeys. From stage to stage, you can visualize the effectiveness of your sales process, as shown in Figure 15-1. They provide an excellent reporting overview that your team can monitor regularly.

REMEMBER

Funnels are useful for sales and marketing alike, as both interact with leads and contribute to the buyer journey at different times and in different ways.

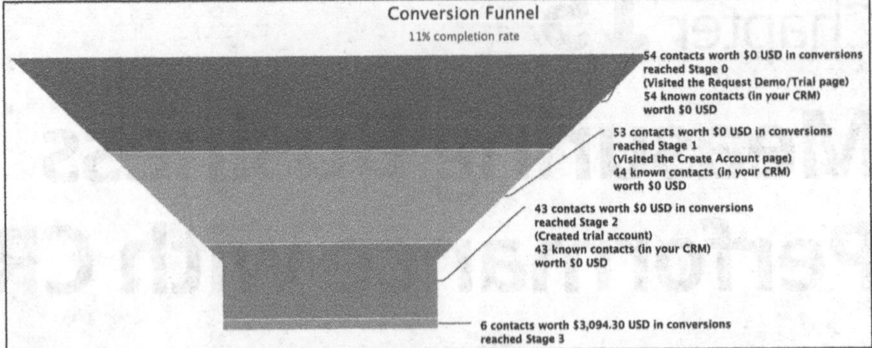

FIGURE 15-1: A typical funnel.

Tracking sales progress with conversions

Generally speaking, sales are divided into two types: business-to-business (B2B) and business-to-consumer (B2C). B2B sells to companies and generally has lower sales volume thresholds, but higher-dollar products and services. B2C sells to the general public and is volume driven.

B2B and B2C both benefit from using funnels to track sales processes. Because B2B sales are more complex and generally take more time, CRM platforms have a special tracking mechanism called an *opportunity* to store everything about that deal. B2C sales are usually faster and don't require the level of detail for each individual sale made. Tracking the buyer journey for a B2C sale tends to be more automated.

Defining the stages of a conversion

Every sale has a process, a buyer journey. Along that journey, you set up specific gates to define stages of the sales process. As leads move from stage to stage, you can measure how long they take and what percentage of leads drop out of the journey.

When you set up your funnels, have specific, defined criteria to determine when a lead moves to the next stage. Often with B2B opportunities, these gates are when a lead takes an action, such as agrees to a demo, accepts a proposal, or signs a contract. With B2C, stages in the funnel might be when a lead visits a specific page on your website, downloads a whitepaper, or purchases a product.

REMEMBER

It's important that everyone on the sales and marketing teams understands what each stage represents and can easily identify when someone doesn't advance to the next stage. Oftentimes in modern selling, a lead backtracks in your sales process, deciding to take more time to make a decision, or passing off responsibility for the purchase to someone else. When backtracking happens, your CRM must track this movement.

Figure 15-2 shows an example of how you can define stages in a conversion process.

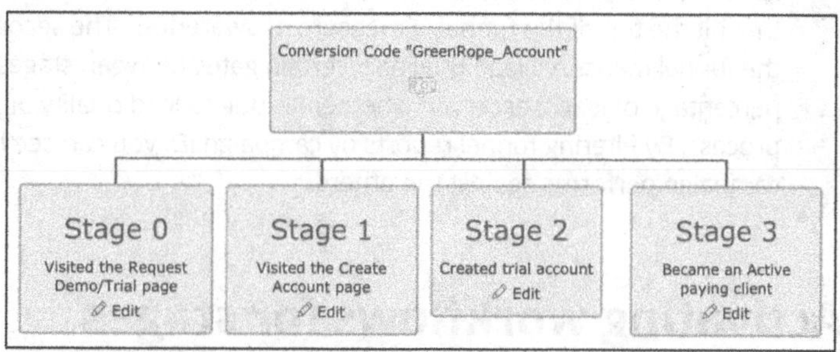

FIGURE 15-2: Defining stages of a conversion.

Measuring time and dropout rates for each stage

Funnels provide two very useful metrics to help you understand your sales process — time in stage and dropout rates. When you see your funnel, your CRM should display these key statistics for you. You should establish goals and measure long-term averages as benchmarks. If you're starting and have no context, you can start with industry benchmarks.

TIP

Watch the final stage of conversion. For example, the software industry standard is generally 10 to 15 percent with many competitors in the crowded market, and my company sets a benchmark of 30 percent. If your numbers show significant deviation from your industry standards or goals, find out why.

Every month, your sales and marketing teams should look at your funnels to determine the performance of your overall sales process, as well as how each salesperson is performing. You can learn from these key factors:

- **Campaigns:** Are any of your campaigns bringing in higher quality leads? If leads spend less time in the funnel to become clients, or if a greater percentage of leads become clients, you're seeing better leads and those campaigns should get more investment.
- **Sales benchmarks:** Are your salespeople hitting conversion percentage goals and sales quotas (numbers of conversions)? If the bottom of the funnel is more human-intensive, examine how each salesperson is doing. More sales training may be required if you see recurring patterns of low conversion rates by some of your sales team.
- **Marketing benchmarks:** Wherever marketing is involved, track overall and specific performance in the funnel. One metric is the total number of leads that hit the top of the funnel, a measure of awareness. The second stage in the funnel measures lead quality. If certain gates between stages filter a large percentage of leads, ascertain whether it's due to lead quality or your sales process. By filtering funnel reports by campaign ID, you can see how each campaign performs against the others.

Activating workflows for stages

Leverage your CRM's ability to track the progress of your leads. Activate workflows to encourage leads to progress through your sales process and funnel. As you analyze your sales process, examine how and why people advance to the next phase. Bring together your sales and marketing teams to assess whether activating a workflow when a lead hits that gate helps the sales process.

Figure 15-3 shows how you can set workflows to be activated automatically when an opportunity reaches a given stage. Another option may be to set a fixed percentage for chance to close the opportunity when that opportunity reaches a given stage.

TIP

Look at your process abandonment strategy. If a lead gets stuck in a stage for too long, activate a workflow as a way to push that lead to advance. For example, you can send a lead a discount code if you feel leads lose interest due to price.

Phase Number (Order)	Phase Name	Automatically Set Close %	Activate Workflow
1	New Lead		
2	Qualified Lead		
3	Prospect		Demo follow-up
4	Proposal	50 %	
5	Proposal Evaluation		
6	Closed - Deal Lost!	0 %	
7	Closed - Deal Won	100 %	

Phases Available (Edit)

FIGURE 15-3: A funnel stage automation configuration screen.

Analyzing Website Visitors

You can learn a lot about your business from what people do on your website. With good web analytics, you can learn about key elements of your marketing strategies and how they're performing:

- Where your best lead sources come from (geography, campaign)
- Exactly who your best leads are (with CRM integration)
- What your leads and clients care about most
- What strategies and tactics work best to get leads to fill out forms and engage with your sales team

In the following sections, I cover which metrics are useful to track and what you need to look for when reviewing your data.

Measuring unique visitors and page views

The two most common metrics to track web traffic are

- **Unique visitors:** The number of specific individuals who are on your website in a 24-hour period
- **Page views:** The total number of individual pages visited by all your users

Figure 15-4 shows these metrics on the same plot, with the top one including unique visitors to the website, and the bottom being contacts who are in the CRM.

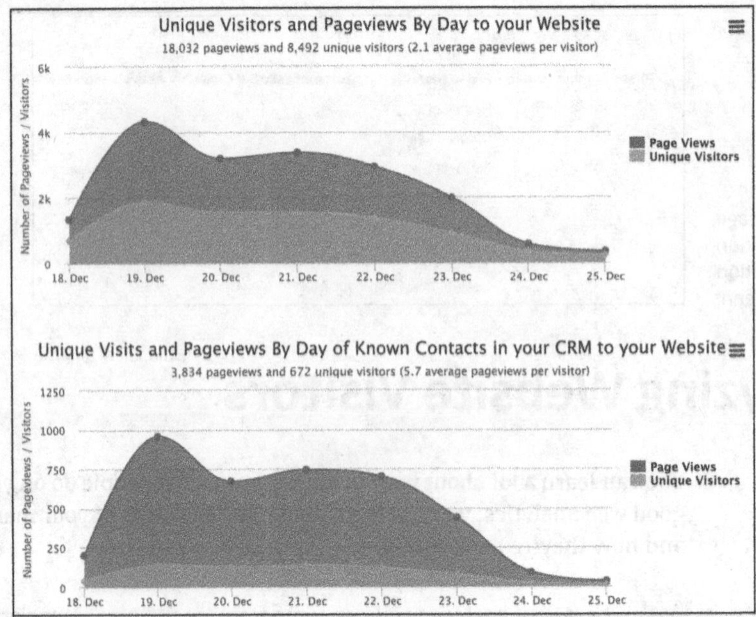

FIGURE 15-4: Comparing page views and unique visitors for all visitors and known contacts.

Three timeframes are useful when examining your website traffic:

» **By hour:** A by-hour metric gives an indication of where people are, or what their buying habits are, as shown in Figure 15-5. For example, if your customers are most active during the late afternoon, there may be a reason they're interested in your product at the end of their workdays. Correlating traffic by time of day may indicate something about their use of your product.

FIGURE 15-5: Page views by hour.

» **By day:** Daily visits to your website are a simple statistic, but can provide insight into how your marketing is doing. If you have an increase in traffic on a particular day, you may have had a successful ad campaign or someone may have written a popular blog post about your company. Regular days with highs and lows in traffic may indicate customer preferences around how your products and services are perceived, as shown in Figure 15-6.

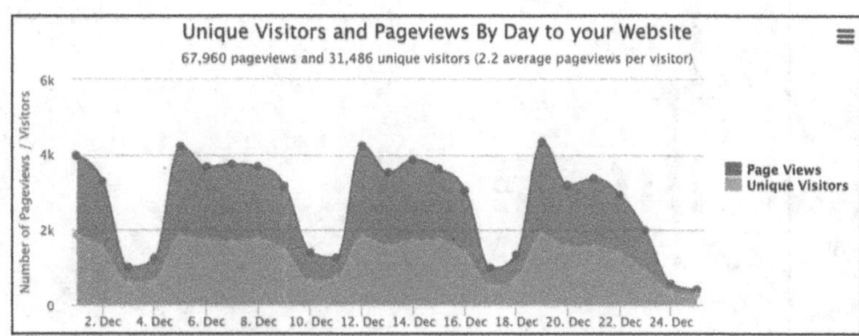

FIGURE 15-6: Page views and visitors by day over several weeks.

- **By month:** Monthly trends are a long-term measure of overall growth. As your brand gains strength, your overall number of visitors and page views increase, as shown in Figure 15-7. If you see overall monthly numbers decreasing, look at your SEO strategy and the efforts your marketing team is making to put content on the Internet that brings people to your website.

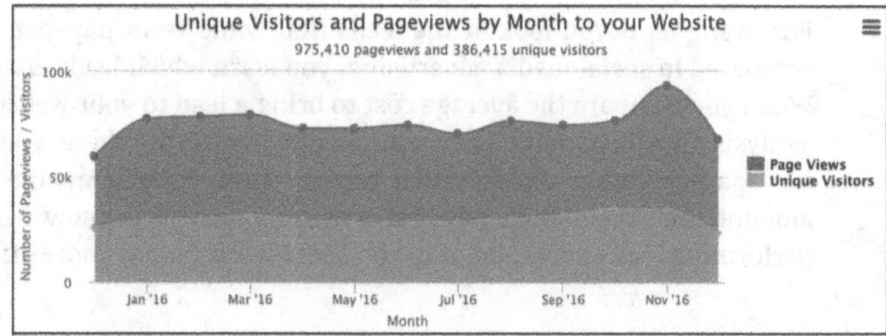

FIGURE 15-7: Page views by month over a year-long span.

Tracking referral sources

Referrals sources are webpages that have links to your website. Most web analytics packages, such as Google Analytics, track the source of all those inbound links. Your analytics software can show which domains drive the most traffic to your website, as shown in Figure 15-8, which gives you insight into how people find you.

Your CRM should reflect this referral data, allowing you to see which contacts arrived from these different referral sources. You can then see which referral sources provide the most revenue, closing the loop on your advertising.

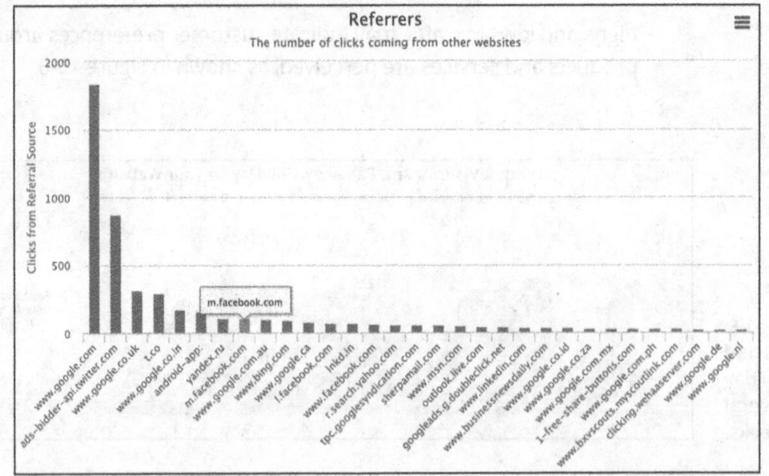

FIGURE 15-8: Different referrers and how many inbound clicks they generate.

TIP

Attach unique campaign identifiers to each of your inbound campaigns to see which campaigns perform best. Figure 15-9 shows a chart of the number of contacts that came from campaigns. Campaign IDs also enable you to create unique buyer journeys. (See Chapter 5.) The better you segment your customer experiences, the deeper your insight into the types of customers that comes from each campaign.

For example, if you look at the leads that come from pay-per-click advertising compared to social media advertising, you learn which leads are of higher quality. When you compare the average cost to bring a lead to your website, you can do an analysis on which method is most cost effective. From there, you can measure the average percentage of leads that convert from each campaign and the average amount each population pays for your products. You know which is the better performing lead source, helping you spend your money more effectively.

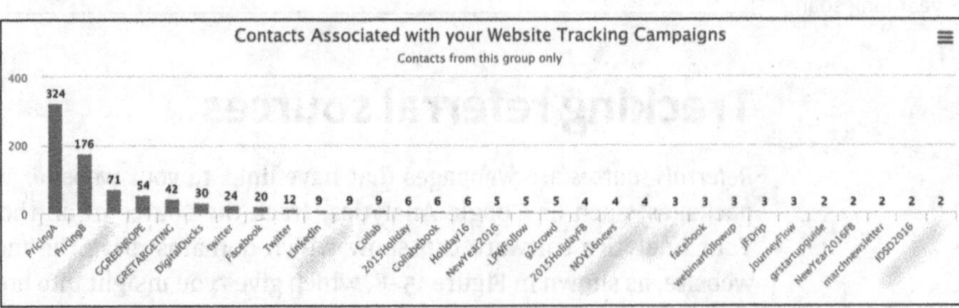

FIGURE 15-9: The number of contacts in a group by campaign ID.

Measuring bounce rate

The bounce rate is the percentage of people who leave your website after viewing only one page, as shown in Figure 15-10. This rate is an indication of traffic quality and the quality of content on your website. If you analyze your campaigns for bounce rate, you can see how many individuals land on your website and immediately leave, telling you the percentage of people who are not interested in your products or services.

Make reducing bounce rate an important goal for your marketing team. This goal crosses different disciplines, as you must examine your campaigns, your website design, and the content on your site. High quality leads should visit high quality content on your site to start the process of engagement and lead nurturing.

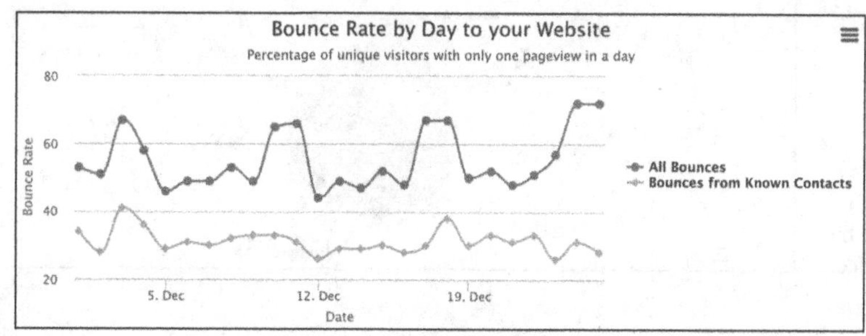

FIGURE 15-10: Bounce rate by day.

Keeping a tally on devices that visit your website

You can also learn a lot about your market by observing what devices people use when they visit your website, as shown in Figure 15-11. If you see an overwhelming majority of mobile devices, or types of devices, you can infer some things about the users of those devices.

Providing a seamless buyer journey regardless of the device your leads are using is called *omnichannel marketing.* A lead may see an ad on a mobile device, visit the mobile version of your website, and request more information using your mobile optimized lead capture form. In other words, a lead can complete his journey without switching to a different device.

Watching where your visitors come from

If you're a global brand, you're no doubt interested in seeing how many people are on your website from various parts of the world. Even if you are a domestic brand, geographic distribution of your leads and clients tells you a lot. It may indicate your increasing popularity with new demographics and the success of certain campaigns. Learn from the locations that bring you leads, and consider making localized campaigns for those regions.

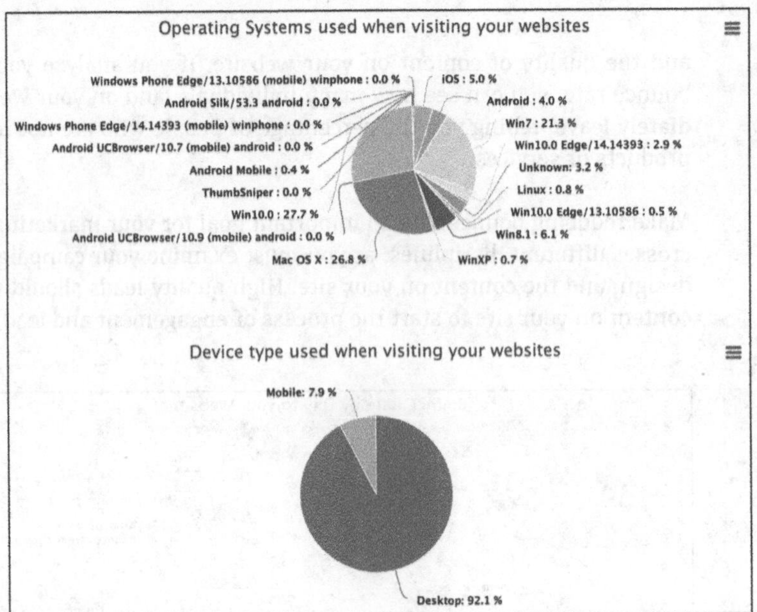

FIGURE 15-11: Visitors to a website by device.

Figure 15-12 shows a chart that tells where contacts come from. This information can tell you a lot about the geographic interest in your products and services.

Measuring time on site

Looking at the amount of time people spend on your website is another useful indicator of interest. People who spend a lot of time clicking around are probably more likely to become customers than those who don't. Look at how much time people spend on your individual pages as an indicator of overall interest in the content on those pages.

Analyzing individual pages

When looking at individual pages on your website, you may be interested in comparing average time spent on various pages, the number of people who are visiting, and where they're coming from. When you isolate common threads of how people reach a particular page, you can put yourself in the mindset of a visitor and understand why he's taking that path.

The expression "walk a mile in someone's shoes" applies to how you think about your website's visitors. When you look at the links people click that bring them from page to page, you can understand why people are motivated to buy from you.

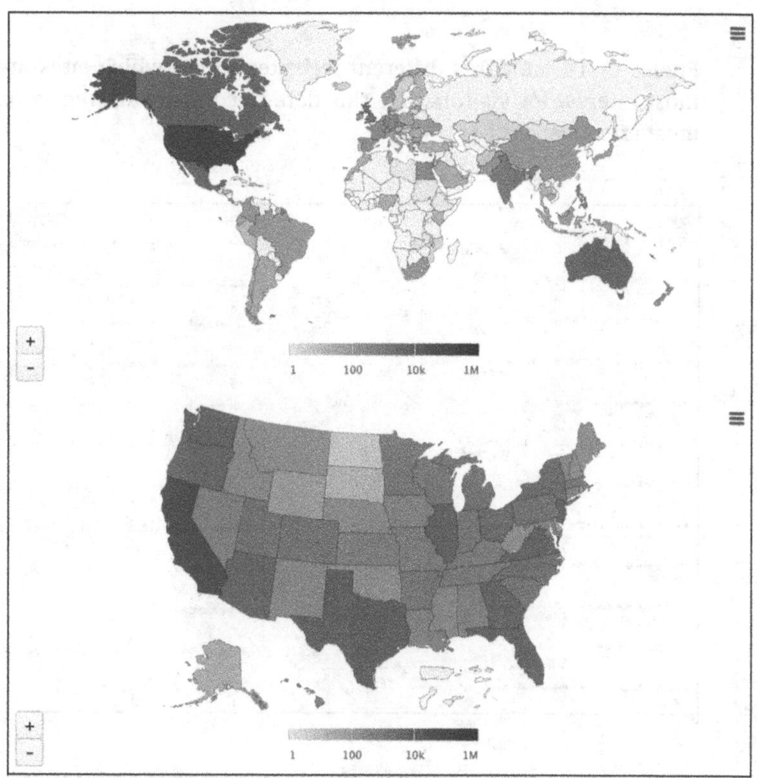

FIGURE 15-12: Darker countries and states represent more traffic from there.

Figure 15-13 shows the kind of intelligence you can gather by looking at individual pages on your website. You can measure time on each page, where people come from, and how popular each page is.

Figure 15-14 shows the traffic that is hitting a particular page, which may indicate clicks to landing pages or popularity of that page on your website. This particular page is the landing page for a campaign that was launched in the middle of the date range selected.

Comparing your website properties

If you have different websites, comparing what happens between them can illustrate how one web property may be doing business better than the others, providing a model for you to work from.

TIP

Looking at the average number of page views and average total time on site for each website can tell you which website is doing a better job of engaging with customers. Diving deeper into the analytics can tell you why. It's worth having someone in marketing do this analysis, as it can impact the entire sales and marketing process.

Figure 15-15 compares different websites to see which sites are generating the most interest for visitors. Use this data to compare strategies to see what works most effectively.

Page	Visits	Uniques	Last Page	Time on Page	Weighting
www.greenrope.com 756 referring clicks from www.google.com 337 more	9644 pageviews	4246 unique	37% last page	1:48 average on page	1 points
www.greenrope.com/crm-pricing.html 507 referring clicks from www.greenrope.com/ crm-pricing.html 54 more	820 pageviews	569 unique	4% last page	1:48 average on page	1 points
www.greenrope.com/antispam.html 11 referring clicks from outlook.live.com 113 more	769 pageviews	689 unique	7% last page	0:59 average on page	1 points
www.greenrope.com/blog/blog147/the-growing-relatio... 107 referring clicks from www.google.co.uk 109 more	651 pageviews	491 unique	5% last page	3:28 average on page	1 points
www.greenrope.com/livedemo 68 referring clicks from www.google.com 215 more	604 pageviews	465 unique	4% last page	1:10 average on page	1 points
www.greenrope.com/special-new-year-offer 120 referring clicks from t.co/ bwYXtoedFF 105 more	424 pageviews	387 unique	4% last page	1:36 average on page	1 points
www.greenrope.com/politics 19 referring clicks from android-app:// com.twitter.android 162 more	404 pageviews	337 unique	4% last page	1:21 average on page	1 points
www.greenrope.com/crm-pricing 288 referring clicks from www.greenrope.com/ crm-pricing 19 more	366 pageviews	310 unique	2% last page	1:29 average on page	1 points
www.greenrope.com/marketing-suite 46 referring clicks from www.greenrope.com/ sales-suite 30 more	344 pageviews	228 unique	1% last page	1:12 average on page	1 points
www.greenrope.com/blog/blog444/benefits-of-custome... 28 referring clicks from lnkd.in 145 more	278 pageviews	226 unique	2% last page	2:03 average on page	1 points
www.greenrope.com/sales-suite.html 76 referring clicks from www.greenrope.com 35 more	259 pageviews	199 unique	1% last page	0:58 average on page	1 points
www.greenrope.com/marketing-suite.html 68 referring clicks from www.greenrope.com 43 more	253 pageviews	197 unique	0% last page	1:11 average on page	1 points

FIGURE 15-13: Comparing different pages.

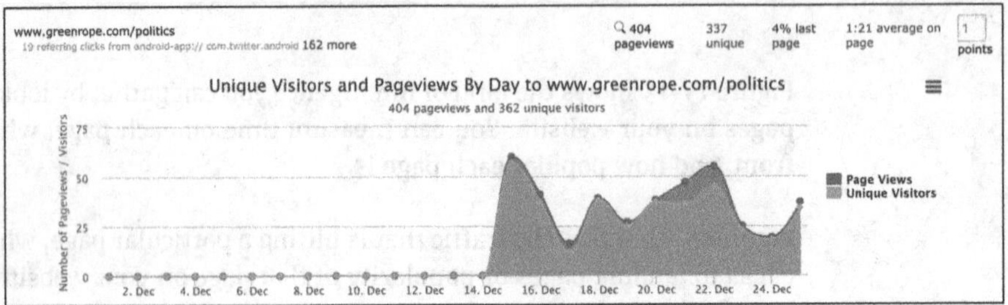

FIGURE 15-14: Traffic to a specific webpage.

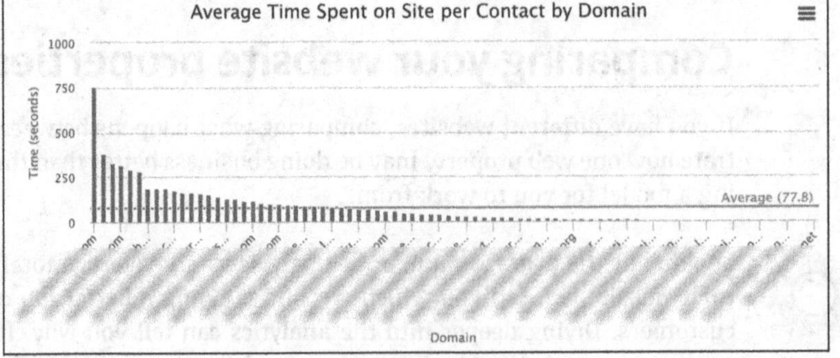

FIGURE 15-15: Average time on site by domain.

Comparing and contrasting campaign performance

Isolate and compare your website analytics from different campaigns. Seeing the average number of page views by campaign ID can tell you which campaigns drive the most interested traffic. If you can break down this number by day, you have insight into market trends, recent news, or other reasons why a particular campaign may have been more successful.

When you look at your conversions, you can then see which campaigns are driving more revenue. Compare costs you are spending on each campaign and each campaign's ROI.

Figure 15-16 shows two different campaign-driven analytics charts. The top is showing overall traffic by campaign ID. You can see the daily volume tracks to total volume, but with differing contributions by the various campaigns that are running.

The bottom chart of Figure 15-16 shows the performance of the visitors who are coming from the various campaigns being tracked. A spike in performance means that on average, more people click around on the website. Staying on a website and looking around generally correlates to interest in your products and services.

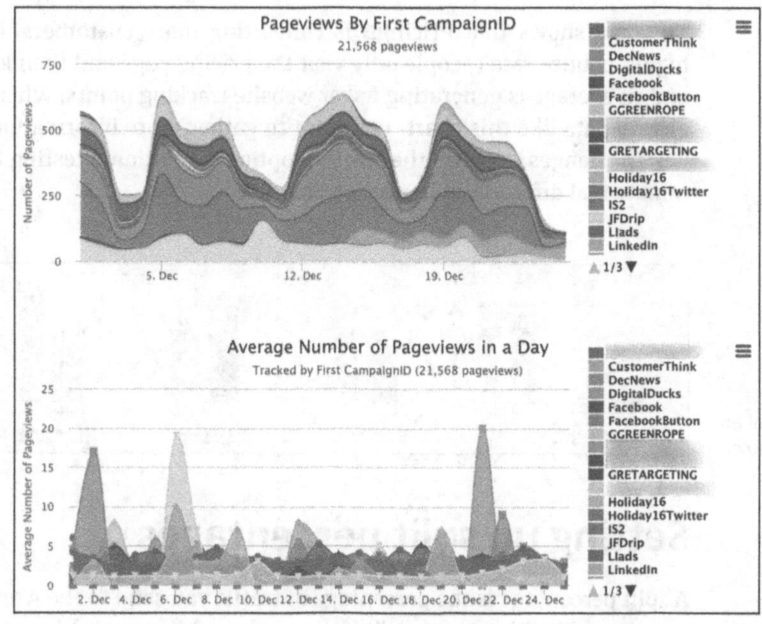

FIGURE 15-16: Campaign performance as it relates to visits on a website.

A/B Webpage Testing

A/B testing, also known as *split testing,* compares two different ways of marketing to a lead or client. The purpose of A/B testing is to see which version performs better, so you can optimize your marketing around the better performing design and get maximum engagement from your campaigns. Your marketing team conducts A/B testing for your webpages, email campaigns, social media posts, and ad campaigns to get the most ROI.

Generally you only want to compare two marketing functions at a time, and with only one difference — say a color — between the two. If you change more than one element, you won't be able to attribute the reason for one outperforming the other.

When you set up an A/B split for two webpages on your website, automatically redirect traffic to one page or the other. Then follow what people do after they reach each page, to measure interaction and purchases from you.

Figure 15-17 shows an A/B split test with live data collected from a website. Sometimes the results are not necessarily conclusive, where one clearly outperforms another. Other times, one option is the clear winner. This particular test compares two pricing pages, one with decreasing prices (PricingA) and one with increasing prices (PricingB).

The data shows that PricingB is converting more customers, but that it has a higher bounce rate (people only visit the pricing page and then leave the website) and on average is generating fewer website tracking points. When you see contradictory data like this chart, you want to gather more information or try different design changes between the two A/B options. Additional testing is needed to illuminate real differences in user preference.

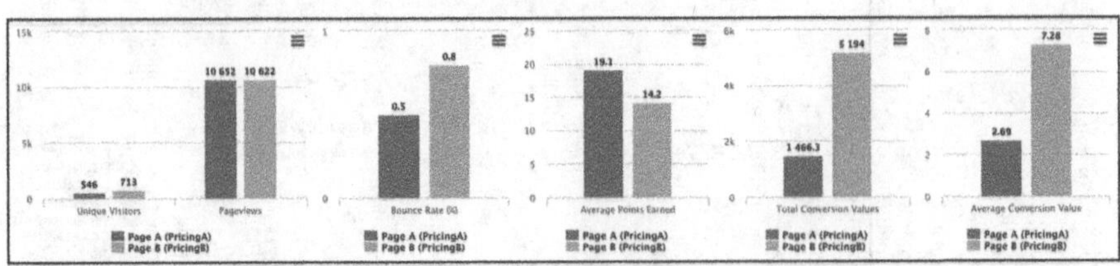

FIGURE 15-17: The results of an A/B split test.

Setting up split percentages

A split percentage is the percentage of traffic you send to the A or B page. You may want to start with a 50/50 split if you are launching something entirely new. If you have an established brand, start with what you know works, and only deviate 10 percent of the traffic to your test web page.

Determining the best criteria for a split

In figuring out how to split your two pages, limit how much variation between pages you show your visitors. Changing a color scheme, a high-level layout, or calls to action are all places to start to determine what your leads and clients like.

On the analysis side of things, measure the average number of page views, average number of lead scoring points, and average conversion values per visitor. A combination of these attributes tells you which A/B split performs better.

Adjusting split percentages automatically

Smart web marketers learn quickly from the data they collect. Sometimes that can be a challenge with the amount of data getting aggregated, so software tools can help you adapt to campaign performance.

You should be able to automatically adjust your A/B split tests so traffic is routed to the better performing pages. Doing so allows you to quickly and easily set up an A/B test with the intelligence to take advantage of the data you gather, without having to do any data analysis or manual adjustment to your website.

Figure 15-18 shows a simple management interface to set up automatic split traffic learning.

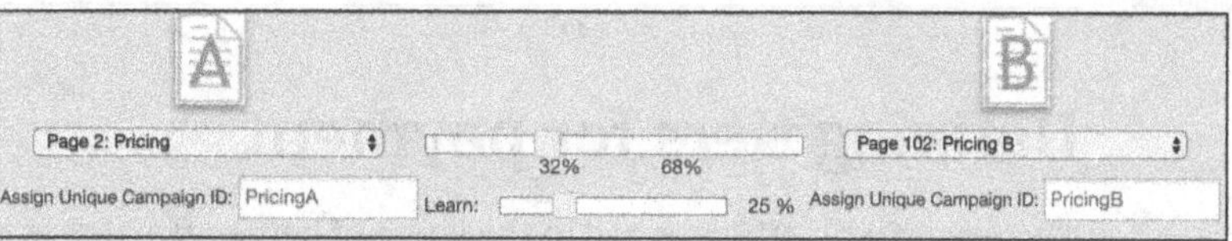

FIGURE 15-18: Setting up A/B split rules should be simple and straightforward.

Managing Affiliates

Affiliate marketing is using other people, companies, and websites to drive traffic to your website in exchange for paying for those referrals. Sometimes affiliates are paid for each inbound link; sometimes they're paid when those leads become paying clients. In either case, you must have an affiliate tracking system so you can pay for those leads.

Affiliate marketing can be a powerful way to bring new clients to you. Many affiliate management systems track people who refer you business, and then can attribute sales to them.

Connecting campaigns to affiliate codes

Associating campaigns to affiliates gives you the ability to track more than just sales. Affiliate tracking can be done in the same way you manage campaigns, assigning campaign IDs to each affiliate. These campaign IDs connect website traffic, buyer journeys, and conversions to individual contacts in your CRM. This connection then associates all your sales and marketing tracking data with your campaigns, and therefore your affiliates.

By tracking conversions and connecting them to campaigns and affiliates, you can easily calculate how much each affiliate should be paid. You can also view the rest of the traffic associated with contacts who came from that affiliate, as shown in Figure 15-19. You get a more precise overview of the quality of leads coming from that affiliate source.

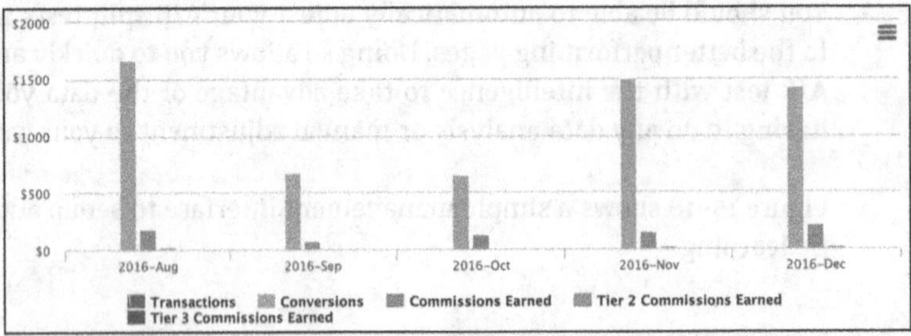

FIGURE 15-19: Tracking payout by campaign ID.

Defining tiers for payment

The reason why affiliates are in the game of being affiliates is so they can be paid to refer you business. It's pretty straightforward to calculate payment from an affiliate when you offer a simple commission (for example, 10 percent of every dollar paid to you by clients they refer for the first six months).

Paying in tiers gives you the flexibility to pay an affiliate based on whom they've referred. In other words, an affiliate can refer another affiliate and receive another payment based on all the revenue brought in by that new affiliate. This multi-tiered payment is useful for bringing in larger groups of affiliates to promote your brand.

Measuring Email Marketing

I cover email marketing in detail in Chapter 10, but more than just watching individual campaigns, measure how your email marketing is performing over time. If your messages are getting more or less effective, you want to know and take action.

TIP

After you understand how your email marketing drives revenue, use your knowledge to predict when your emails create action from your contacts. Because your CRM is tied directly to your email marketing system, you can analyze your database and see which demographics bought more from you. If you know men over the age of 50 performed well in a campaign, look at the design and ascertain why. You can use this knowledge for future campaigns.

Watching read and click rates over time

When you look at overall performance, you're accumulating a lot of data from what your contacts do with the emails you send them. Watching read and click rates over a prolonged period tells you whether you're hitting the mark on a holistic level.

Reads and clicks are the best indicators of interest in your large-scale email communication. When you measure this data, you need to average the daily variations and see how you're doing as a whole. You need to undergo statistical analysis to understand true long-term performance.

To accurately measure long-term email marketing effectiveness, take your daily volume into consideration and do some data smoothing. It prevents small volume days and statistical noise from skewing your results. With good statistical modeling, you can see whether people are taking more interest in your messages and whether you're getting better at convincing them to engage with your emails.

Figure 15-20 is a summary of reads and clicks over a three-month span. Daily reads and clicks have variations, because during low volume days, email sent is triggered by workflows. Automatic email has a lower overall effect on total read and click rates, however, because it does represent much less volume.

Comparing performance to benchmarks

One question I hear a lot is whether a client's read, click, or bounce rates are "good." The answer is always "it depends," much to the frustration of the person asking.

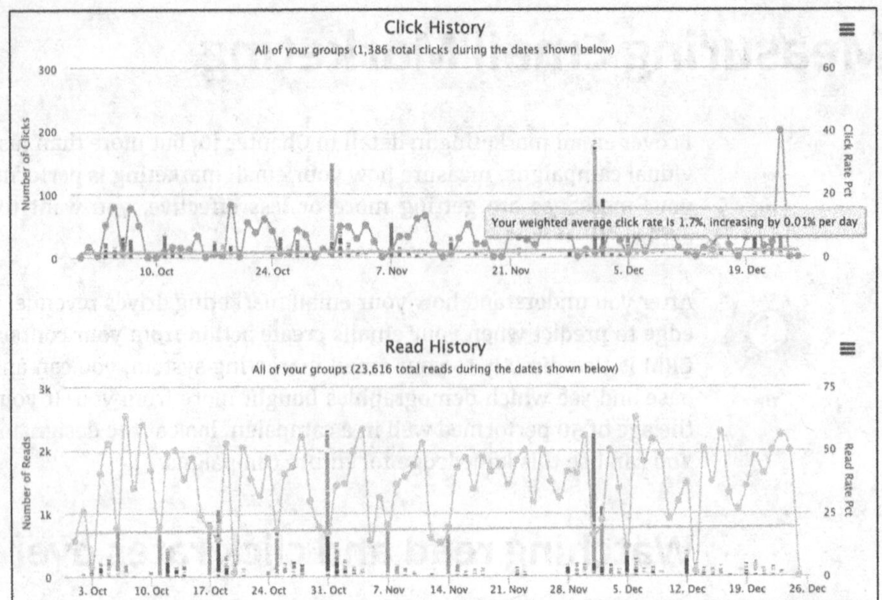

FIGURE 15-20: Trending reads and clicks over time.

Many studies have been published over the years, with differing statistics available based on industry, list size, and email frequency. What I've found is that list size is the strongest driver of email interaction. This statistic isn't much of a surprise, as larger lists are often associated with less personal, less meaningful relationships between the brand and the individual.

Your email service provider or CRM vendor should provide you with benchmarks you can use to compare your performance against similar clients, as shown in Figure 15-21. Industry benchmarks are a good indicator of your effectiveness compared to others in your market.

Measuring conversions from email campaigns

Conversion tracking requires your CRM to track people all the way from when they received your email to the conversion itself. You can tag links in your email with campaign IDs, which can then track back to your individual campaigns. You may also consider using a CRM that does this segmentation for you automatically.

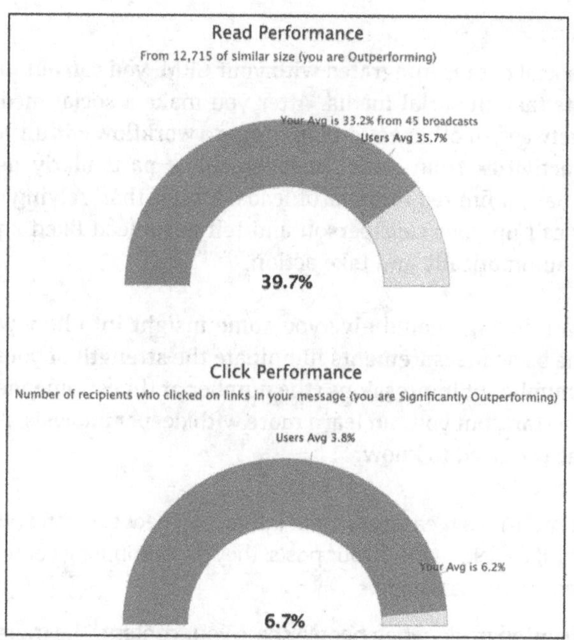

FIGURE 15-21: Read and click benchmarks for a broadcast.

Tracking Social Media

Social media is a powerful platform for communicating with a large number of people and expanding your reach. One significant challenge for marketers is that the bulk of the data collected about the use of social media is kept in the hands of the social media companies. Good social media measuring tools help extract that data.

To make the most of your social media marketing, your primary objective should be to drive people from the social media websites and applications to your website and applications. Social media is a means to start people on your buyer journeys. This connection between social media and your CRM is sometimes called *social CRM*.

Measuring impressions and actions

All social media channels provide some level of analytics. Some social media networks give you more insight into these analytics, allowing you to connect activity on those social networks with your CRM.

TIP

Whenever you post anything in social media, tag inbound links to your website with campaign IDs. You can then track *attribution*, a connection between a source campaign and a contact in your CRM. You can see which social media channels contribute to new leads and conversions.

When your social data is integrated with your CRM, you can automate actions that your contacts take in social media. After you make a social media connection, a like, share, retweet, or other action can trigger a workflow within your CRM. Scheduling CRM activities from social engagement is particularly useful when your salespeople have a limited number of leads. Rather than relying on your marketing team to call up your salesperson and tell her a lead liked a post, she can be alerted to it automatically and take action.

Social media tracking should give you some insight into how well you're doing overall. Some basic measurements illuminate the strength of your brand on social media. The number of impressions (the number of times someone sees something you post) is a start, but you can learn more with deeper analysis. A few key metrics tell you what you need to know:

- **Conversation** is a measurement of interaction between you and your contacts. If people reply to your posts, they're contributing content to your brand and your messaging.
- **Amplification** tracks when people share your content. The more sharing, the greater your reach and the more brand credibility you're establishing.
- **Applause** measures when someone likes or favorites one of your posts. This statistic tells you the level of empathy and agreement you have within your audience.
- **Impact** is an overall measurement of engagement with your audience.
- **Interest** is a summary of clicks that your audience has done with your content. More interest means more clicks, which often can be traced to an ROI.

Figure 15-22 displays all these metrics together on the same chart. Spend the time to see how your social media posts impact your business.

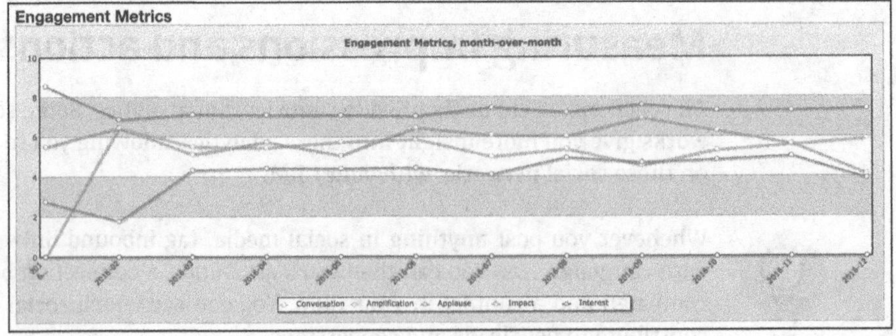

FIGURE 15-22: A chart measuring these key metrics over time.

Calculating influence and lead qualification

Third-party data sources can connect social media data to your CRM. FullContact (`www.fullcontact.com`) is one such provider, allowing you to learn more about the contact and his sphere of influence through *data appending*. Based on a contact's email address, you can learn a lot of additional information that is useful to people in sales and marketing, such as number of followers on Twitter, topics blogged about, or the contact's LinkedIn page address.

With FullContact (or a similar vendor) data available in your CRM, you have the power of information at your fingertips. The easier it is to discover important information about leads, the more successful your sales team can close them.

Taking a Global View

A true Complete CRM gives you a view of everything happening in your business in marketing, sales, and operations. Visualizing all that data can be a challenge.

Your CRM platform should give you a tool to help you see what is happening in your business in real time. Figure 15-23 shows how a CRM can show you current events in your company. In this chart, darker colors are more recent. Different colors represent different activities, such as website visits, email reads/clicks, forms filled out, conversions completed, and more.

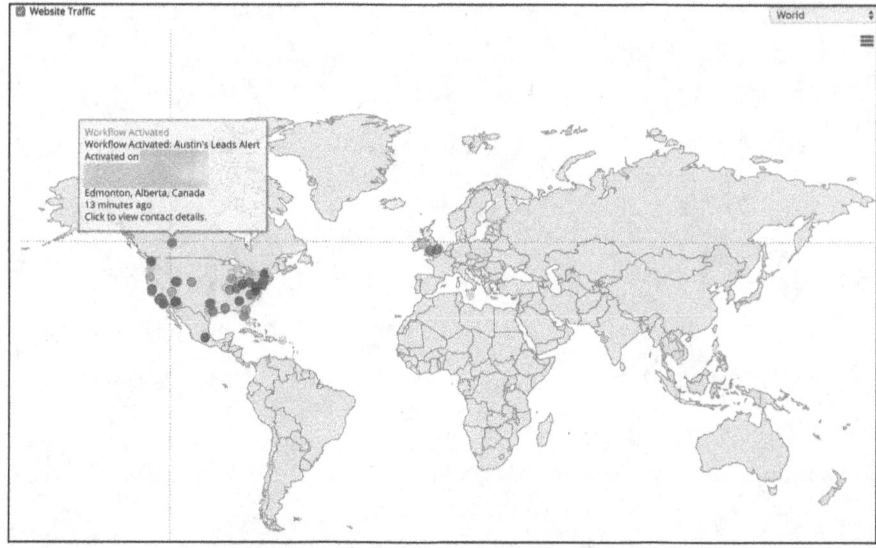

FIGURE 15-23: Real-time view of everything happening in a business.

IN THIS CHAPTER

» Surveying customers

» Resolving customer issues with ticketing forms

» Setting up live chat to communicate with clients

Chapter 16 Gathering Feedback and Supporting Customers

Providing the best customer experience is really about listening. Website forms are passive, opening the door for feedback and requests for help. Surveys represent a proactive way to listen to what your leads and customers want. With the right incentive, you can use all these methods to gather specific and general trends of what your target market wants.

When your contacts know you're listening, they're confidant in your brand and the people behind it. An emotional connection is made whenever a customer successfully engages on a personal level with your brand. This engagement must get into your CRM so you can make the most of it.

The three tools covered in this chapter — surveys, ticketing forms, and live chat — are powerful tools to help improve the customer experience. Connecting each to your CRM gives your sales and marketing teams data they can use for targeting messaging and building relationships. In the end, the more ways you satisfy customers, the better your brand, and the stronger your growth.

Sending Surveys

Surveys have been around for a very long time. Today, with easy tools that can send surveys by email to a large group, you have an unprecedented ability to learn how to better serve your market. Surveys provide immediate feedback and can either be anonymous or connected to individual contacts in your CRM. This insight is gold for any business interested in improving customer satisfaction and gaining market share.

Applying surveys to the right situations

Surveys are a powerful tool, but not one that can be used too frequently. They request individuals to invest considerable time in their busy days for what they perceive as your benefit. You can use surveys in a few ways to effectively target your contacts:

- **Ask for feedback.** In a generic sense, you can ask for feedback on how you're serving your clients. Ask how they like the product you're selling or whether they can find information on your website. Questions like these may point you in the general direction about actionable steps to improve the customer experience.

  REMEMBER

  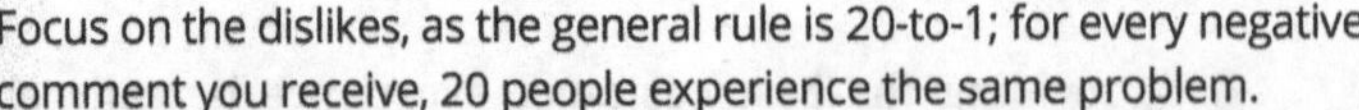

  Focus on the dislikes, as the general rule is 20-to-1; for every negative comment you receive, 20 people experience the same problem.

- **Ask for direction.** Getting your customers involved in the product development roadmap of your product or service can give you insight into what your market needs. If you open the door for customers to tell you what they want, you can use that information for your product development team or your service offerings. You may hear a new way to use your product or service, new potential markets interested in your company, or performance of key staff that influences your brand's perception in the market.
- **Assess client knowledge, skills, or preparation.** Use surveys for client education and onboarding. Ask questions that tell you how easy or difficult clients find your products or services. Learn from the answers so you can tailor education and onboarding to best fit your clients' needs. Your new clients likely come from a wide variety of backgrounds, and they most likely use your products and services differently. For example, if you send a survey that indicates a client has a lot of experience in your product, you can start with an advanced version of your training program. You gain insight into your market segments and the demographics of experienced customers with these kinds of surveys.

The NPS is a very useful metric for your business as a whole (see the next section). By looking at how likely someone is to recommend your business, you get an overall feel for the quality of the customer experience when interacting with your brand.

When designing your surveys, focus on what's most important. Studies show that your surveys should take less than 5 minutes to complete if you want to get the maximum number high-quality results from your survey recipients.

Developing the questions people answer

Writing survey questions is an art form; you must make what you're asking clear, and give the client an easy way to give a helpful response. The more specific your questions, the more you understand.

The Net Promoter Score (NPS) is a question that is specific and helpful. It simply states "How likely is it that you would recommend [brand] to a friend or colleague?" It's answered on a scale from 1 to 10; the higher the score, the more likely a customer willingly recommends your company.

Use the NPS to get a feel for the overall customer experience. Follow up with anyone who gives a low NPS, and you likely uncover areas where you need to focus your attention.

REMEMBER

The key to asking survey questions is to minimize *cognitive friction*, the mental energy a survey taker needs to understand your questions. The answers should also be easy to choose. If you're asking an open-ended question, make it clear what you're asking the survey respondent to write about.

Building logic into survey structure

When you build a survey, some questions are tailored to specific responses. For example, if a "yes" answer means that the next several questions apply, you want to show those questions; on the other hand, if the answer is "no," you want the survey to automatically jump the survey taker ahead to the next relevant question.

This branching logic allows you to build a personalized experience for the user, as shown in Figure 16-1. Guiding people to provide you with more details relevant to their answers encourages thoughtful, actionable responses.

Logic with surveys is a helpful part of onboarding and training. In assessing someone's abilities, you can find where your training team needs to focus its efforts. You can work more efficiently and shorten your training cycle for both new employees and new users of your products.

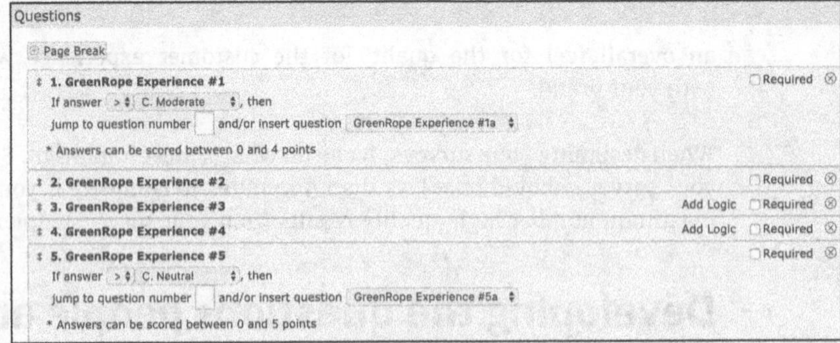

FIGURE 16-1: Building logic into the questions visible in a survey.

Scoring survey responses

Scoring surveys is a lot like school tests. When done as a skill or knowledge assessment, a scored survey gives you the ability to make a judgment on someone's proficiency. You can learn what skills your contacts have and how they're positioned to use your products and services.

TIP

If you're a consultant who offers services, consider giving leads or new clients a free "assessment" of their company's readiness or the respondent's skills. People who score high may be good candidates for your advanced program, while people who score low get your beginner's curriculum. This assessment creates engagement and the perception that you're listening and customize your services for each individual.

Scoring your survey responses can help you identify groups of people for easier targeting and follow-up. Figure 16-2 shows how you can assign points to different answers. After points are assigned, you can set up automation around various score bands. For example, if someone scores more than 20 points, she gets a different message selling advanced services than someone who scores under 5 points who is in more need of basic help.

FIGURE 16-2: Getting points for answering questions.

Triggering workflows from surveys

Tying your surveys to your CRM is a must. With CRM integration, you can leverage a particular response to a survey question by having that response activate a workflow. You can then personalize interaction between your company and your contacts. (See Chapter 5 to set up your workflows.)

Some answers to your surveys require you to take action. For example, when someone is extremely dissatisfied, you want to know why and have a customer representative follow up. A workflow is a great way to ensure the follow-up happens, preventing the issue from going unnoticed. You head off a potential negative review about your company and can turn that dissatisfaction into a learning experience for you and the dissatisfied individual.

You may also want to activate a workflow based on the total score a contact earns from filling out your survey. If, for example, you're measuring someone's knowledge or experience in a subject and her score is low, you can trigger a workflow for an onboarding specialist to have a preliminary call to help a potential problem client.

Figure 16-3 shows how a specific score activates a workflow through the CRM.

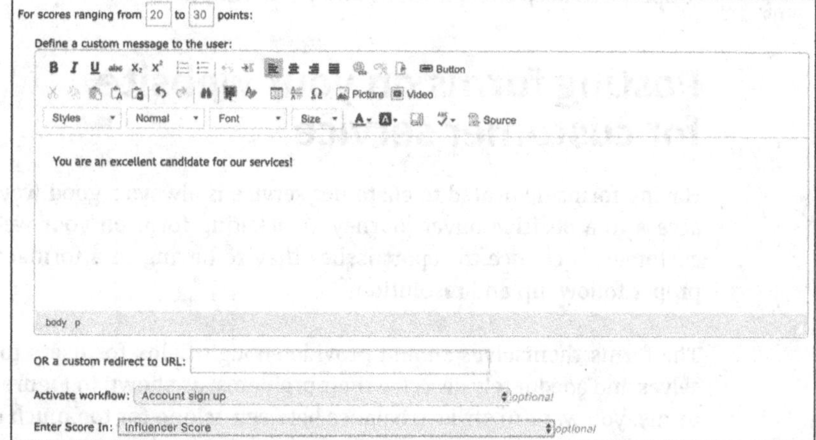

FIGURE 16-3: Survey scores trigger workflows and update the CRM automatically.

Connecting survey responses to your CRM

Complete CRM — where you measure the entire relationship between your brand and your leads and clients — involves tight integration between surveys and your CRM. Every response should be stored, and where applicable, responses should update custom data fields within the respondent's CRM record. The responses can contribute to your lead scoring and predictive analytics engines.

Surveys are another tool that can positively impact customer experience, sales, and marketing. Your sales and marketing team can use survey responses to better understand whom they're selling to. Better understanding means more precise personalization and marketing that resonates, driving engagement and positively impacting sales.

Supporting Clients with Ticketing Forms

In Chapter 8, I cover how to use a ticketing form to capture leads. The other main use for ticketing forms is for managing customer service issues. A ticketing system integrated with your CRM is a surefire way to make sure issues that your customers face are resolved and resolved quickly. Every business manager fears problems falling through the cracks, where an issue is brought up and everyone assumes someone else is taking care of it. Ticketing systems prevent that from happening, which ultimately has a positive influence on the entire buyer journey.

Design your customer service forms the same way you design sales and lead generation forms. Focus on pertinent fields, make the Submit button large and easy to spot, and keep the questions and fields simple.

Posting forms on your website for customer service

Having forms dedicated to customer service is always a good way to provide easy access to a positive buyer journey. A ticketing form on your website gives your customers a chance to report issues they're having in a format that guarantees proper follow-up and resolution.

The forms themselves should provide enough fields for users to identify themselves and adequately describe their problems, as shown in Figure 16-4. Like most forms, you want to strike a balance between asking for too much information and not asking enough. If you ask for too much, you may not get the feedback you need, but if you ask for too little, your customer service team has to spend time going back and forth asking questions.

Include the capability to upload images in your ticket forms. An uploaded picture or screenshot saves time in the back-and-forth of asking questions to get an understanding of what the problem really is.

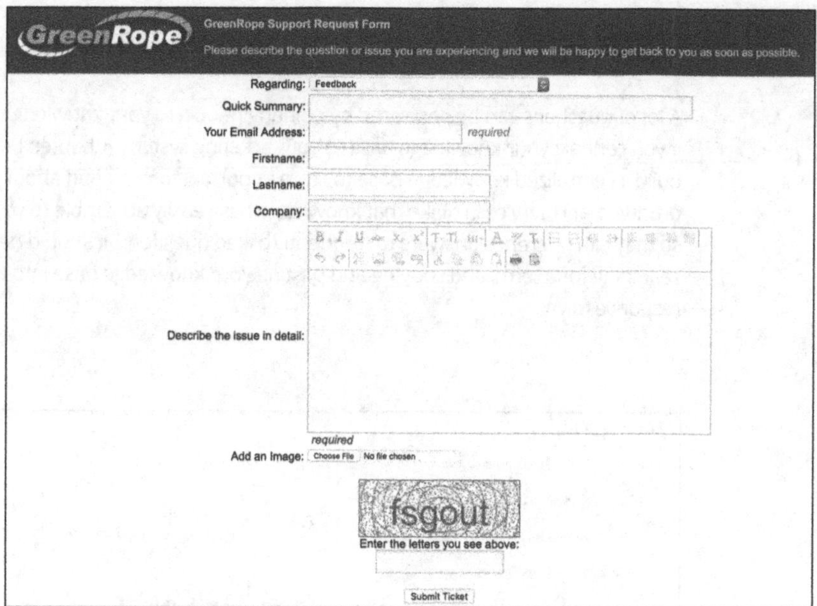

FIGURE 16-4: Support ticketing form available on the Help screen.

Automation with ticket forms

When someone fills out a support request form, it automatically generates a ticket. This ticket remains open until someone on your team closes it.

Each time someone updates the ticket, all parties working on that ticket should be automatically notified, most likely by email. You can also build in automation and workflows around your ticketing forms. Connect your ticketing form to your CRM, so you can identify or create a record in your CRM for the person making the support request.

When a ticket is opened or closed, consider activating a workflow as a follow-up. You can find out whether the user is happy with your response and that any problems he had are resolved. At the very least, use the opportunity to ask for feedback.

Setting up automation around a ticket submission should be straightforward, as shown in Figure 16-5. Note all the options and how they can customize the customer experience.

USING YOUR KNOWLEDGE BASE

A lot of questions can be answered by pointing people to your knowledge base — that is, if you connect your knowledge base to your ticketing system. (Chapter 12 covers how to build a centralized knowledge base to store important information about your company, products, and services.) Make that knowledge base easily accessible to your support team, so they can reference answers to frequently asked questions. It should be as easy as searching for a term, and copying and pasting your knowledge base into the ticketing response form.

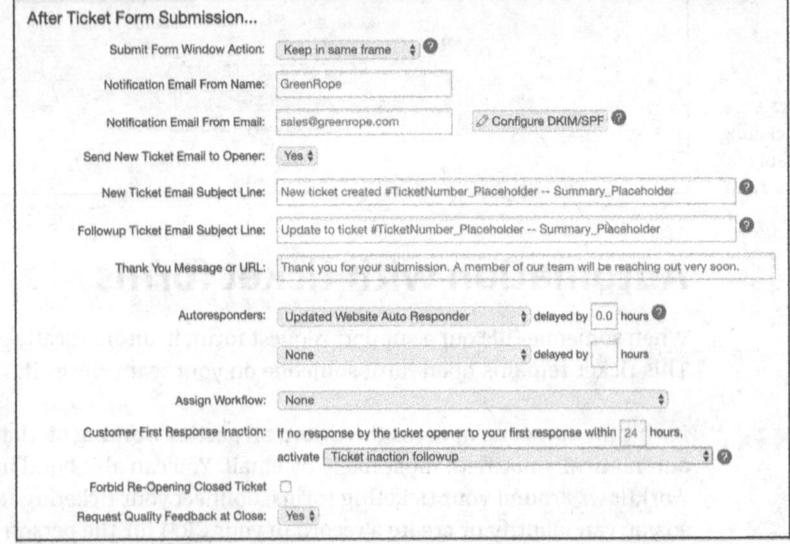

FIGURE 16-5: Action and automation after the ticket is submitted.

Setting standards and goals for your support team

Responding accurately and quickly should be your primary goal for customer service. The people who review new and ongoing tickets must have sufficient knowledge to give the right answer. The goal of their responses is to make your customers feel confident and happy that their issue is resolved or resolved shortly.

Another goal for quality customer service has to do with the tone of your communication. Your customer service team must be respectful, never condescending to anyone who fills out a ticket. Acknowledge that the customer has a problem and work together to solve that problem. When both sides act on the same side of an issue, the result is a positive customer experience. Set standards to ensure this communication always happens.

Another important goal is to set reasonable expectations for the client. If you need to escalate an issue to someone who won't be in the office for a few days, explain that to the client. Setting expectations and meeting them is honesty that pays off later.

Measuring important metrics

With customer service and support ticketing forms, your management can review a few metrics to ensure you're offering high quality service:

- **Client satisfaction:** This rating usually goes from 1-5, where the client fills out a form after the ticket has been closed. The client can express his or her overall feeling of the experience, along with any details you can take action on.

  An individual ticket and the ticket manager can be tracked within a ticketing system, as shown in Figure 16-6. This data should be linked directly to the contact records of the ticket opener.

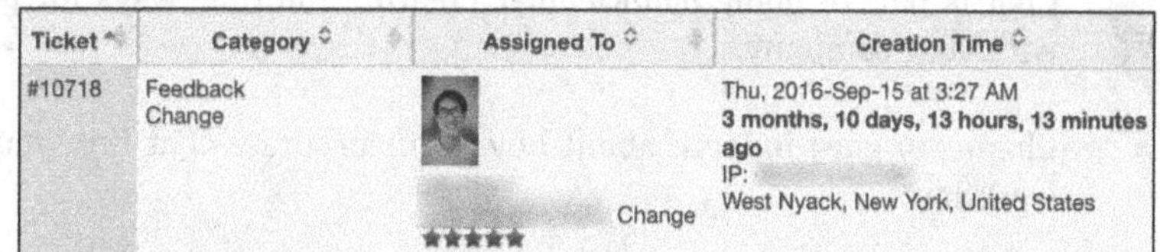

Ticket
Category
Assigned To
Creation Time
#10718
Feedback
Change
Change
Thu, 2016-Sep-15 at 3:27 AM
3 months, 10 days, 13 hours, 13 minutes ago
IP:
West Nyack, New York, United States

FIGURE 16-6: A 5-star rating for this customer service manager.

- **Response time:** Response time is the amount of time from when the ticket is opened to when someone on your team picks it up and responds to the client.
- **Number of tickets opened:** This number gives you a sense of how many open issues your support team is facing. You find trends and themes that impact the way you do business, so pay attention to how and why tickets are opened.
- **Number of tickets closed:** Watching how many tickets your various support team handles can tell you how busy they are and who your best support team members are. Over time, the ticket complexity averages out, giving you a sense of your own resource utilization. If your people answer many tickets in a day, you may want to look at your product or service, or examine your internal processes.

Figure 16-7 shows a dashboard widget that measures the overall performance of the support team.

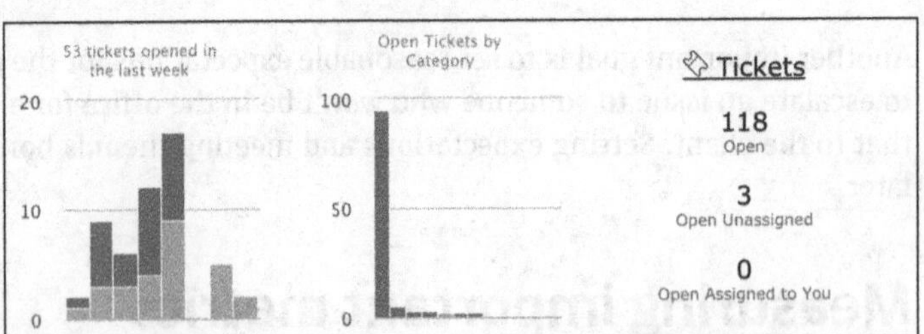

FIGURE 16-7: Tickets opened summary widget.

Chatting with Leads and Clients

Live chat services are a great way to offer support for your customers, as shown in Figure 16-8. A lot of people are either too shy or busy to pick up the phone and talk to you and would rather connect by chat. It shows customers that you're interested in hearing what they're thinking and willing to solve problems they might be having. Another benefit of chat is that a customer can multitask while chatting.

REMEMBER

Chat is part of being *omnichannel*, creating multiple ways for people to interact with your company.

Chapter 9 goes indepth about how to incorporate chat into your CRM and your workflows.

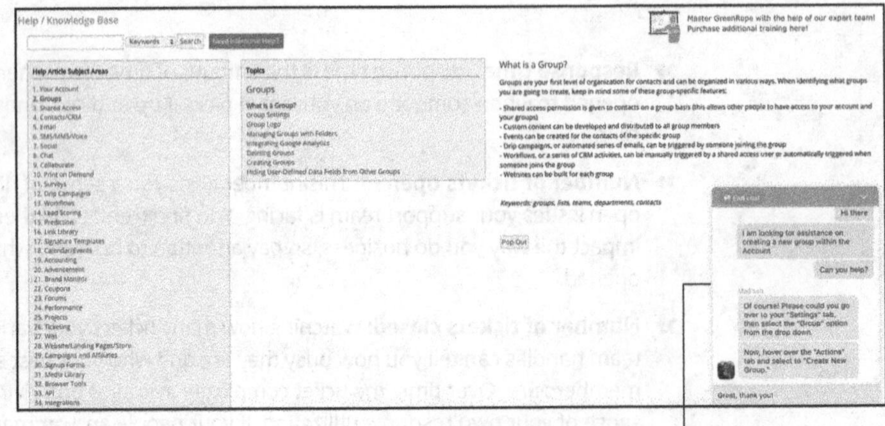

FIGURE 16-8: Use chat to offer help to customers.

IN THIS CHAPTER

» **Reporting on the relevant information you need to use**

» **Turning data into action to improve your business**

» **Building strategies for lead scoring that impact sales**

» **Using predictive analytics to focus your energy on the right initiatives**

Chapter 17
Using Analytics the Right Way

Gathering a lot of data isn't enough. You have to know how to use it and you need to know what impact that data has on the way you do business. The analytics you derive from your Complete CRM can guide your strategies and decisions. Without a complete picture of your business's performance, you can easily make the wrong decisions and invest in the wrong initiatives, costing time and money. With Complete CRM in place, you can have the confidence and the ability to adapt to market conditions.

In this chapter, I talk about setting the right key performance indicators for your business as a way to help monitor overall health and performance. Leverage your website analytics data, your lead scoring, and your predictive analytics results to illuminate the best path ahead for your business.

The strategies you adapt as you learn about your market and your business present a constant force of change in your organization. In a free market, this change is good and keeps your business competitive. Embrace this change and maintain a culture of agility and constant learning. Your business remains competitive and sustainable as market forces change and your business grows.

Defining Your Key Performance Indicators

Key Performance Indicators (KPIs) are high-level metrics that you use to measure the overall performance of your organization. Metrics are related to

- **Sales:** Measure revenues and how they relate to your sales funnels.
- **Marketing:** Look at how effectively you're generating leads, engaging with those leads, and up-selling to your existing clients.
- **Operational:** Help you examine customer service, events, HR, and other day-to-day interactions with your leads and clients.

Overall, your KPIs tell you how your business is growing, and how good a customer experience you're offering. At a high level, when you see significant departures from the norm, you can then drill down into your CRM to see why.

Knowing what to measure and why

Your CRM should provide these KPIs in your dashboard, or have them easily accessible with a custom report, as shown in Figure 17-1:

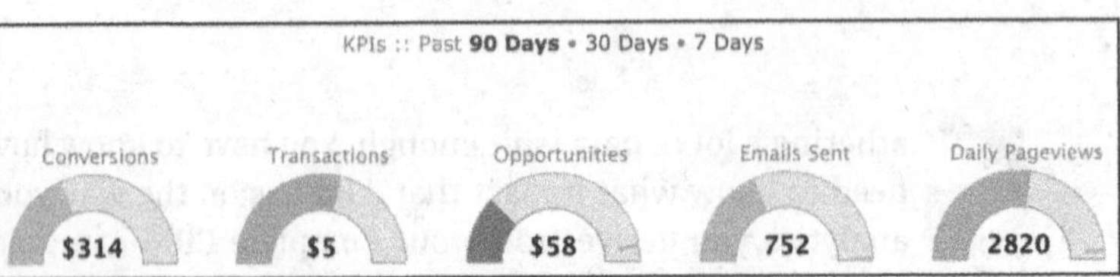

FIGURE 17-1: A KPI dashboard widget.

- **Total revenues:** You should review top line revenue weekly, monthly, quarterly, and annually. Compare those figures to a baseline value or growth goal.
- **Opportunities closed:** If you're a B2B organization, opportunities likely track closely to total revenue, but if you have a mixture of B2B and B2C products and services, isolate your opportunities and their performance from the rest of your revenue generation.
- **E-commerce sales:** If some of your revenue comes from an e-commerce storefront, break those sales out. Investigate sudden deviations from goals or averages for changes in strategy or store design.
- **Specific funnels:** Isolate a few key funnels that are critical to your business. Visually inspect how the funnels are performing and drill down to see key conversion rates and average times in each stage of the funnel.

- **CRM activities:** See how many activities your team completes on a specific day. Drill down to see who is doing what to get a granular picture. Some sales managers like to see a minimum number of calls, email, or other engagements per day, and a daily or weekly report can keep management on top of your team's activities.
- **Sales leaderboards:** Review who your best salespeople are and come up with ways to publicly recognize your top performers.
- **Emails sent:** Gauge the total number of emails sent to ensure your marketing is staying consistent and no one is forgetting to keep continual, steady, but not overwhelming interaction with your contacts.
- **Webpages viewed:** If you see sudden increases or decreases in traffic to your website, you want to know about it. Your lead generation strategy and customer interactions are primary drivers to this metric, and visitor activity directly correlates to your business.
- **Calendar:** Get an overview of what is happening in your business on any given day. If you're hosting events, see how many people are coming. Get an overview of CRM activities and email campaigns scheduled to be sent.
- **Tickets opened:** Tickets are useful for sales and support, so measure performance by how many tickets are created and how effective your team responds to those tickets. Incorporate opening a ticket into a sales funnel to track stages of a buyer journey.
- **Signup forms:** If you're using signup forms to gather interest in your newsletter, take a look at how many of those forms are filled out. If you have several forms on your website, pay attention to which forms are most popular. Your most popular forms are indicators of which pages are better designed and which pages address the needs of your target market.
- **Contact demographics:** You get a general sense of your contacts. Pick a few key fields that give you insight into your data. For example, you can list the top five countries your contracts are from or rank contacts by a custom data field.
- **Group growth:** Watch trends in the sizes of your groups, as shown in Figure 17-2. To track what drives change in your database, measure how your lead capture, workflows, and sales teams impact your business. If adding a contact to a group is part of a campaign, you can easily see what the effect of your sales and marketing has on your market segments.
- **Aggregate lead scoring:** A complete picture of your lead scores gives you insight into which campaigns drive interaction with your brand by leads and clients. Spikes can occur with this scoring based on successful campaigns you're running, so watch for that.

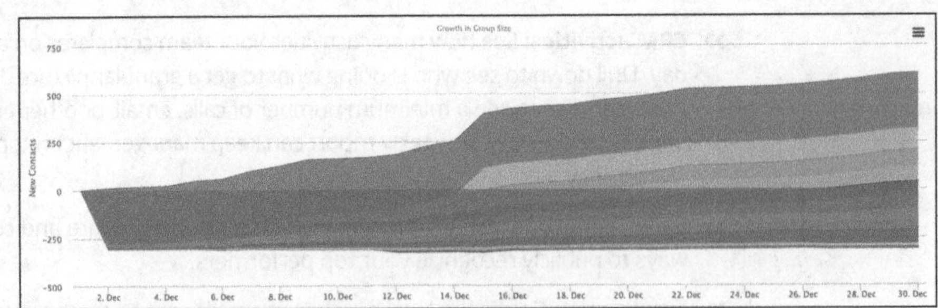

FIGURE 17-2: Group growth over time.

Setting reasonable standards

When you develop your KPIs, it's important to establish a baseline for each one. That baseline may be a running average, or a minimum value that you need to feel comfortable that your business is running properly. I like the longtime running average, as deviations from that can show you when business is improving or hitting snags.

REMEMBER

You also need to establish the "what if" scenarios if those numbers are not met. Always have someone responsible for that KPI. If a decrease in performance rears its ugly head, talk to that person and hold that person accountable to understand how and why. Be sure you have a plan to correct it.

If KPIs are indicating strength or growth, remember to publicly commend the people responsible. Being data driven, KPIs are the quantitative, unbiased result of the success of teams of people working on and in your business. No one can argue with numbers, so the more you rely on them for praise and recognition, the more your team values everyone's contributions.

Reporting your KPIs

For all KPIs, there is some amount of analysis before you determine what's important and what to use in terms of measuring your success. Your CRM pulls all the data from the various sources to build the KPI charts and reports you need. Your KPI charts should be available in real time and on demand. To make those charts useful, design your CRM so your management team can drill down to see supporting data. Use your CRM to send daily and monthly summary reports that you can review. Regular reports in your inbox are a good way to augment your KPI charts.

The importance of using KPIs to measure the health of your business is clear. The hardest part is getting all that data into a single system, which is why Complete CRM is useful. You need to bring your data and your team together, and it requires your vision to see why your KPIs are important to everyone you work with.

Developing policies for exceeding standards or failing to meet them

KPIs are designed to be independent of opinion or qualitative judgment. They're data streams rolled up into useful, concise charts and reports. If KPI standards aren't met, or you see a decline in overall performance, be sure you have a plan in place to change that.

Declining KPIs may be the result of different influences, and as a manager in your company, you have to investigate to find the real root cause. Are market forces shifting? Are your products having more defects? Are more competitors bidding against you? Is your management being too hands off or too restrictive? Is morale suffering?

REMEMBER

Understanding downward trends of a KPI requires investigation into the entire ecosystem that supports that KPI. You can only evaluate what you can measure, so your CRM must incorporate everything to identify what may be broken.

On the flip side, improving KPIs may be the result of internal or external factors. Are processes making your team more efficient? Do you have leaders who are motivating your team and increasing morale? Has manufacturing come up with a better mousetrap that the market loves? Give reward where reward is due, and let the numbers guide you.

Sharing performance with investors and employees

Not all KPIs are for public consumption. You may not want to share every piece of data with your entire team. In my experience, however, the more you share, the more your team can understand where your company is going. Management hiding something tends to breed mistrust among employees.

I recommend sharing KPIs and daily reports with your entire team. They may choose to ignore the reports, but you can never be accused of being deceptive. You then build morale and put accountability for the success of the business on everyone's shoulders. Transparency is something everyone appreciates and understands.

Analyzing Your Website Traffic

Web analytics can be complicated to dive into, but your marketing team should be able to distill important factors in your marketing that can guide your strategy and policy.

Assessing SEO and PPC performance

Search engine optimization (SEO) and pay-per-click (PPC) advertising are two top-of-funnel marketing-related activities that directly influence sales. Each can be tagged with campaign IDs so you can see what kinds of leads they're driving to you.

When you're looking at SEO, evaluate the strength of keywords on search. Google, and to a lesser extent Bing, send you traffic based on what they perceive your reputation and relevance to be. Work with an SEO expert to come up with the right keywords and content for your pages. To the extent you can see what kind of search words bring traffic to your site, work with your web development and marketing team to make sure you're targeting the right people and maximizing clicks from those important market segments.

SEO is as much about what you put on your website as it is what other websites publish about you. When high quality sites link to you, they tell search engines that you're relevant and important. Be sure your SEO strategy includes both aspects.

PPC gives more control to you as the advertiser. You can bid on different keywords, adjust how much you spend on them, and evaluate the success of those campaigns.

Comparing campaigns and their impact

In Chapter 15, I talk about setting up web analytics and assigning campaign IDs to your advertising. Your marketing team should look at the different campaigns you're running to assess how your campaigns are performing. Invest more money into the better performing campaigns and test new variations on those. Continually adjust and perfect your ads, landing pages, and follow-up strategies. Use A/B testing (also discussed in Chapter 15) in conjunction to see what kind of content resonates best with your target market.

Tag your campaigns with IDs, so you can see how your website traffic is performing with each campaign. Take a look at the average number of webpage views your visitors generate with each campaign. More page views generally indicate greater interest, which usually results in more revenue, but not always. Be sure you track conversions, which you can trace back to different campaigns. Evaluate cost associated with bringing in a lead to access which campaigns are most effective. This cost per lead (CPL) calculation is good for comparing raw numbers of people entering your sales funnel.

With any campaign, your goal is to minimize the cost of generating a new lead while maximizing both the chance of converting that lead and the revenue generated by that lead. Structure your reporting to look at these factors and focus on the best campaigns you're running. Ask your marketing team to determine *why* your better-performing campaigns are more successful so you can learn from what works and capitalize on it.

When your CRM tracks interactions across multiple channels, you can generate a report like that shown in Figure 17-3. When one channel or campaign significantly impacts brand interaction, you can see it visually in a report like this.

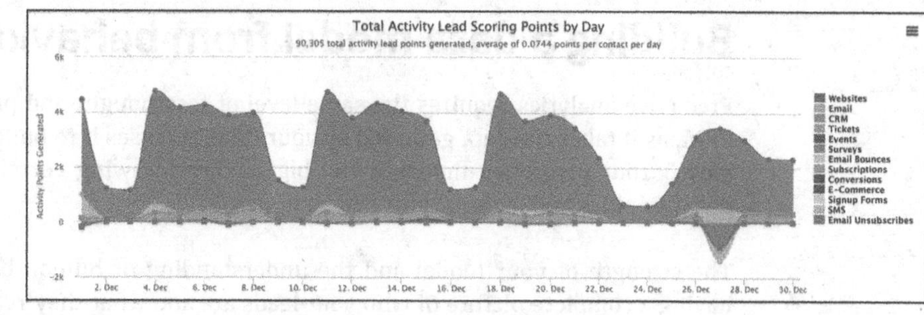

FIGURE 17-3: Measuring the impact of multiple channels in the same report.

Scoring Your Leads and Clients

In Chapter 6, I describe strategies for building lead scoring rules. The rules you generate are constantly evolving, along with your business model and market forces. Review your lead scoring every few months to see whether you need to adjust actions and demographics.

TIP

Assign a qualitative letter designator to a lead. For example, an "A" lead is the best kind of lead, with a responsive, interested client who can bring in significant revenue. A "D" lead is likely not going to convert and represents little value to your business. "B" and "C" leads fall in the middle, with the salesperson making the assessment of where those lead categories apply.

Predictive Analytics

Predictive analytics uses a mathematical model to predict what people will do before they do it. By learning from behavior, you can draw statistical correlation between demographics and actions.

Predictive analytics can sound intimidating, but technology has gotten to the level where it no longer needs to be. The science of predicting human behavior has been around for a long time, but not until recently has the technology had the capability to collect and process data fast enough to make it useful.

Predictive analytics has two primary components: building the data model and applying the model to contacts. You must first build the model by collecting data, which correlates certain attributes or behaviors to purchases. After you have the model built, you can then apply it to contacts to see who is likely to purchase from you.

Building a data model from behavior

Predictive analytics requires the same level of forethought and planning as your CRM, as it takes the data gathered by your CRM and uses it to build your *predictive model*. Your predictive model is the big picture, drawing correlations between demographics and actions with conversions.

The strength of your model and the understanding of human behavior rely on having a complete picture of who your leads are and what they're doing — which is the whole point of Complete CRM. The concepts of Complete CRM — building a comprehensive understanding of the leads and contacts in your CRM — are centered on gathering data from as many channels as possible.

REMEMBER

If you're gathering incomplete data about your leads and contacts, your predictive analytics model is also incomplete, and it may point you in the wrong direction. For example, if you don't collect data from your social media campaigns and posts, you won't know if someone liking your Facebook page has any influence on the buying decision. If it's significant, you know something about your market and how you should be communicating to your leads and clients.

Your predictive model is built around finding statistical significance between actions and conversions. Because your Complete CRM is measuring every action taken by a contact and then correlating those actions with individuals buying from you, the data is available to connect the dots between contacts and conversions.

Some of the data your CRM gathers is demographic and some is behavioral. You may find that certain interests or characteristics of individuals are greater predictors of buyers, which in turn influences how you define your buyer personas. From this, you can then target your markets more effectively. (See Chapter 4 for more information on creating and using buyer personas.)

You may also find that certain key actions taken by leads are strong predictors of conversions. If a phone call or a demo or visiting a particular webpage is strongly correlated to a lead converting into a customer, focus your marketing efforts on getting the lead to take that action.

When you build a predictive model (see Figure 17-4), you can draw correlation strength between demographics/actions and conversions.

Existing Prediction Model for GreenRope_Account		
Visited	*www.greenrope.com*	correlates 0.66
Visited	*www.greenrope.com/pricing.html*	correlates 0.54
Campaign	*PricingA*	correlates 0.42
Visited	*www.greenrope.com/features.html*	correlates 0.42
Visited	*www.greenrope.com/livedemo*	correlates 0.41
Opened ticket	*I would like a live demo*	correlates 0.35
Opened ticket	*I would like a trial account*	correlates 0.28
Visited	*www.greenrope.com/trial*	correlates 0.26
Visited	*www.greenrope.com/crm*	correlates 0.25
GreenRope Account Status (User160) is	*Trial*	correlates 0.23
Campaign	*PricingB*	correlates 0.21
Visited	*www.greenrope.com/contact.html*	correlates 0.17
Visited	*app.greenrope.com/app2/create_account.pl*	correlates 0.16
Visited	*www.greenrope.com/marketing_automation*	correlates 0.16
Visited	*www.greenrope.com/email_marketing*	correlates 0.15
Visited	*www.greenrope.com/comparison.html*	correlates 0.15
Visited	*www.greenrope.com/pricing*	correlates 0.14
Activity	*Follow Up*	correlates 0.13
Visited	*app.greenrope.com/app2/login.pl*	correlates 0.13
Visited	*www.greenrope.com/greenrope_crm_and_website_analytics*	correlates 0.13
Referrer	*www.google.co.uk*	correlates 0.12

FIGURE 17-4: A predictive data model based on demographics and actions.

Adjusting your model

After you build your model, revisit your data on a regular basis to confirm nothing significant has been influencing buyer behavior. You may also want to rebuild your predictive analytics model after you make a significant change in your business model, such as changing pricing or sales processes. If you find different things influence buyer behavior after such a change is made, you may need to adjust your sales and marketing tactics accordingly.

Connecting your predictive model to lead scoring

When you build your predictive model, you see the characteristics of a person that are most strongly correlated to successfully completing a conversion (becoming a customer). Seeing those characteristics, you can then adjust your lead scoring model accordingly. (See Chapter 6 to set up lead scoring.)

TIP

If you learn that a particular action, such as visiting a webpage, watching a video, or downloading a whitepaper, is a strong influencer for a lead to become a customer, assign a high number of lead scoring points to that action. You can then set up automation around those individual key actions or on activity scores that trigger communication or schedule CRM activities for your sales staff. Immediately, your sales and marketing is timely, relevant, and targeted right where it should be.

REMEMBER

With a more accurate lead scoring model, your salespeople can better gauge the quality of each lead. They can then be more effective and target their best leads, which improves conversion. More conversions mean more revenue for your organization, something your entire team can get behind.

Applying your predictive model to leads

The other half of predictive analytics is using your data model to predict when people are going to do something. When you do this, you can target your sales team's efforts on those most ready to convert (shown in Figure 17-5) — or, as salespeople like to say, "the low-hanging fruit." This assessment is based on quantitative data, driven by all the work you've done in the past to build your data model.

Just as activity lead scores decay, ensure your predictive model builds in decay on significance of actions. Lead scoring and predictive analytics must account for the declining propensity for someone to convert over time. If a lead has all the ear-marks of becoming a client, but disappears for a week or two or longer, the chance of conversion drops with that delay. This setting should be automatic, making it easy for you to do predictive analysis and provide the results to your sales team.

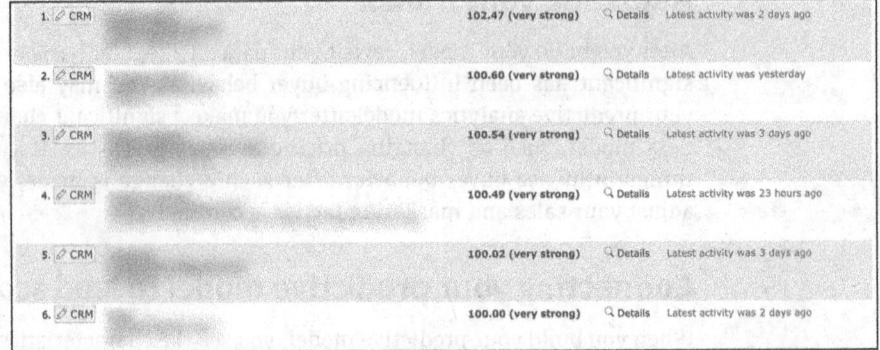

FIGURE 17-5: Top leads found by predictive analytics.

Applying your predictive model to your business model

When you build your predictive model, you see what correlates to conversion. These indicators show where you should invest your resources. You can use a few types of indicators to adjust your business processes:

- **Webpages:** If specific webpages drive people to convert, review what is on those webpages. Your target market may be looking for specific content. Or leads are clicking specific links that lead to or from your website. Review whether other webpages connected to that highly converted webpage are also strongly correlated with conversion. This process helps you understand the buyer journey and can tell you why certain campaigns are more effective, which directs how you spend your advertising budget.
- **Email clicks:** If you send emails via drip campaigns or workflows to people in your lead funnel, there may be a history of calls to action that resonate with your leads. Look at why that is; either the content is interesting, or the call to action in the message itself influences buyer behavior.
- **Social media actions:** Social media interaction may indicate a public desire for a potential contact to engage with your brand. If particular channels tend to drive people to become clients, you're building social proof and giving opportunity to reach out to others on that social network. Consider running additional campaigns on that network to build likes or shares.
- **CRM activities with an individual:** You may find that certain individuals in your organization act as particularly powerful brand ambassadors. They're likely to be useful in closing bigger deals so take note of how they interact with clients. Take any opportunity you can to get them on video talking about your business.

Sharpening your team's skills

There is no such thing as a salesperson who has nothing to learn. Get feedback from all members of your sales team to see how your predictive analytics model "feels." If they agree with what the data provides, they may have input into marketing strategy. The converse is also true — the marketing strategy educates your sales team on what your target marketing is looking for. Learning from conversion rates and statistics helps your salespeople close better.

This kind of cross-functional communication is why Complete CRM is so revolutionary for your business. When different parts of your business can share feedback that is backed by data, the entire organization benefits.

5 The Part of Tens

IN THIS PART . . .

Ten review sites to compare CRM solutions.

Ten tips to ensure success with Complete CRM.

Chapter 18

Ten Top-Notch Software Review Websites

You can visit a number of review websites that help you discover the right CRM platform for your business. However, when it comes down to it, no system is one size fits all, which is why it's important that you understand your business requirements.

REMEMBER

Be careful when you give your information for a free trial or demo through these review sites. They tend to take your information and sell it on to other vendors.

Expert Market

www.expertmarket.com

Expert Market provides resources to search for, explore, compare, and learn about the best products and services for your business. Expert Market is different from the other review sites because it focuses on more than just software and acts as a hub for anything and everything a business needs to get up and running.

The website is modern and easy to navigate. It provides expert guides and other content to help you learn about your options. The discovery phase is easy. It takes you through a guided series of questions to help filter the results based on your business needs, as shown in Figure 18-1. You can customize your request and select the features that you want to narrow your options and help find the right solution for you.

After you specify exactly what you're looking for, the knowledgeable and friendly team sends quotes from the top four providers that match your requirements, along with recommendations for other products or services you might need.

Expert Market is perfect for any business owner who wants to act quickly with as little complexity as possible.

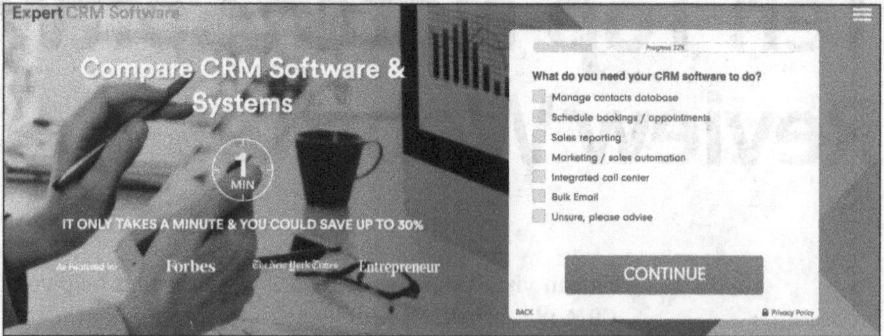

FIGURE 18-1: Expert Market helps define what you need in CRM software.

G2 Crowd

https://www.g2crowd.com

G2 Crowd is software focused and provides reviews, comparisons, and in depth descriptions of platforms in a number of different categories, as shown in Figure 18-2. Each quarter it releases a report called *The Grid* that identifies top performers, niche platforms, high performers, and so on. It includes almost all the vendors you could possible choose from, and the site is pretty easy to sift through.

You can search by category or for a specific platform. The depth of each vendor profile largely depends on the vendor and/or whether the vendor subscribes to the G2 Crowd lead generation program. Some vendor profiles allow you to watch a live demo, ask the vendor a question, or request a demo. If you see a vendor that you like that does not have any of those options, do not rule it out. Simply visit its website and request more information.

G2 Crowd currently has over 140,000 user reviews; however, the site favors the software companies that purchase one of its branding packages. If a vendor purchases a branding package, G2 Crowd does a review campaign and other bells and whistles to help the vendor's profile stand out.

That being said, it still remains one of the most highly used and trusted software review sites. I would just keep in mind that because of its business model, some vendors might seem to stand out or be more accessible than others.

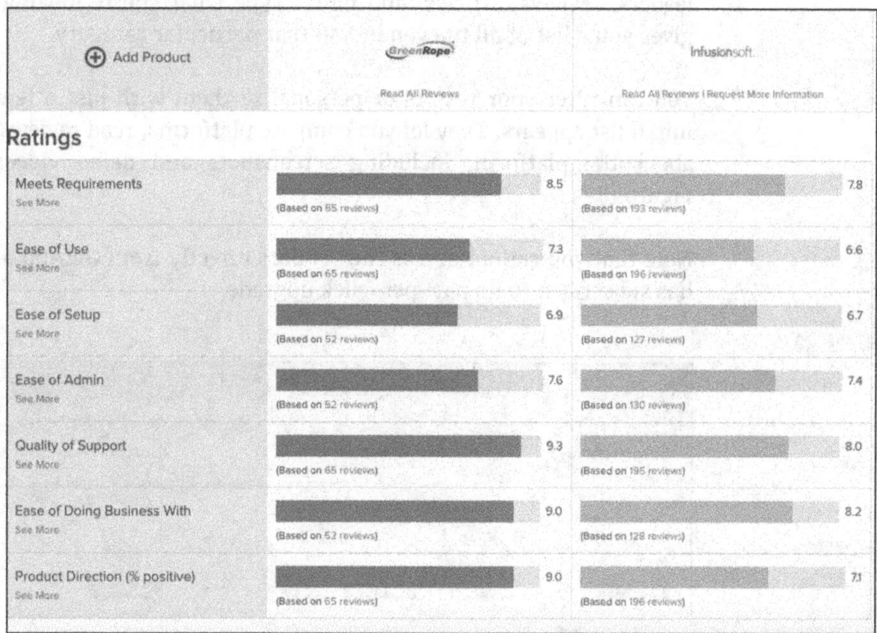

FIGURE 18-2: The G2 Crowd's CRM product ratings.

SaaSGenius

`www.saasgenius.com`

SaaSGenius is a SaaS directory where you can explore, review, and compare business tools to help you grow your business. Like the other sites, you can filter through your results, compare platforms, and access content such as blog posts, guides, and so on.

This site is fast growing, but does not yet have the vendor diversity of some other review sites. Any vendor can set up a free listing, but SaaSGenius offers a premium package to vendors that gives them premium listing placement and other lead generation benefits.

GetApp

www.getapp.com

GetApp is another frequently used and highly rated software directory and review site. The company is owned by Gartner, one of the world's top technology research firms.

The site has all the content you need, including buyer's guides, category leaders, reviews, articles, and more. Type what you're looking for and GetApp gives you a list of all the vendors in that particular category.

You can filter your results or personalize them with just a few clicks after the initial list appears. They let you compare platforms, read reviews, and learn more about the platform, including screenshots and demo videos, as shown in Figure 18-3.

Note that you cannot access the vendors directly from GetApp unless the vendor has subscribed to its pay-per-click upgrade.

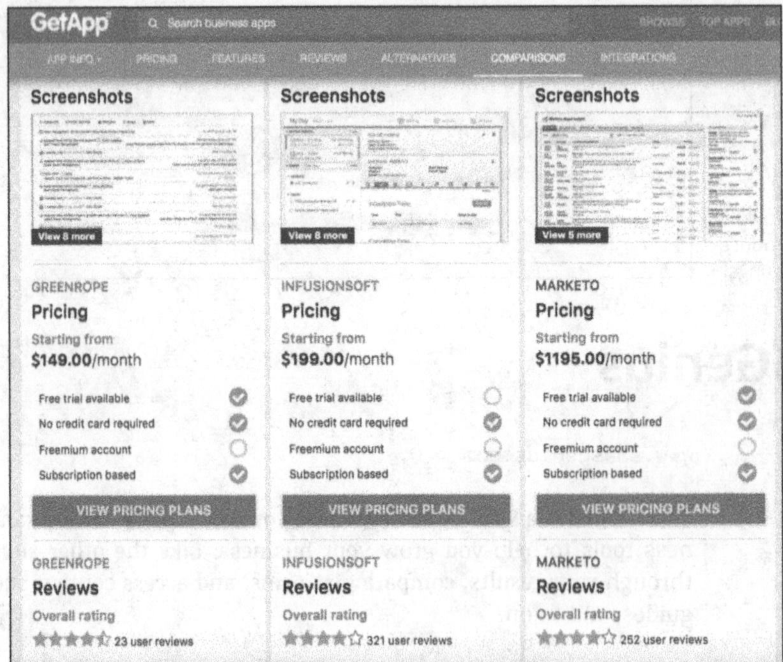

FIGURE 18-3: The GetApp comparisons.

Technology Advice

technologyadvice.com

TechnologyAdvice is a small technology directory. Just like the other review sites, you have access to reviews and comparisons for all the vendors listed. Because the site is smaller than the rest, the vendor selection is limited and so are the reviews.

Software Advice

www.softwareadvice.com

Software Advice is also owned by Gartner. (GetApp and Capterra being the other two featured in this chapter.) However, Software Advice takes a consultative and research based role in your discovery process.

If a vendor upgrades to its Leads program, Software Advice sends your information to the vendors directly so that they can contact you directly.

Software Advice matches you to the best software for your needs through a telephone qualification process and in-house matching. Vendors do pay per lead; however, Software Advice claims that equal representation is given to each vendor. That being said, the vendor isn't provided with your information unless the vendor pays for that service.

Figure 18-4 shows how you can review a software platform's ratings in an easy-to-read format.

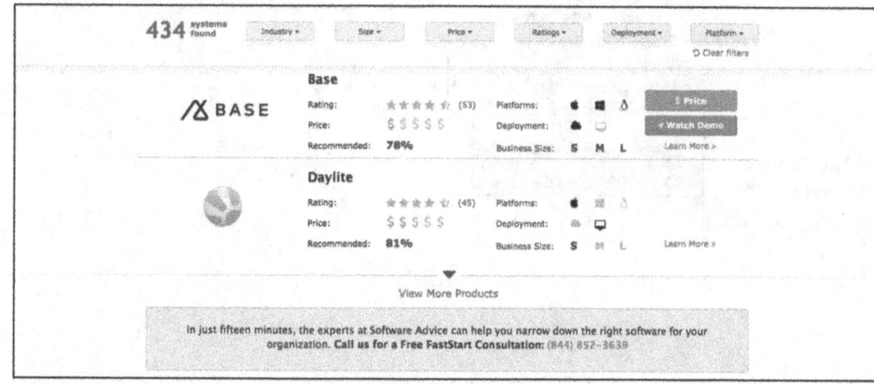

FIGURE 18-4: The Software Advice software ratings.

Capterra

www.capterra.com

Capterra is another Gartner-owned software listing and review site and works in much the same way as the others.

You can easily compare systems, filter results based on your needs, and view screenshots of what the platform looks like, as shown in Figure 18-5. It provide an easy to read summary of the reviews and a snapshot of key features. Capterra, like GetApp, does not offer the depth of G2 Crowd, but is great if you're looking for a quick and accurate snapshot of the platforms.

Capterra also runs on a PPC business model, so only those vendors that subscribe to this upgrade have a Visit Website link in their profiles.

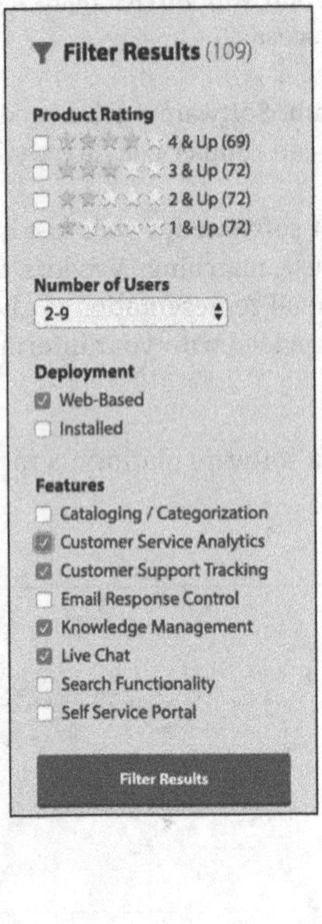

Filter Results (109)

Product Rating
4 & Up (69)
3 & Up (72)
2 & Up (72)
1 & Up (72)

Number of Users
2-9

Deployment
Web-Based
Installed

Features
Cataloging / Categorization
Customer Service Analytics
Customer Support Tracking
Email Response Control
Knowledge Management
Live Chat
Search Functionality
Self Service Portal

Filter Results

FIGURE 18-5: The Capterra filters and results.

Finances Online

`financesonline.com`

FinancesOnline is a small, robust software review site and arguably one of the fastest growing marketplaces. Its focus is on finance-focused software; however, the vendor selection spans across all categories.

This website is great because it provides a lot of great content for you to consume. Vendor listings are filled with information, ratings, and reviews all in one place. It does offer premium services, so some vendors may have more prominence than others. Keep this in mind as you review featured vendors.

TrustRadius

`www.trustradius.com`

TrustRadius is a software listing and review site. Its site has quickly gained a large number of reviews and monthly website visitors. The website is easy to use, provides in-depth descriptions of platforms, and offers more content and information than the Gartner sites (GetApp, Capterra, Software Advice), as shown in Figure 18-6.

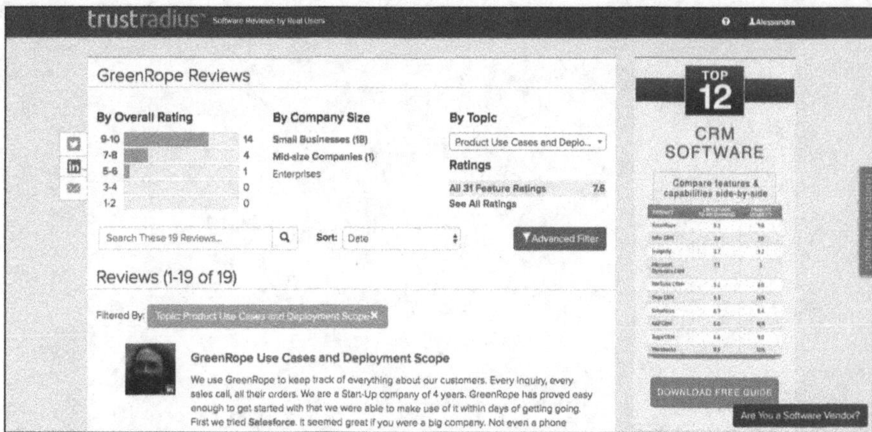

FIGURE 18-6: Software reviews on TrustRadius.

This review site is more similar to G2 Crowd in both functionality and the level of accessible information about each vendor. Like the rest of the review sites, TrustRadius also offers vendors different upgrade options to help drive leads and fill the vendor's funnel. It offers review campaigns, cost per lead, advanced software reports, and more.

If you're looking for a more in-depth look at each vendor, TrustRadius is a great place to start. It offer plenty of free buyer's guides as well as top charts.

Marketing Automation Club

`www.marketing-automation.club`

Marketing Automation Club is a software comparison website, and hones in on providing users and marketing tech buyers with unbiased information on the best marketing automation platforms for businesses of all sizes and verticals.

The site allows you to compare three solutions at a time, so you can focus on the features you need most. Site visitors can find useful information about marketing automation as well as what to look for in a vendor. Instead of ranking each vendor, it bases the comparisons on customer experiences, features, and services offered, among other criteria. It does offer services to help buyers choose the right software, but does not offer sophisticated pay-per-click programs like some of its competitors, making this site more objective.

Chapter 19

Ten Common CRM Mistakes

The best way to build a successful CRM strategy is to be ready for the things that can derail your progress. CRM requires vision, foresight, and a lot of hard work. With this chapter, you can prepare for obstacles that have tripped up other people.

Not Getting Buy In from Your Team

CRM is a team effort spanning across all departments. To succeed with CRM, your entire team must be onboard and take ownership of the process. When one person tries to force the CRM vision on everyone else in an organization, resentment ensues. And resistance kills a CRM implementation. Everyone must participate and believe in the *why* behind the CRM.

Believing CRM Is about Software

CRM is a mindset and a strategy. Everyone has to change the way he or she thinks about business, and your culture must be one of open communication. Installing your CRM software doesn't magically solve your business's problems. Everyone must make the effort to learn and use the software every day. Each team member takes responsibility for going through onboarding and training.

Not Doing Your Homework First

You can't just jump into a CRM and expect it to "work." You have to take the time to understand your business. You need to build your own data structure, define your processes, and segment your customers. If you don't take the time to do upfront work, you'll have to go back and rework everything you started with your CRM.

Not Listening to Expert Advice

Rely on experts who are familiar with CRM technology to guide you through the setup of your CRM on your chosen CRM platform. Your CRM provider should be able to offer you that expert advice or connect you to someone who can. Your CRM vendor has people who have helped many businesses just like yours get CRM working. Regardless of your experience level, getting feedback and bouncing ideas off people who do work with CRM every day is a good idea. If you know CRM experts, talk to them.

Take the time to read articles and reviews about the CRM software you use. Look at what people say and why.

Not Going through Vendor Software Training

CRM is complicated, any way you look at it. Most businesses have complex processes that have to get cataloged in a CRM, which means understanding process, information, and the people who use them. Your vendor needs to understand all these things and help you set up your CRM in a way that is usable and makes sense for your team. Take the time to watch instructional videos, read how-to guides, and participate in interactive training.

Not Setting Up DKIM and SPF

This seemingly small step impacts your ability to deliver email. Many alerts in your CRM and outbound communication to your leads and clients rely on email. If those emails land in the junk folder, your voice is never heard. Setting up DKIM and SPF is a 10- to 15-minute process. Your vendor should have videos you can watch or be available to help walk you through the process.

Buying Lists

If you buy lists of people to contact, never use email to prospect them cold. You gain a reputation as a spammer, and it affects your ability to deliver emails. Don't fall into the trap of instant gratification through email. The penalties to your deliverability and brand far outweigh any short-term gain you may see from clicks.

Your ability to communicate relies on getting your messages to the inbox. Don't jeopardize that by spamming people who don't know you. ISPs such as Google and Yahoo are good at filtering spam, and a bad reputation follows you. Instead, use a lead nurturing process of driving people to you through advertising and capture them with effective landing pages and forms.

If you do buy a list, have your team contact leads by cold call and ask them for permission to email. Successful calls can start each lead on your customer journey, with targeted messages and ads that drive people to convert.

Relying Only on Cold Calling

Some people believe cold calling is the only effective way to generate leads. If it's your preferred method to generate business, be sure you measure the cost and lead quality generated by those cold calls. Your CRM tracks the success rate. You may find better success using different methods of attracting leads, so diversify to include different methods of acquiring leads and compare your ROI from each lead generation channel.

Not Journey Mapping First

Use a journey mapping tool to model your process flow before you start designing your CRM and identify the problem you're trying to solve.

When you can look at a diagram that shows you who does what, you can build your data model, set up your market segments, and design your workflows. Some of the processes are internal (done by your team) and some are external (done by the lead). Do your best to capture and anticipate as many actions and decision points as you can.

Focusing on One Requirement

Complete CRM is an all-inclusive solution, one that spans your entire team. Include all your functional areas and people in coming up with your needs and wants. If you require specific functionality, be careful using that one requirement to qualify or disqualify a CRM vendor. Avoid qualifying or disqualifying a vendor based on this one requirement. Remember your bigger picture.

When you look at your strategy and the functionality the vendor offers as a whole, you get a bigger picture of what the CRM can do for you. If you like a particular vendor that doesn't have a specific functionality you need out of the box, consider the effort required to work around that and build it into your decision-making criteria.

Appendix A

CRM Decision Matrix

The best decisions are made both quantitatively and qualitatively. The criteria listed in this chapter are a starting point, but are by no means exhaustive. Adapt the list according to the specific needs of your organization.

Ask your short list of vendors these questions and rate their responses. Get a live demo with the vendor representative to see the system in action. It should inspire confidence that the software is stable, reliable, and capable of meeting your needs.

Vendor

- Given the current number of contacts, users, and emails sent per month, what is the expected monthly payment now? In one year? In three years?
- How long has the company been in business?
- What kind of training resources are available?
- Is a trial account available? For how long? How is it limited?
- Is support included? Are there limitations?
- What kind of response times can be expected?
- Is support in-house or outsourced?
- What kind of customer reviews are there?
- How often is the software updated?
- How is your data secured and protected? Can the vendor share it in any way?
- Do you agree with the principles the company stands for? Its mission/vision statement?

CRM

- **Users**
  - How many users can the account hold?
  - What is the cost, if any, to add additional users?
  - How easy is it to limit access of users to certain areas of the system?
- **Contacts**
  - Does the contact view show the user everything he needs to see?
  - Can the contact view be customized?
  - How many custom fields can be attached to a record?
  - Can custom fields be attached to individual contacts, as well as companies?
  - Can changes to custom field data trigger automation?
- **Opportunities**
  - How easy is it to set up and advance opportunities?
  - Can you customize products associated with opportunities?
  - Can you customize the phases of the opportunities?
  - Can you set quotas and forecast?
  - Can you attach multiple contacts to an opportunity?
  - Can you attach workflows to opportunities and have them act differently than if attached to a contact?
- **Dashboard**
  - What data can be seen on the dashboard?
  - Can you customize the dashboard?
- **Gamification**
  - Can you set targets for team activity?
  - Can team members view each other's activities and performance?
- **Real-time collaboration**
  - Can your team members communicate with each other in real-time about issues?
  - Are they alerted when new posts are made?

» **Lead scoring**

- Can you score both demographically and with activities?
- Can you set a decay rate for activity lead scores?
- Can you see your most active contacts and segment them by groups or tags?
- Can you set both hot and cold automation?
- Can you attach lead scores to contact record custom fields?

» **Workflows**

- What can workflows do when they're activated?
- Can you move/assign groups or tags?
- Can you send emails, text messages, and print campaigns?
- How easy is it to set up drip campaigns? Is there campaign-level performance measurement?

» **Email marketing**

- Is it easy to build an attractive, responsive email within the system?
- Can you mail merge recipient data in the message?
- Can you use rules-based mail merge to build the message on the fly for each recipient?
- Does the system automatically handle bounces, unsubscribes, and forwarding?
- Can you track scores of people interacting with your email campaigns?
- Can you review the reputation of the IP addresses that send your emails? What is the sender score(s) of the IP addresses you would send through?
- Does someone monitor your messages?
- When people click the "Report This As Spam" button in their email client, does it automatically unsubscribe them from your list?
- How comprehensive is the tracking available?
- Does email behavior automatically show up in the CRM for each contact?

» **Lead capture**

- Can your forms gather all the information you need and automatically put it into your CRM?
- Are forms protected from spammers/bots?

- Can you use both single and confirmed opt-in forms? Why or why not? Does it affect your deliverability?
- Can you customize your user experience and confirmation emails?
- Can you set up auto-responders? How many?

» **Live chat**

- Can you install a live chat module on your website?
- Do chat transcripts automatically get added to CRM records?

» **Support ticketing**

- Can you set up a ticketing/case management system for your support staff?
- Can ticket submission trigger workflows?
- Do ticket issues and resolutions automatically get added to CRM records?

» **Social media**

- Can social media actions trigger workflows in the CRM?
- Which social media networks can you connect to?
- Are the connections visible in contact records within the CRM?

» **Video tracking**

- Can you measure when someone watches one of your videos?
- Can you track how long someone watched?
- Can video watching trigger a workflow?
- Does the CRM automatically record when someone watches a video?

» **Web analytics**

- How easy is it to install the tracking scripts on your webpages?
- What kind of data does it collect about who is visiting your website?
- Can you easily track campaigns from the inbound clicks?
- Can you compare performance between different campaigns?
- Can you see website visit data in real-time in the contact records in your CRM?
- Can you track affiliates and set up affiliate marketing programs?

» **Website Content Management System (CMS)**

- Does your website content management system integrate with the CRM?
- Can you easily build a membership website for a group of contacts in your CRM?
- Can you password protect your website?
- Can you sell products and services? Subscriptions?
- Is it easy to build a landing page?

» **Calendars**

- Can you share calendars of events and meetings?
- Can you publish calendars and embed them on websites?
- Can you set up a booking calendar?

» **Events**

- Can you manage events with registration?
- What kind of registration options can you set?
- Can you collect registration payments?
- Can you trigger workflows based on event attendance?
- Does attendance information automatically connect to contacts in the CRM in real time?

» **Phone/mobile**

- Can you click-to-call from within the CRM? Are those calls recordable? Are they automatically attached to the CRM record?
- Are inbound calls tracked? Are they recordable? Are they attached to the caller's CRM record?
- Can you send SMS and/or MMS messages?
- Can contacts opt-in via text messages?

» **Surveys**

- Can you send surveys to your contacts?
- What kinds of questions can you ask?
- Can surveys be connected to workflows or other automation?
- Can you score surveys and trigger workflows based on individual responses or sum scores?
- Are survey responses stored for contacts in the CRM automatically?

» **Project management**
  - Can you manage projects within the CRM?
  - Is it easy to assign tasks in projects, track hours, and know when updates are made?
  - Can you calculate billing and measure resource utilization (the percentage of billable hours worked)?
» **Knowledge base**
  - Can you build your own knowledge base for your team within the system?
  - How easy is it to restrict access to the knowledge base?
  - Can certain articles be made public?
» **Learning Management System (LMS)**
  - Can you set up a program to train or onboard new clients or employees?
  - Can completion of LMS modules trigger automation?
  - Is progress stored in the CRM automatically?
» **Media library**
  - Can you store images, files, and other content in a central repository?
  - How easy is it to access that content? Embed in landing pages or emails?
» **Integration**
  - Does the software support a secure application programming interface?
  - Does the software integrate with a third-party application clearinghouse such as Zapier?
  - What other custom integrations are available?
  - Are costs associated with using the API?
  - Are there limitations on access to the API?
» **Overall system**
  - How user-friendly is the platform?
  - Is there contextual help inline that gives you insight into best practices?
  - Is there an overview screen where you can visualize the automation processes you build?

Appendix B
Self-Assessment

This appendix gives you a series of questions; the answers can give you a sense of how far along you are in the setup of your CRM. If you can't answer a question, consider whether a Complete CRM strategy and software can provide a benefit in that area.

How you answer these questions determine where you should focus your energy in building your Complete CRM. If you don't have ready access to these answers, find out why. People in your organization should be responsible for them and should report on them on a regular basis.

Who is your ideal customer?

How big is your market?

What market segments are you pursuing?

Who are your buyer personas?

What competitors exist?

How many contacts are in your database?

How often do you send email newsletters?

What are the average read/click rates for your newsletters? Are the interaction trends increasing or decreasing?

How many people visit your website?

How many contact forms have you built on your website? Do they work well?

Have you set up auto-responders for your forms?

Do you have support ticketing and lead capture built in to your website?

Do you have live chat installed?

Are you advertising online? How much are you spending? How many people visit your website from your ads every month?

What is your average cost-per-impression (CPM) for your advertising?

What is the average cost-per-new-client acquisition (CPA)?

Which campaigns have the lowest CPA?

Which campaigns generate the highest average conversion values?

Are your salespeople set up with a CRM? How often do they use it?

Can your salespeople see email marketing and website traffic data in the contact records in their CRM?

Are you managing offline events, such as meetings and trade shows? Does attendance data automatically get into your CRM?

Have you designed and defined internal company process?

Have you designed and defined your buyer journeys?

Do you have lead scoring set up? Demographic and activity?

Do you have hot and cold automation workflows built?

Do you have drip campaigns built for market segments?

Do you have predictive analytics built?

Can you identify actions and demographics that correlate to conversions?

Index

A

B

C

D

E

J

K

L

M

Q

R

S

T

U

V

W

Y

Z

About the Author

Lars Helgeson has been in the Internet marketing space since 2000, when he cofounded one of the world's first email service providers, CoolerEmail. As a pioneer in responsible email marketing, he grew CoolerEmail to a global software company specializing in marketing communication with over 1,500 clients. In 2010, after spending several years designing and implementing a more comprehensive way to meet the needs of small and mid-sized businesses, he launched GreenRope. GreenRope is the world's first and only Business Operating System, a cloud-based platform that simplifies and consolidates a company's sales, marketing, and operations. GreenRope currently provides technology solutions to over 3,000 companies worldwide.

Lars earned Bachelor of Science and Master of Science degrees in Mechanical Engineering from Rensselaer Polytechnic Institute in Troy, New York. He also has an MBA from the Robert Anderson School at the University of New Mexico. He served in the United States Air Force for four years, working in the Air Force's space test program, Air Force Research Laboratory, and Ballistic Missile Defense Organization. He enjoys travel, stand-up paddleboarding, mountain biking, and ice hockey, and practices yoga whenever the forces of the universe are not aligned to keep him at his computer.

In the past several years, Lars has been a finalist multiple times for the *San Diego Business Journal*'s Most Admired CEO and Information Technology Executive of the Year, and a finalist for *San Diego Magazine*'s Top Tech Exec Award. Lars has also been named a Top Ten Most Inspiring Leader in Sales Lead Management Software by the Sales Lead Management Association for the second consecutive year.

Dedication

Dedicated to Mom, who always stood by me.

Author's Acknowledgments

I'd like to thank the people who directly contributed to this book: Alessandra Ceresa for reviewing my drafts, Madison Potter for putting the charts together, Ivana Smesna for the illustrations. I'd also like to thank the entire team at GreenRope, who supported the creation of the book and are the driving force behind the vision of Complete CRM. I'd like to thank my family, who always were there to provide emotional support through all the ups and downs. Thank you to my close friends who were there at the ice rink, on the golf course, and in the surf, helping me blow off steam. And last, but not least, Little Buddy, my Boston Terrier, who happily went on stress-relieving walks and was always up for a game of hide-and-seek during those long nights of writing.

Publisher's Acknowledgments

Acquisition Editor: Amy Fandrei
Project Editor: Rebecca Senninger
Technical Editor: Michelle Krasniak
Editorial Assistant: Serena Novosel
Sr. Editorial Assistant: Cherie Case

Production Editor: Antony Sami
Front Cover Image: ©ThomasVogel/iStockphoto

Leverage the power

Dummies is the global leader in the reference category and one of the most trusted and highly regarded brands in the world. No longer just focused on books, customers now have access to the dummies content they need in the format they want. Together we'll craft a solution that engages your customers, stands out from the competition, and helps you meet your goals.

Advertising & Sponsorships

Connect with an engaged audience on a powerful multimedia site, and position your message alongside expert how-to content. Dummies.com is a one-stop shop for free, online information and know-how curated by a team of experts.

- Targeted ads
- Video
- Email Marketing
- Microsites
- Sweepstakes sponsorship

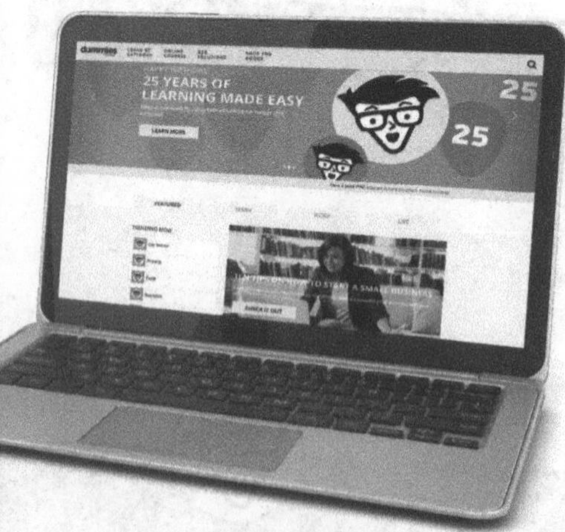

20 MILLION PAGE VIEWS EVERY SINGLE MONTH

15 MILLION UNIQUE VISITORS PER MONTH

43% OF ALL VISITORS ACCESS THE SITE VIA THEIR MOBILE DEVICES

700,000 NEWSLETTER SUBSCRIPTIONS TO THE INBOXES OF *300,000* UNIQUE INDIVIDUALS EVERY WEEK